Created and Directed by Hans Höfer

INSIGHT GUIDES
GREEK ISLANDS

Edited by Martha Ellen Zenfell
Updated by John Chapple

Editorial Director: Brian Bell

HOUGHTON MIFFLIN COMPANY

APA PUBLICATIONS

Writing about Greek islands is the opposite of visiting Greek islands. The very qualities which make destinations like Mýkonos shimmering holiday centres are the same qualities which give journalists sleepless nights. Deadlines on a Greek island? Dedicated accuracy from a shepherd tending his flock? An island that spells its name three different ways and has a ferryboat once a week, if you're lucky?

Such challenges are nothing new to the *Insight Guides* series, created in 1970 by **Hans Höfer**, founder of Apa Publications and the company's driving force. Each of the 190 books encourages readers to celebrate the essence of a place rather than tailor it to their expectations and is edited in the belief that, without insight into people's character and culture, travel can narrow the mind, not broaden it.

Endorsing that view was this book's project editor, **Martha Ellen Zenfell**, an American living in London and now one of Apa's senior editors. As a veteran of several travel guides to the islands, she was aware of the immense logistical problems. For one previous book, she travelled to more than 50 of the islands, armed only with a typewriter, a notebook and a waterproof pen. The memories are still clear.

She was severely bitten by mosquitos on Zákynthos and ate grey gruel for days when fresh food ran out on Telendos. Her motorbike broke down in a storm on Skopelos and tears were shed in the Dodecanese when the third ferry in as many days was, again, six hours late. "But why do you want to leave Leros?" asked a fishman who found her weeping on the beach. "Is this not the most beautiful island in the Aegean? Come and stay with my family, and write your book here."

The kindness of strangers is the flip side of travelling alone and extensively in Greece: the unknown man who lent 2,000 drachmas from his own pocket when she was stranded on Chálki, the farmer's wife on Náxos whose invitation prompted a stint as a wailer at an island funeral.

Zenfell began the task of assembling a crack team of reporters and photographers to share the tribulations and the satisfactions of producing a book on these islands. **Rowlinson Carter**, an English journalist and historian who has since become a frequent contributor to *Insight Guides*, was one of the first to be recruited. His journal of a year-long stay in the Sporades forms the basis for several essays on contemporary island life.

Another early recruit turned out to be **Mark Mazower**, who wrote the history section. He was born in 1958 and educated at universities in Oxford and Bologna. Mazower lived in Athens and contributed to *Insight Guide: Greece* before moving to England to become a Research Fellow of Christ Church, Oxford, specialising in Greek history.

Marcus Brooke, whose major written contribution is the Crete section and who also supplied many of the photographs, is a Scot who wanders around the world with typewriter and cameras. Aeons ago, when leading a less peripatetic life, Brooke was seduced hook, line and sinker by Greece. Since then he has lived, on various occasions, on Crete, Rhodes and Hydra.

Rhoda Nottridge, a writer from Brighton, England, gave up her holiday time to cover the dubious delights of Corfu. Her plea to save the turtles on Zákynthos is a reminder that tourists can play an active, rather than a passive role, in preserving the islands.

Journalist **Stephanie Ferguson** has been a regular traveller to, and writer about, Greece since the late 1970s.

Höfer

Zenfell

Carter

Mazower

Brooke

Ferguson

She sees herself as a visitor, not a tourist, and likes to get involved, from learning to belly-dance on Lésvos to dishing up snails and chips with the shepherds of Chálki, to staying in the monastery on Symi. Brought up in Wales, she has written for a variety of British newspapers and keeps an up to the minute eye on the islands.

David Glenn's job is all about sailing. As deputy editor of the magazine *Yachting World,* Glenn was well-placed to write about cruising the Med, with all its pitfalls and pleasures. His article should be read by anyone who contemplates hoisting a sail.

Kerin Hope, a former archaeologist, wrote the sections on Athens and Piraeus. She was at the time the Athens correspondent for the Associated Press and later represented the *Financial Times* in the same city.

It fell to **Carol Reed**, a freelance writer based in Athens, to put the vexed question of tourism management into perspective. What can we expect from the islands, not only now but well into the 21st century?

John Carr's contributions combine two of his specialities. As Athens correspondent of the *Wall Street Journal,* Carr was in an informed position to write the essay on shipping and cruising. As a drummer in a rock band when he first arrived in Greece, he studied the cadences of Greek folk music and contributed to *Billboard* magazine, so he was the natural person to approach for the article on island music. He has lived in Athens for a quarter of a century.

Carr

Anthony Wood spent a year studying traditional agricultural farming, specifically related to a Greek island. **Jane Cocking**, who wrote the piece on island crafts, is a research fellow of Darwin College, Cambridge. Her PhD was on the folk textiles of Crete. **Nile Stanton**, an American-born lecturer at the Faltaits Museum was, during his first winter on Skýros, the only English-speaking person on the island.

Anita Peltonen, a US-born journalist, has variously worked in Montreal, Manhattan, Helsinki and London. She writes: "There is no middle ground when travelling in Greece; it's an experience always imbued with passion. It's a place to find exotic husbands – and diseases. The islands are not the neatly wrapped touristic trinkets they appear to be, and this is what I love about them. You can be in the throes of shamelessly European gratification one day and pitched into an unforgiving wilderness the next."

More than a dozen photographers gave this book its distinctive look. Special thanks must go to **Pierre Couteau, Markos G. Hionos, Michele Macrakis** and **David Beatty**.

Peltonen

This edition has been completely overhauled on the spot by **John Chapple**, an American who has lived in Greece since 1969, working as a writer and editor of books about Greece for Lycabettus Press in Athens. He summoned a team to check the islands out from top to toe. **Diana Farr Louis** is a writer who has lived in Greece since 1972, and is author of a travel guide to Corfu and the Ionian islands. **Nikos Stavroulakis**, a native of Crete, is a former director of the Jewish Museum of Greece and now teaches Byzantine and Ottoman history in Athens.

Jeffrey Carson has lived on Paros since 1970 and teaches art history at the Aegean Center for the Arts. **Marc Dubin**, a well-travelled American, has a house on Samos, contributed many photographs to this book and thoroughly explored the islands for this edition. He has a number of travel books to his credit and has kept *Insight Guide: Greece* up to date.

Dubin

CONTENTS

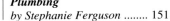

CONTENTS

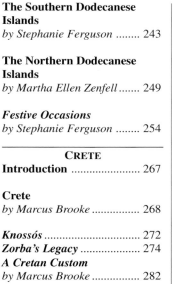

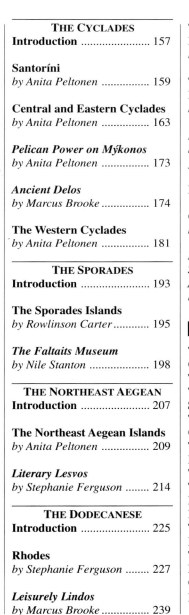

TRAVEL TIPS

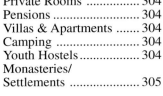

"Island" is one of those words which psychiatrists might use to trigger an automatic response from patients stretched out on the couch. The response may be influenced by childhood recollections of Robinson Crusoe, in which case islands are possibly associated with the idea of escape from a complex universe into a private, more manageable world which offers individuals control over their own destiny. Crusoe becomes comfortable in his reconstructed womb, and it is a surprise, when rescue is at hand, that he doesn't tell his saviours to push off.

"Greek island" would probably add some specific touches to the imagery: a cluster of blisteringly white buildings against a shimmering sea, donkeys slowly carrying their burdens against a backdrop of olive groves, weather-beaten fishermen repairing nets, and tavernas full of *retsina*, *moussaká*, shattered plates and an endless supply of *Never on Sunday* and *Zorba the Greek*. Accurate as far as it goes, but any worthwhile generalisation about the Greek islands – anything, that is, more adventurous than the staringly obvious – would almost certainly be wrong.

Inter-island relations: Although the islands are classified as members of one group or another, they have a strong sense of separate identity and invariably an idiosyncratic history to back it up. Often, the feeling between neighbouring islands is mutual suspicion bordering on loathing, although this is something visitors would seldom be aware of unless they made a point of going down to the local *ouzerié* and chatting to the old boys entrenched there. Conditioned by long winter nights when nothing much happens, the old boys have developed the knack of waffling on about any subject under the sun, and a new face in the audience is welcome.

As an example of inter-island relations, Skiáthos and Skópelos in the Sporades have never been able to see eye to eye on the matter of ice. The origins of the dispute are buried in history, but it may spring from days

when making ice depended on clanking contraptions which were partly home-made and therefore the focus of parochial pride. Neither side in the respective *ouzerié* will volunteer what is wrong with the other island's ice. Uncharacteristically, questions are turned aside, but hopeless shaking of grey heads hints at a truth so awful that they cannot bring themselves to utter it.

The telephone directories on Skiáthos and Skópelos reveal some of the same surnames. Could the families by any chance be related?

The inquiry seems to hit a nerve as painful as the ice business.

Only in one area, if the old boys are to be believed, are the two islands in full agreement, and that concerns Skýros, the largest island in the chain. Skiáthos and Skópelos are within full view of one another, a distasteful but undeniable fact, whereas Skýros lies below the horizon. According to the miraculously united old boys, that means, luckily, that Skýros may not exist.

Such theories are expounded with twinkling eyes and guffaws; even if they should not be taken too literally, they are great fun, and the opportunity to move among neigh-

Preceding pages: a church in the Cyclades; a boat on Mýkonos; a priest on his way to work; sailing into the sun. **Left**, men playing cards on Chíos. **Right**, on the look-out for swordfish.

bouring islands in order to compare notes should not be missed.

It is sometimes said that if against the odds two islands struck the curious visitor as being practically identical, those islands would necessarily be at opposite ends of the Aegean. Apart from the natural tendency for small island communities to be staunchly independent, there is a historical basis for their individualism.

From the Phoenicians onwards, the islands have been tossed around like loose pebbles in the cultural tides which have surged backwards and forwards through the eastern Mediterranean, and none has emerged from that experience quite like any other.

require more diligent research than most visitors would be inclined to conduct while staying there on holiday.

Beginning in the 11th century, Corfu was ruled successively by Normans, Sicilians, Genoese, Venetians, Greeks ("the despotate of Epirus"), more Sicilians, Neapolitans and then by the Venetians again. On this occasion the Venetians stayed for 400 years. Then the procession of foreign rulers resumed: France, Russia and the Ottoman Empire, Britain, Greece, Italy, Germany and finally, after World War II, Greece again.

Dedicated scholars could probably assemble a jigsaw, with pieces extant in Corfu, that would reflect each and every one of these

Momentous events were taking place on Crete and some of the Cyclades as early as 3000 BC. The golden age of Athens under Pericles lay as far in the future then as, for us, it now lies in the past – more than two millennia either way. Settlers from Mesopotamia landed with the skills which developed into the Minoan civilisation.

Intruders: To look at the history of Corfu merely from the 11th century is therefore to pick up that particular story a long way down the line. Nevertheless, the record from that date reveals an amazing cavalcade of intruders to the island, all of whom must have left a mark, even if the traces today would

waves. The evidence does not necessarily consist of archeological ruins or excavated objects. Corfu extrapolated from one small chapter of its convoluted history an abiding passion for cricket. It is still played on the square in the middle of the town, albeit with local variations which would raise the eyebrows of traditionalists in England.

Other islands got almost as much unwanted outside attention as Corfu. Piracy was a perennial problem, and that accounts for the number of citadels (kástra) on high ground to which the island population retreated when danger threatened.

Determined pirates: The defences did not

always keep determined pirates like Khair-ed-din Barbarossa out, but they did mean that the pirates had to summon the effort instead of lazily helping themselves to everything of value when they happened to be cruising by.

Crete and Rhodes have by far the richest and most thoroughly documented sites for historically-minded visitors, but on any island there is bound to be something to pick over, even if it isn't marked on the map. A good tip for amateur archaeologists would be to ask themselves where, taking into account security, prevailing winds, terrain, water supply etc., they themselves would have chosen to build something – and then

ment to observe, however, that the "Greekness" of the islands is variable. Italy did not cede the Dodecanese to Greece until 1947, and the inclusion of Crete as part of Greece was once an issue nearly as hot as the present one over Cyprus. Some islands were deeply affected in the 1920s when Greece and Turkey exchanged large numbers of their respective ethnic expatriates.

The topographical differences among the islands are worth considering. If some of the islands look like mountain peaks, it is because much of the area now covered by the Aegean was once a solid land bridge between Greece and Asia Minor, which eventually fractured and "sank". These islands

start looking for evidence of past peoples.

Invasions of self-contained communities in the confined space of a small island would naturally be more disruptive than they would be on a relatively amorphous mainland. In extreme cases, invaders wiped out the existing population completely and started all over again. Modern Greeks are ultra-sensitive to the suggestion that the country has been overrun by outsiders so many times that they are not remotely connected with their distinguished ancestors.

It is not to become embroiled in that argu-

Left, and above, the church plays a social role.

are the tips of what used to be ranges encroaching from either side.

The largest mountain ranges in mainland Greece caused famous military bottlenecks at places like Thermopylae where, in Xerxes' time, there was only the narrowest of passages between the mountains and the sea. Since then the sea has receded, so what used to be a death trap, where Spartan defenders calmly bathed and combed their hair (according to Herodotus) while waiting for the Persian onslaught, is now a coastal plain 5 km (3 miles) wide.

The contours of submerged mountains and valleys extending from the area around

Thermopylae caused the seabed around the islands to drop precipitously to 1,800 metres (6,000 ft). On the Turkish side, the sea is generally much shallower, and it is the shallows which can cause the Aegean, quiet and bather-friendly one moment, to be transformed into a lethal cauldron within the space of an hour or two.

Anyone hiring a boat on holiday should never leave port without consulting the islanders. For thousands of years, lives have depended on accurate weather predictions, and local knowledge handed down is often more reliable than official forecasts carried on the wireless or in newspapers.

If the purpose of a visit to the islands is

nothing more than to settle on a stretch of agreeable beach and live cheaply, visitors should be lucky on both counts. Greece has about 2,000 islands altogether and these, plus the islets, add up to technically the longest coastline of any country in Europe. Basic commodities, including restaurant meals, are price-controlled. They may rise with inflation, but against major foreign currencies the Greek drachma usually goes down, so the net result for foreigners is constant good value for money.

Advanced androgyny: The one exception may be Mýkonos, which in recent years seems to have cornered a market in advanced androgyny. The islanders used to ask themselves why there were so many churches on Mýkonos (hundreds of them); they now tend to say (stoically, while pocketing the money) that the birds of paradise who descend on them in summer are undoubtedly in urgent need of every one of them.

Mýkonos would not have been allowed to develop its exotic reputation under the puritanical military junta, when even topless sunbathing was discouraged. Since the overthrow of the glum colonels, what bathers choose to wear or discard has been a personal decision, and there is usually at least one beach on an island where nudity is tolerated even if it is not official.

There is nothing ambivalent about the attitude towards drugs, however, and the more popular islands are subject to close undercover surveillance. Some humdrum medicines sold without prescription elsewhere may be illegal in Greece, and as the legal system seems to rest on the principle that the slightest suspicion warrants a spell in prison before the proceedings proper begin, it is wise to err generously on the side of extreme caution and leave nothing to chance.

The best way to enjoy the islands is to arrive with a certain attitude of mind. By all means, begin by uncritically enjoying the cluster of blisteringly white buildings against a shimmering sea, donkeys with a backdrop of olive groves, and so on – the vista, indeed, seared into the senses by piles of island holiday brochures.

Do not shrink, either, from personally smashing a few plates. They are a special, unglazed type not intended for any other purpose. When the novelty wears off, or perhaps earlier, examine each island as if it were an onion, and start stripping off the skins. If not a long-standing dispute about ice, some other unexpected aspect is certain to be revealed.

How to strip the onion is a large part of what this book is about. It hopes and tries to show by example. A book that says everything about 2,000 islands will never be written. The learned Helidorius once tried to set out all he had learned about the monuments of Athens – as they existed in the second century BC. Fifteen volumes later…

Left, family group at Ambelaki, on Salamis. **Right**, preparing the evening meal.

What distinguishes the course of Greek history from that of her Balkan neighbours is the impact of the sea. The sea diffuses cultures, transfers peoples and encourages trade – and until our own times it was invariably a swifter means of transmission than overland. Nowhere in Greece is the sea as inescapable as on the islands.

Foreign incursions: The poverty of the arid island soil has forced inhabitants to venture far afield for their livelihood. At the same time, the islands have been vulnerable to foreign incursions whether by Arab pirates, Italian colonists or modern tourists. All have played their part in transforming local conditions; some have had an even wider impact.

Phoenician traders, for example, appear to have brought their alphabet to Crete in the early archaic period, which the Greeks then adopted and changed. At the same time, Egyptian influence was leading island sculptors to work in stone. It is no coincidence that the earliest examples of monumental Greek sculpture are all to be found on the islands.

On Crete, the Bronze Age had produced the first urban civilisation in the Aegean: this was the age of the Knossós and Phaistós palaces, erected in the centuries after 2000 BC. Other islands, too, such as Santoríni, flourished at this time. Thucydides' account of how King Minos of Crete established his sons as governors in the Cyclades and cleared the sea of pirates certainly suggests considerable Cretan control of the Aegean.

This control, if it ever did exist, disappeared with the eclipse of Minoan society in the 15th century BC. The settlement on Santoríni (Thíra) was wiped out by a volcanic explosion, but why the rest of Minoan control disintegrated remains a mystery. In any event, the Aegean was not to be dominated by a single sea power for another millennium until the rise of the Athenian empire.

Considerable wealth: Before this, however, communities of Greeks had begun to flourish on most of the islands, exploiting local quarries and mines, and developing indigenous political systems. Some communities achieved considerable wealth, notably on Sífnos, whose gold and silver mines had made her inhabitants reputedly the richest citizens in the Cyclades by the 6th century BC. Some reflection of this wealth can be seen in the ruins of the marble treasury which Siphniots dedicated to Apollo at Delphi.

It was in the 6th century, too, that the inhabitants of Santoríni began to mint their own coinage, a physical manifestation of the island's powerful status in the Aegean. At one point Santorini's influence was to extend, not only to Crete, Mílos, Páros, and Rhodes, but as far west as Corinth and as far east as Asia Minor.

During the 5th century BC, the islands' independence was curtailed as Athens used anti-Persian fears to manipulate the Confederacy of Athenian leadership. The Confederacy had been formed in 478 BC as an alliance between equal partners to form a strong naval power in the Aegean. But Athens soon controlled the Confederacy and used its resources in a series of wars against rivals such as the naval power of Aegina.

Athenian intrigue: It was Athenian intrigues with the Corinthian colony on Corfu, however, that led to the Peloponnesian War which was ultimately to cripple – and break – Athens forever.

In the Hellenistic period the islands remained turbulent backwaters, prone to internecine struggles which made them easy prey for their more powerful neighbours. By the middle of the 1st century BC, Rome had established herself in the Aegean; Crete became the centre of a province which included a part of North Africa.

Under Roman guidance roads were laid, aqueducts constructed, new towns and grand buildings erected. It has been estimated that the islands' population in Roman times was probably greater than it is today.

Despite this prosperity, the Aegean as a whole remained in the background in Roman times. Little is known of conditions of life in the islands either then or after AD 395, when they passed under the control of the eastern Roman Empire. Only with the onset of the Arab raids in the 7th century does the historical record become more complete.

Preceding pages: 17th-century map of Ancient Greece. **Left**, marble idol, Early Cycladic II era.

With the decline of Roman power in the Mediterranean, the islands faced a long period of instability: for more than a millennium they were attacked by invaders from all points of the compass. From the north, briefly, came the Vandals and Goths; from the south, the Arabs, who established themselves on Crete in 827 and proceeded to plunder the rest of the Aegean for over a century; from the west came Normans in the 11th century, followed by the Genoese and Venetians; finally, from the east came the Ottoman Turks, who succeeded in dominating almost all of the islands in the Aegean between the 15th and 18th centuries.

Other groups, too, played minor roles – quite apart from powers such as the English, French and Russians, who all shared an interest in the Greek islands. There were always pirates to contend with, too – a notoriously mixed bunch. A 13th-century Venetian report on piracy mentions corsairs of the following backgrounds: Genoese, Venetians, Lombards, Sicilians, Provençals, Catalans, Spaniards, Greeks, and Slavs.

The impact of these various peoples on the islands was complex and tangled, making it awkward to generalise about the historical experiences of the islands themselves. Only by considering the main island groups individually may things fall into place.

The Ionian Islands: On the eve of the 1821 Greek uprising, an English traveller to Corfu noted: "The natural weakness and position of the Ionian islands, and all their past history, demonstrate that they must ever be an appendage of some more powerful state; powerful at sea and able to protect them as well as to command." Close to the Greek mainland, vital staging-posts on the voyage from western Europe to the Levant, it was inevitable that the Ionian islands should be a source of constant conflict.

Corfu had suffered brief attacks during the 5th century from Vandals and Goths, the destroyers of the Roman Empire in the West, but it was not until the eastern Empire lost its possessions in southern Italy that the Ionian islands again became vulnerable to invasion. This time the predators were the Normans. At the time when William the Conqueror

was establishing Norman control over England, Robert Guiscard, Duke of Apulia, defeated the Byzantine army and its emperor, before dying of a fever at Cephalonia. His nephew Roger, King of Sicily, occupied Corfu in 1146 and held it for six years. As the Byzantine hold over the islands weakened, the Venetians came in as reluctant allies.

These allies soon proved to have territorial ambitions of their own. The islands were situated on important trade routes to the eastern Mediterranean, and commercial interests led to the desire for political control.

After the sack of Constantinople in 1204 during the Fourth Crusade, the islands were divided into fiefdoms among noble Venetian families. Not until 1387 however, were the islands brought under direct Venetian rule, which continued through a succession of Ottoman attacks down to 1797 when under the new order created by Napoleon's conquests, the islands went to France.

During these four centuries, the Ionian islands were ruled by local nobility and by administrators sent out from Venice. The influence of the Republic was felt in the introduction of cash crops such as olives and currants, in the repressive regime under which the peasants worked and in the Italian language which the nobility affected to speak.

At first Venetian rule was energetic – so that, for example, after Ottoman raids had left Zákynthos virtually uninhabited in the late 15th century, vigorous resettlement policies soon created the basis for new prosperity. Zákynthos had only 36 families in 1485, but 752 families by 1516, and her revenues increased forty-fold in 30 years thanks to the introduction of these valuable crops.

Corrupt: By the 18th century Venice had lost her possessions in the Aegean and the Peloponnese; in the Ionian islands, her last remaining stronghold, Venetian rule was corrupt. The islands were ravaged by pirates based on Paxos and the Albanian coast;

imperfect themselves, were rendered wholly null by the corruption of the judges".

The end of Venetian rule was bloodless: when the French invaders arrived, they discovered the fortress guns rusting and the garrison without any gunpowder. Napoleon himself had written in 1797 that "the great maxim of the Republic ought henceforth to be never to abandon Corfu, Zante..." However, British troops managed to establish a foothold in the minor islands in 1809. After Napoleon's defeat this was extended and the new Septinsular Republic was placed under British protection.

The British found a backward society at least by their lights: wheeled transport was virtually unknown on several islands owing

internally, blood feuds and political assassination made life precarious.

Henry Holland wrote in 1812: "The governors and other officers sent to the island were usually of noble family and often of decayed fortune; men who undertook the office as a speculation of interest and executed it accordingly. Bribery and every mode of illegal practice were carried on openly; toleration for a crime might easily be purchased; and the laws, in many respects

Left, Dionysios Solomos, national poet and the Ionians' most famous son. Above, a watercolour of Ithaki harbour.

to the appalling roads; the superstition of the priests was such that they opposed the introduction of the potato to the islands on the grounds that this was the apple with which the serpent had tempted Eve in the Garden of Eden. At the same time, the inhabitants of these islands were demanding the most modern of political institutions. Sir Thomas Maitland, the first Lord High Commissioner – in the words of a Victorian historian – "reconciled these incongruities by establishing a Constitution which, possessing every appearance of freedom, in reality left the whole power in his hands".

Autocratic British rule brought the islanders the benefits of improved roads, drainage schemes and, not least, the game of cricket. But it could not satisfy the islanders' desire for freedom from foreign rule, a desire which intensified after the creation of the Kingdom of Greece in 1832.

The Cyclades, Sporades, Saronic Islands: The Cyclades, unlike the Ionian islands, were a commercial backwater: main trade routes passed through Crete and the eastern Aegean islands to Smyrna and Aleppo. While they remained a lure to pirates, they were never of comparable interest to major powers. Until the rise of the seafaring Italian city-states in the 11th century, most trade in the Aegean was in the hands of Greeks.

However, the weakness of the Byzantine navy was underlined by a series of Arab raids against the islands and the Greek mainland. By the 12th century a British chronicler noted that piracy had become the curse of the Aegean: many of the islands were abandoned, while others – Skýros in the Sporades, for example – became pirate lairs.

The sack of Constantinople in 1204, which brought the Ionian islands under Venetian control, also brought new masters to the Aegean. The unimportance of this group of islands to them meant that the Venetians were content to leave the task of occupying them to private citizens. Of these, the most successful was Marco Sanudo, a nephew of the Doge Dandolo, who equipped eight galleys at his own expense and sailed to the Aegean where he founded the Duchy of Náxos in 1207.

Náxos itself became the capital of a fiefdom of some islands, and on it Sanudo built a castle, erected a Catholic cathedral and provided solid fortifications for the town. Other adventurers helped themselves to islands such as Andros and Santoríni. The Ghisi family obtained Tínos and Mýkonos, as well as the islands in the Sporades, establishing a dynasty which clashed with the Sanudi until both were overwhelmed by the Ottoman navy in the 16th century.

Traces of the Venetian presence are to be found both in the Catholic communities which survive on Sýros and Tínos, and also in local family names which betray a strong Italian influence. The Duchy of Náxos lasted over 350 years, and only ended with the death of Joseph Nasi, the Sephardic Jewish favourite of Selim II, upon whom the Sultan had be-

stowed the islands after their capture from the Sanudi.

But the exceptional longevity of the Duchy of Náxos should not be allowed to obscure the turbulence of life in the Aegean in these centuries. Piracy had increased in the late 13th century, with Greek corsairs from Monemvasiá or Santoríni, Sicilians and Genoese – and had led, for example, to the inhabitants of the island of Amorgós to emigrating *en masse* to Náxos whose fertile interior was relatively inaccessible.

In the 14th century, Catalan mercenaries, brought in for the conflict between Venice and Genoa, ravaged some of the islands and raided others. Ottoman troops landed on

Náxos and took 6,000 captives. The Ottoman forces often consisted of recent converts to Islam, and were led by renegade Aegean Greeks such as the notorious brothers from the island of Lésvos, Khair-ed-din and Amrudj Barbarossa.

Local rulers began to complain of depopulation: Andros had to be resettled by Albanian mainlanders; Ios, virtually uninhabited, was replenished by families from the Peloponnese. Astypálaia was repopulated in 1413, abandoned in 1473 and only inhabited once more after 1570. In the 16th century, the islands suffered a series of attacks by the Turkish navy and by mid-century Venetian influence was on the wane. Within 50 years, most of the islands had been brought under Ottoman rule, though the last, Tínos, only succumbed as late as 1712.

Conditions of life did not improve under Ottoman rule. Piracy, famine and fatal disease remained the perennial problems. In the 18th century, the plague decimated the islands on four separate occasions, continuing into the next century, well after the disease had died out in most of Europe. Thus the Ottomans, like their predecessors, were forced to repopulate.

Early visitors: Often the new colonists were not Greeks. Tournefort reported in the early 18th century that most of the inhabitants of

Antiparos were descended from French and Maltese corsairs. He also noted that villages on Andros were "peopled only by Albanians, dressed still in their traditional style and living their own way, that is to say with neither creed nor law".

It was the Albanians who were to play a major role in the struggle for Greek independence. Waves of Albanians had been colonising the islands of the Aegean since the 14th century. They were concentrated on the Saronic islands – the eminent Koun-

Left, detail of Skýros embroidery, probably 17th-century. **Above**, watercolour of Náxos, 1795.

douriotis family, for example, moved from Epiros to Hydra around the year 1580. By the late 18th century, Hydra, with a largely Albanian population, possessed one of the largest and most powerful shipping fleets in the Aegean, which played no small part in defeating the Ottoman Turks after 1821.

The importance of these islands was underlined by the choice of Aegina, for a short time, as the first capital of the new Greek state. Refugees flocked here when it was the seat of government, only to leave again when Nafplion replaced it. When Edouard About visited the town in 1839 he reported it "abandoned – the homes that had been built tumbled into ruins, the town once more became a village; its life and activity fled with the government".

The Northeast Aegean Islands: Although the east Aegean islands shared the experience of Arab raids with the Cyclades, the two areas developed differently as the rivalry between Venice and Genoa increased after the Fourth Crusade. As allies of the resurgent Byzantine Empire against her Latin enemies, the Genoese were given trading rights in the Black Sea and granted permission to colonise the eastern Aegean.

A Genoese trading company controlled the *mastic* plantations of Chíos from the beginning of the 14th century. In 1333 Lésvos passed into the hands of the Gatteluso family, who eventually extended their control to Thássos and the other northern islands. However, as in the west Aegean, the power of the Ottoman navies simply overwhelmed these local potentates, and with the fall of Chíos in 1566 all the islands of the east Aegean passed into Ottoman hands.

Lésvos had been conquered by the Ottoman Turks as early as 1462, and most of the inhabitants emigrated. In 1453 the inhabitants of Sámos fled to Chíos, but returned to the deserted island in the 16th century. Belon du Mans, who visited the island around 1546, wrote: "It is striking that an island like Sámos must remain deserted. The fear of pirates has rendered her uninhabited so that now there is not a single village there, nor any animals".

Despite the islands' proximity to the mainland, they attracted only a small number of Muslim colonisers, and the bulk of the population remained Greek, supplemented by the inevitable Albanian immigrants. Only on

Lésvos were Muslim settlers to be found farming the land; elsewhere they stayed close to the towns.

The 1821 insurrection sent shock waves through the islands. Sámos was first; the unrest then spread to Chíos where, in 1822, the Ottomans brutally suppressed a rather uncertain revolt. Fustel de Coulanges wrote in 1856: "Any person aged more than 32 years whom one meets today on Chíos was enslaved and saw his father slaughtered". It was little consolation to know that the massacre on Chíos had aroused the attention of European liberals, and strengthened philhellene sentiment.

Refugees fled westwards, transporting the

were bought by middle-class Greeks who became an increasingly powerful force in the aging Ottoman Empire.

By the end of the century the Ottoman hold had become tenuous: Sámos, for example, had maintained a certain autonomy under a traditionally Christian prince. And on Thássos the Oxford don Henry Tozer found in 1884 that there were no Muslims there apart from the governor himself and a few soldiers. Since the people had to pay neither the "head tax" – universal elsewhere in the Ottoman Empire – nor Ottoman trade duties, it is not surprising that they appeared content with their system of government.

The Muslim islanders, on the other hand,

island's traditional *loukoumi* industry (the making and selling of Turkish Delight candy) to Sýros in the Cyclades, whose port of Ermoúpolis became the busiest port in the new Greek state. Other refugees settled in Alexandria, Trieste, Marseilles and as far north as Amsterdam.

Elsewhere in the east Aegean, the changes were just as great. The Ottoman authorities were only able to suppress the rising with the aid of Mehmet Ali and his Albanian mercenaries who had as little respect for the local Muslim notables as they had for the Greeks: many Turkish landowners sold up and emigrated to Anatolia, while their properties

continued to leave for the mainland. Even before the Greco-Turkish population exchange in 1923, the Turkish communities on Chíos and Lésvos had dwindled away. Their place was filled by a mass of Greek refugees from Anatolia.

The Dodecanese Islands: The 14 or more islands, misleadingly known as the "Dodecanese", (*dódeka* means "12") suffered as elsewhere from the collapse of Roman authority. They were repeatedly attacked and plundered. When the Arabs occupied the island in AD 654, they broke up the remains of the Colossus of Rhodes and sold the bronze for scrap on the mainland. The Byzantine hold remained firmer here than it did in the west, but after 1204 these domains were also ceded to Frankish adventurers in return for nominal acknowledgement of Byzantine sovereignty.

By the beginning of the 14th century, Venice had helped herself to those two crucial stepping stones to the East, Kássos and Kárpathos. At the same time, Rhodes, which was held by Genoans and Venetians, was bartered away to the Knights of St John, a military order which, after the loss of Jerusalem in 1187, had been based in Cyprus since 1291. Fulke de Villaret, the first Grand Master of Rhodes, reconstructed the city.

But, although the island had thus been able

The island's inhabitants were compelled to leave the town of Rhodes and settle outside. But because the Ottomans never made up more than one-third of the population, their overall influence was never that strong. Since the land on many islands was difficult to farm, the islanders looked elsewhere for their livelihoods.

Many became seamen, while on Kálymnos and Sými the tradition of sponge fishing prospered. In 1521, the islanders of Kálymnos paid homage to Suleiman II with sponges and white bread to demonstrate that "sponge fishers do not cultivate corn, but buy flour – and only of the best quality". During the 19th century, the sponge fishers went interna-

to withstand a siege by the Ottomans in 1480, not even the Knights of St John could hold off the Ottoman threat indefinitely. In 1521 they were outnumbered by a massive Ottoman force over 100,000 strong, and after a siege lasting several months the starving defenders were forced to capitulate. With the fall of Rhodes, the position of the neighbouring islands was undermined, and by 1537 they had all been incorporated into the formidable Ottoman Empire.

Left, the sea battle of Sámos; watercolour from 1824. **Above left**, the Colossus of Rhodes. **Above right**, 19th-century drawing of Kássos girl.

tional opening agencies in London, Frankfurt and Basle.

Unexpected liberation: But these developments, typical of the growing Greek middle class, did not lead to union with Greece until late in the day.

The islands had been intended for the new Greek state in 1830, but were retained at the last minute by Turkey in return for the mainland island Euboea. Liberation from the Ottoman Empire came unexpectedly through the occupation of the islands by the Italians during their war with the Turks in 1912.

At first, the islanders welcomed the Italians. A congress on Pátmos passed a resolution thanking the Italian nation for delivering them from the Turkish yoke. However, another resolution at the same congress calling for unification of the islands with Greece was less satisfactory to the local Italian commander who broke up the congress and forbade such public meetings.

The Italians did not intend to hold the islands permanently but, with the dismemberment of the Ottoman Empire, their dreams of establishing a foothold in Asia Minor led them to renege on a promise made in 1920 to return the islands to Greece. Mussolini sent groups of reluctant administrators to turn the islands into a fascist colony. In the early 1930s, many islanders emigrated to the main-

their brief and very brutal occupation, to exterminate the ancient Jewish population, much against the evident wishes of the islanders, the Italians and even some of their own soldiers.

It is understood that now, only three survivors of the Jewish community remained on Rhodes. Just a few months after the Jews had been deported, the islands were occupied by the Allies, who finally handed them over to Greece in 1947.

Crete: The "Great Island" has had the most violent history of all: its strategic position, agricultural riches and, not least, its inhabitants' fierce and unbroken tradition of resistance to foreign oppression have all ensured

ΣΚΗΝΗ ΕΝ ΚΡΗΤΗ ΚΑΤΑ ΤΟ 1866.

land, Egypt and Australia.

For those who remained, life had to be endured under the farcical prohibitions of a totalitarian regime: an extensive secret police network guarded against nationalist activity; the colours of the Greek flag – blue and white – were prohibited in public; all shop signs had to be painted in Italian. Slogans such as "*Viva la Duce, viva la nuova Italia imperiale!*" were daubed on the walls of recalcitrant shopkeepers.

But the process was brought to an abrupt halt by World War II. Once Italy surrendered in 1943, the islands were taken over by the Germans who managed, in the course of

this. From AD 823, when it was conquered by Arab freebooters out of Alexandria, who made it the centre of the slave trade and a springboard for pirate raids throughout the Aegean, the strategic importance of Crete has been obvious.

Around 3000 BC, a prosperous civilisation spread its influence throughout the Aegean. The Minoans, whose rituals have filtered down to us through the legend of Theseus and his labyrinthine struggle with the Minotaur, left proof of their architectural genius in the ruined palaces of Knossós and Phaistós. Daring soldiers, they appear to have preferred commerce to agriculture. They established outposts in the Peloponnese and made contact with the Egyptians.

By 1500 BC, Cretan civilisation had reached its zenith. But then the island was shaken by a series of disasters: a stupendous volcanic eruption on the island of Santoríni (Thíra) unleashed a tidal wave that damaged settlements along the north coast, and barely a generation later, most of the important sites in central and southern Crete were destroyed by fire. But the causes of the wider disintegration of Minoan control remain a mystery. Only Knossós continued to be inhabited as Cretan dominance in the Aegean ended.

In the early 13th century, Venice and Genoa tussled to wrest the island away from the helped pass on ideas from Crete to enrich the renaissance in western Europe.

Though the Venetians developed the towns and fortresses on the north coast, they knew how little they were loved by the Cretans. In 1615 a certain Fra Paolo Serpi had warned that "the Greek faith is never to be trusted," and he had recommended that the people "must be watched with more attention lest, like the wild beasts they are, they should find an occasion to use their teeth and claws. The surest way is to keep good garrisons to awe them". Under such a regime the peasants were probably worse off than under the Turks on the mainland.

Occasionally, as in 1263 and 1571, there

waning Byzantine Empire. Although Venice ultimately turned Crete into a prize possession, Byzantine influence remained strong. The old Greek noble families survived, while ties with Constantinople were reflected everywhere in church art and secular literature.

This strong Byzantine tradition became crucial after 1453 when the island gave refuge to exiles fleeing the Turks, and briefly became the centre of a renaissance of Byzantine culture: artists such as Dom. Theotokapoulos, otherwise known as El Greco,

Left, oil painting of the 1866 Cretan Revolt. **Above**, Irákleion at the turn of the century.

were major uprisings which the Venetians harshly put down. After one such revolt, 300 people were executed and many exiled, their villages were burned and razed, their property confiscated and other severe penalties exacted. In 1538 the coasts were laid waste by the pirate Khair-ed-din Barbarossa. On top of all this, the inhabitants faced other – natural – terrors such as the famine which in 1626 reduced the population of the island by one-fifth. In these circumstances it is not surprising that the Venetian presence on the island remained small and that Roman Catholicism never became widespread.

Venice kept its hold on Crete long after

most of her other Aegean possessions had been surrendered. But, in 1645, the town of Chaniá fell to the Turks and, in 1669, after a siege lasting two years, Irákleion fell too and the entire island came under Ottoman rule. By this time, the Ottoman administration had lost much of its early vigour: in the early 18th century one commentator described Irákleion as "the carcass of a large city… little better than a desert".

Cretan converts: In an effort to escape the burdens of Ottoman rule many Cretan families converted to Islam, especially during the 18th century, on a scale unknown elsewhere in the Aegean. But these converts continued to speak Greek, drink alcohol and had names

such as Effendakis and Mehmedakis, which were a bizarre jumble of Greek and Turkish elements. Villages continued to be called by their Greek names even after all their inhabitants had converted.

From 1770 onwards, a series of revolts broke out against Ottoman rule. But it was to take more than a century before they succeeded in their aim of independence in a Greek state; nevertheless these insurrections altered the balance of power on the island as many Muslim farmers sold out to Christians before moving, first to the coastal towns, and then, at the turn of the century, away from the island altogether.

These revolts also had a catastrophic effect on the island's economy. Passing through the interior shortly after the 1866–69 insurrection, Tozer noted: "Every village that we passed through, and all that we could see along the hillsides, had been plundered, gutted and burnt". Even today, abandoned villages are not an uncommon sight in the countryside inland.

In 1896, when the next major revolt broke out, the inadequacies of Ottoman rule were so evident that the European powers stepped in. For example, on the whole of the island there was just one short stretch of carriage road which went from from Chaniá to Suda Bay; and as William Miller reported in 1897, in Irákleion, the largest town on the island, there were no carriages at all "for the two that used to exist were last employed for the conveyance of the admirals on the Queen's Jubilee last year, on which occasion the bottom of both vehicles fell out, and the distinguished officers had to walk inside the bottomless machines".

Troubles in Ottoman Crete in 1897 provoked a wave of sympathy on the mainland. Greek naval forces were sent to the island while the army marched northwards – only to be checked by the Ottoman forces who pushed back down into Greece. This defeat was humiliating for the Greeks, but it proved only to delay the future enlargement of the kingdom for a while.

The following year the island of Crete was made an independent principality under Ottoman sovereignty. The new prince was, significantly, a member of the Greek royal house. The writing was on the wall and within a few years union with Greece had finally been achieved.

In 1909, political change was once again forced through by military means. Junior army officers staged a revolt against the political establishment in Athens and, at their invitation, a new politician with a radical reputation, Eleftherios Venizelos, came to Athens from Crete to form a new government. A consummate diplomat and a man of great personal charm, Venizelos channelled the untapped energies of the Greek middle-class into his own Liberal Party, which dominated Greek politics for the next 25 years.

Left, a watercolour of urban Cretan costume.
Right, a naïve painting of Eleftherios Venizelos.

The islands did not all become part of independent Greece at the same time. Only the Cyclades and their neighbours formed part of the original state in 1830. The Ionian islands were added in 1864, Crete and the Northeast Aegean islands in 1913, the Dodecanese only in 1947. Since several of the islands were wealthy ports at a time when Athens was still a village, it is scarcely surprising that their influence on developments in the new state was enormous.

In politics, the Hydriot families of Voulgaris and Koundouriotis, the Metaxas dynasty on Corfu, not to mention the Cretan Eleftherios Venizelos – in many ways the founder of the modern Greek state – all typified the vigour which the islanders brought to the political scene. Nor did their influence stop here: Greek literature was marked by the Ionian islands' close links with Italy, while Lésvos has produced both the Nobel Prize-winning poet Odysseus Elytis and the naïf painter Theophilos.

The islands' economic influence has also been profound, especially before the Balkan Wars of 1912–13 added the fertile regions of northern Greece to the impoverished state. The shipping fleets of the Aegean islands, currant and oil exports from Zákynthos and Kefaloniá, emigrant remittances from islanders scattered across the globe – from Romania to Australia to Florida – have all helped to bolster the periodically enfeebled economy of the mainland.

But islands had other uses, too. Límnos, under Turkish rule, was used as a place of exile for political offenders. Henry Tozer, who visited the island in 1884, learned that a former Grand Vizier had been living on the island for eight years and was "almost forgotten at the capital."

This policy did not cease when the islands became Greek. The dictator Metaxas in the 1930s sent his opponents to forbidding islands. During the civil war (1947–49), in which left-wing forces, which had formed a strong resistance to the occupying Nazis,

were suppressed, several barren islands off the Attica coast held prison camps for political detainees.

Fortunately, this was less the case when the Colonels came to power in Greece on the morning of 21 April, 1967. The junta was driven by a mixture of self-interest and hazy nationalism. In their policies and attitudes the Colonels drew on earlier traditions – with peasant or lower middle-class backgrounds, they symbolised a provincial reaction to a new world of urban consumers. Thus they

laid great stress on the need for a return to traditional morality and religion. They closed the frontiers to bearded, long-haired or mini-skirted foreigners – at least until they realised the implications for Greece's tourist trade.

Islands for outcasts: But other outsiders *were* confined to islands: one of the more magnificent relics of Aegina's moment as capital of Greece is the now disused prison, still more or less intact. And the fortress islet of Spinalónga, off the northeast coast of Crete, after a long career as Venetian outpost and Turkish village, was used as a leper colony until the late 1950s.

Today tourists can visit the ruined fortifi-

Left, Cretan peasant, about 1950. **Above**, a pelican once started an inter-island feud between Mýkonos and Tínos.

cations of Spinalónga on day trips from Crete, signalling perhaps a sort of economic progress, as tourists bring in money the islanders once only dreamed about.

These new arrivals indicate the most recent transformation of the islands – into places of pleasure. Mass tourism is one aspect of this, but the trend was seen most clearly in the vogue which began in the 1950s among shipowners to acquire islands for their private use. When Niarchos bought Spetsopoúla in the Saronic Gulf in 1958, he was swiftly imitated by his rivals, and real estate prices for barren islets off the Peloponnesian coast soared. With extensive investment in consumer goods, radar and

police personnel, these rocky outcrops were to become mid-20th century equivalents of Circe's island. How ironic that this vogue should have coincided with an unprecedented wave of emigration from the larger islands. Of course, there had always been movement of people from island to island, but in the 1960s the exodus accelerated rapidly.

Several reasons lie behind this failure to emigrate until the latter half of the 20th century. In the first place, would-be emigrants were constrained by the availability of transport. An extreme case of such isolation was to be found in Gávdos, an islet off Crete. According to Spratt, who visited there in

1865, the inhabitants did not see a boat approach for months on end, and he himself disembarked among naked swimmers who he found were "primitive in their habits and ideas… a mixed and degenerate race." Thus, to some extent, the opportunities for emigration depended upon improvements in transport and communications.

In the second place, several islands initially prospered upon incorporation into the Greek state. Sýros, for example, became the most important port and manufacturing centre in Greece in the first few decades after 1830. Even after the rise of Piraeus it remained an important centre where the standing may be gauged by the fine 19th century villas and warehouses of its capital Ermoúpolis. On other islands, such as Andros and Náxos, the late 19th century was a period of rapid exploitation of mineral resources.

By World War I, however, much of this activity had slowed down, and emigration both to Athens and abroad was increasing. With the collapse of international trade between the wars, this trend was interrupted for several decades, but it gathered pace once more with the European economic "miracle" of the postwar years.

Improved communications: By now, the road and rail links between Greece and western Europe had been modernised. So, too, had links between the islands and the mainland: the first air connection with Athens had been established as far back as 1927 by the Italians, but it was only in the 1960s that aerial links with the Aegean were extended. In the same period, car ferries were introduced. These developments opened up the closed societies on the islands.

Improved communications also opened up the closed island economies – which had come close to starvation during World War II – to a new world of consumer delights. In Athens newcomers from the islands formed closely-knit communities, each with its own clubs and cafés – islands of familiarity in an ugly urban sprawl. Many moved further afield – to Italy and West Germany.

Thus, even as the era of mass tourism brought western Europe to the Greek islands, the islanders themselves had gone off to find western Europe.

Left, fishing boats are hired by tourists in the summer. **Right**, an island washing line.

Early evening on Chálki in the Dodecanese and the sun sets behind the crusader castle, high above the village, turning the sands of Pondamos Beach a deep rose colour.

Michaelis Perakis, 18, leads his donkeys down to drink from the trough in the rocks and fills his plastic containers from the watering hole. Chálki has no fresh water, rivers or springs, and relies on the water boat to bring supplies. Daily life revolves around stocking up cans, filling cisterns (known as *stérna*) and making sure the animals – for many families the only form of transport or wealth – get properly watered.

It's summer and Michaelis, studying to be an electrician in college in Rhodes, is home for the holidays. His mother, Lefkosia, aged 40, one of the island's best cooks, has just opened a small taverna down on the harbour. Once a week during the tourist season she carts her pots and pans, slabs of ice and ingredients by donkey or three-wheel dumper truck up to Chorió, Chálki's deserted village, where she caters to a small group of British visitors who make special evening trek up to the castle.

There's no electricity so Lefkosia cooks by gas by the light of oil lamps in the old school room where she used to attend lessons. It's a real family affair. Michaelis waits on tables, sometimes helped by his 20-year-old sister Katholiki. Their father, Stavros, prepares the charcoal grill for the *souvlákia* and roast lamb, gathering sticks and handfuls of aromatic herbs, while young Metaxas, 12, dragged away from his BMX bike, gets under his mother's feet. He's usually first to sample the food – homemade *taramasaláta*, meatballs, stews, *dolmádes* and fresh fish. Bread is baked to Lefkosia's own recipe in the village bakery.

Stavros, 54, known to everyone as Fanos, has his own fishing-boat. When he's not out laying his nets with Metaxas or bringing in the catch he prepares food and helps his wife in the harbourside taverna.

The Perakis family is well-off by Chálki standards. As well as the new taverna and the fishing boat they keep flocks of sheep in the mountains and make a living selling the wool and meat on Rhodes. Once fertile, the island became barren when seawater seeped into the boreholes. Now the islanders grow nothing except olives, and goats nibble where a dairy herd once grazed.

The soil is rich and if plans to lay water pipes under the sea from Rhodes ever materialise the island could flourish again. Meanwhile, Chalkians rely on all their food and produce coming in by boat, or go on shopping trips to Rhodes.

From riches to rags: Once rich with copper (hence its name) and a major sponge-fishing centre, the island's population has dwindled from around 3,000 in its heyday to a paltry 300. As the sponge industry declined, Chalkians left in droves to seek their fortunes in Tarpon Springs in Florida. Chorió became deserted as people moved down to Emborió, the harbour, when the grand old sea captains' houses crumbled.

In 1987 the Greek government stepped in to bring work to Chálki and under a UNESCO scheme declared it the Island of Peace and Friendship. A hotel was built for foreign tourists in the derelict olive oil factory and local people were given jobs restoring the houses. For the first time package tourism came to Chálki.

"Tourism has brought new life to the islands," said Lefkosia, smashing huge slabs of ice with a meat cleaver to keep her retsina cool. "Before, we were very poor; there wasn't work. But now there are new jobs and new opportunities."

Life on Chálki is unavoidably bound to Rhodes. There's no senior school on the island so for further education children have to go to Rhodes which means, especially in the case of the girls, mother goes too.

Many women have second homes or stay with relatives on Rhodes during term time, returning to husbands and younger children at weekends. Grannies and aunts all help raise the children. While Katholiki was at school Lefkosia lived in Rhodes with Metaxas for four years, working in a taverna and returning home to Chálki in summer. Chalkians are used to this split way of life.

Preceding pages: festive occasion at Olympos, Kárpathos; café society. **Left**, an island family.

But it's expensive and physically wearing. "It's very hard but there's nothing else we can do," said Lefkosia, in between boiling up a feast of snails (and chips) for the local shepherd community.

This morning she rose at 4am and did housework. She fed the sheep near the house, a traditional neo-classical villa at the back of the village. She gave milk to the lambs, fed the chickens, ducks and rabbits, then nipped onto the mountainside to pick *hórta* (wild greens) before going to the taverna.

"I cook all day for lunch and dinner. We usually close about 2am so I might get two hours' sleep if I'm lucky. When I have this group to cater for up here I don't have any

landers, the Perakis family works night and day in summer and spend little time at home.

In autumn and winter it's different. With no tourists around, it's time to pick olives and make the oil, or go fishing for the local equivalent of whitebait. Fanos catches fish for the family and is part of the island's co-operative, but other fishermen sell their wares from loudspeaker vans around the Rhodes suburbs. This affords them the opportunity to visit wives and school-age children based on Rhodes.

Lefkosia pours more coffee into the smart gold and white cups which all bear her name. She then plunges her hands into the *tsatsíki*, mixing the oil into the yogurt.

sleep at all. Tomorrow I'll be exhausted."

Some people manage to grab a nap in the afternoons, but in summer it's often impossible for those islanders involved in the busy tourist trade.

Home is basic by western European standards, quite comfortable by theirs. The kitchen has fitted units and a modern stove – Lefkosia's pride and joy – and there is a simple living room. Up the wooden stairs a vast bedroom houses three beds in a row for the children, a cubicle with a huge double bed at one end for Mum and Dad, and a giant colour TV. There's no bathroom, just an outside lavatory and shower. Like many is-

"It is difficult in the winter," she adds. "Especially if you are taken ill and have to go to Rhodes. If the weather's bad the boat can't sail. One girl had a miscarriage because she couldn't get to hospital on time." In winter she bakes the family's bread outside in the wood-fuelled oven. Lambs, too are spit-roasted outdoors. It's all very medieval. "It takes an hour to get the oven hot and an hour to cook the bread, and I also have to gather the sticks and make food for the animals."

Although Chálki has her own doctor, emer-

Above, in many island villages, bread is still baked in a traditional oven.

gencies and maternity cases have to be dealt with across the water – which is a two-hour trip in rough seas. Sometimes the storms are so bad the sea fills the tavernas, so boats are anchored out of the harbour in case they get smashed up.

Winter's hard for the young people who don't escape to Rhodes. Michaelis says he's lucky. While at college he can enjoy city life, like a trip to the cinema. But he's not a *kamáki* or playboy. He doesn't enjoy discos and prefers traditional Greek music and dance, particularly Chálki's own fast and furious *soústa*. He's the island's champion young dancer, and often leads the circles at any village festivals.

Kafeneíon society: When he comes home in winter, he tends the sheep brought down from the mountain for shelter. He might read at home, play football or go to the *kafeneíon* with his *paréa* (friends) to play cards or to have a go on the Space Invaders machine. The *kafeneíon* tends to be a men-only domain in winter where fishermen, shepherds and soldiers spin out the hours with blue videos and card schools.

In summer you'll see the more liberated Chálki girls in the cafeteria, especially when Greek teenagers from Athens, Rhodes or even America turn up for the holidays. But parents keep a watchful eye on them and you'll often see father whisking a protesting daughter home like Cinderella. In winter girls remain indoors and do embroidery or lace-making and learn to run the home. Some of them fraternise with the soldiers, much to the horror of the villagers.

The girls often see the soldiers as escape routes from a humdrum island life, especially with few Chálki suitors around. The island barracks has national service conscripts from all over Greece and village girls often think if they can land a husband from Thessaloniki, Athens or another big city, life will be rosy.

Dressed in army uniform one girl stole off with a soldier on the early morning ferry. The boatman's son noticed the "soldier" was wearing women's shoes, but didn't give them away. They telephoned her parents from Rhodes who insisted the couple should be married immediately because of the family shame. She was 14. And pregnant. Now the husband wants a divorce and she's back on the island, trapped.

"Girls like her are crazy," says Katholiki, who is training to be a hairdresser on Rhodes. "We all have the same opportunities but they ruin their lives."

Tourism may bring work to the island, but the influx of foreigners with Western ideas can lead to problems, she feels. The old ways and the new clash head on and young Greeks are the victims in the middle. It may be accepted that boys chase after tourist girls but if they have more serious intentions family and neighbourhood close ranks. Parents want their young to marry other Greeks. Not just because of religion: they know the rules and traditions.

"Life is still difficult for women in Greece," says Katholiki. "My generation wants modern things like bikes and personal stereos, and we want to mix with other people. But our parents and grandparents are years behind and don't understand. I think the gulf will narrow in time and the next generation will be free."

Spring is a favourite season for several members of the family. Lefkosia, a keen singer and dancer, enjoys stepping out at the festivals, particularly Easter which is always a time for great celebration.

The house is cleaned inside out on Clean Monday, *Katharí Deftéra*, when blankets and clothes are washed and the house is painted and whitewashed. The family goes on a Lenten fast (no meat or olive oil) and Lefkosia has to prepare pickled vegetables, lentils and special split pea soup.

As Easter approaches, she makes biscuits and dyes hard-boiled eggs red. On Easter Saturday the family's Paschal lamb is killed and she makes *patsás*, a special meal, with the innards, head and feet. On Sunday the lamb is roasted and it's party time.

But, at the moment, it is summer and the height of the tourist season. Down in the harbour at 3am Metaxas and Michaelis are fast asleep in the taverna, stretched out on chairs. Fanos is going fishing, and Lefkosia is washing up.

She isn't going to bed. Tomorrow will be another long day. "If only we had water here," she sighs. "My biggest hope for the future is our own fresh water so we could grow our own vegetables and fruit and have a proper tourist industry and real work for everyone. Yes, life here is very hard. But what can we do?"

ISLAND ELECTIONS

The time was clearly ripe when an island shopkeeper, an amiable old soul who liked poetry and had spoken warmly of his son's help in running the business, had the son by the throat and was spluttering with rage. The son, roughly twice his size, managed to break away and retreated into the road, howling. "The election," the old man explained, staring after him, "he just told me who he's voting for."

The candidates' posters had been going up for several days – as soon as the last of the season's charter flights had left. They showed the incumbent mayor wearing a benign and statesmanlike expression. The potential usurper was younger, had a large moustache, and affected the pose of a visionary. Gossip in the *ouzerié* revealed that "hate" would not cover what they thought of one another. The younger had once been hounded off the island – a suitcase literally thrown after him into a departing boat – for reasons that were never clear. He was back, they said in the *ouzerié*, for his revenge.

It would be difficult to exaggerate the passions aroused by island municipal elections. They are run on national party political lines, a passionate matter in its own right in Greece, but are wonderfully exacerbated by real as well as somewhat enigmatic local issues, the power of future patronage, and private feuds. Almost anything is capable of convulsing small, compressed communities of people who, at the time of the year when elections come round, have nothing else to do, are irascible after the strain of the tourist season, and are looking forward to a state-sanctioned opportunity to get cross.

The elections cannot be totally avoided, even if some islanders did wish to distance themselves from the flying fur. Voting is compulsory unless a voter can prove to have been more than 180 km (112 miles) from home on polling day. Failure to vote may lead to difficulties, for example, in acquiring a passport or having an old one renewed.

A previous election on a neighbouring island gave a foretaste of what might be in

Left, a message for the people: Communist Party posters stuck to a decorative wall.

store. It had been predicted that the result of that previous election would be extremely close, and one of the candidates had arranged a secret weapon – 30 registered voters who were living on the mainland but were willing to come back and vote for him. His opponent uncovered the plot and, in collusion with supporters at the mainland port where the returning voters had assembled, managed to have the ferry services to the island cancelled until after voting.

The Englishman telling this tale had been persuaded to fetch the stranded voters, an operation which involved sneaking away in his boat and collecting the voters under cover of darkness. After numerous complications

particular, the mayor's failure to live up to his promises about new ones.

The interpreter became restless, and if her translations were to be taken literally, all the committee's replies ended with statements like "…and if you believe that, sir, you are an idiot." When the interpreter stormed out, saying that she could stand no more of their lies, she confirmed the suspicion that she might support the other candidate.

Down the road, the opposition was asked what they thought the election was about. Their spokesman reeled off a list which concerned democracy, a caring society, organised crime, human rights. "But what about drains?" he was prompted by a bystander.

of an appropriately Byzantine nature, the small boat returned to the island top-heavy with voters and their baggage with minutes to spare. It tottered into the fishing port to the cheers of supporters and the speechless fury of the opposition. The election result was tipped by the secret voters, with only one vote to spare.

With this incident to draw on, the election committee of the present challenger was approached. "What are the issues?" they were asked through an interpreter, a girl who worked in the shop next door. They went into conference and emerged with a verdict: "Drains." So drains were discussed and, in

"What about drains?" he echoed.

"Well, the other party says…"

"No!" The opposition candidate held up an admonishing finger. A lorry had come to a halt outside the campaign office. A gang of workmen climbed down and attacked the cobbles with pick-axes under the noses of the committee. "You see, no problem with drains. New ones."

Two days before voting, the candidates made their speeches – the challenger down on the quay, the incumbent afterwards outside the church. The general idea was that the audience would move on from one to hear the other. A hugely amplified fanfare announced the start. "Ladies and gentlemen," a voice boomed from behind the as yet empty balcony, "I give you...Dimitris Prevezanos!" Four small boys let off compressed-air hooters to herald the grand entrance.

Dimitris Prevezanos, however, failed to materialise. Another fanfare, another introduction, more hooting – and still no Dimitris Prevezanos. Instead, a water pipe chose that moment to detach itself from a tank above the balcony. Prevezanos supporters, wearing Sunday suits, leapt out of the way.

"The drains," was the reply when asked what's wrong. "His speech was about drains. Now he must talk about something else. Maybe he can't think of something else."

The mayor did not mention drains, presumably because by then most of the main street and the quay had been dug up, as no one on the island could have failed to notice. He concentrated on broader issues like the new airport building and was prepared to stand on his record.

An army contingent arrived on the island for polling day. A man was running a book on the results, with a plastic bag stuffed with bank notes to cover all bets. When asked how much, he winked: four million drachmas. It says something about the island that he felt able to wander off from time to time and leave the bag unattended on a table.

The bets were settled at 8pm when red

It was a partisan opinion although when, third time lucky, the candidate did appear, he *did* have something to say about drains. He may have had other topics but the time taken to repair the pipe had to be subtracted from the time available before the incumbent went into action. When he finished speaking, the audience duly filed up the hill to listen to Kostas Papadoulis, the incumbent. The small boys passed their hooters to another set of small boys who would apply them to the task of getting Papadoulis re-elected.

Left, a political pow-wow. **Above**, two women discuss Greece's economic situation.

flares announced that the result was known: Papadoulis was back in office for four years. He was carried shoulder high around the village while a disappointed Dimitris Prevezanos was said to be packing for a further spell of exile, this time self-imposed, on the mainland.

The following morning, father and son resumed normal relations and – to almost nobody's surprise – the work on the drains ran into "technical difficulties" and ceased. They were not completed for the next big event on the calendar, Easter, and only just in time for the second, the charter flights which signalled the beginning of the tourist season.

The visitor is ambling along some majestic harbour at sunset, with the sea breeze between the masts of the yachts and caiques, and looking forward to a meal of fried octopus, washed down perhaps with a little diluted *oúzo*. What better way to top the evening than with some tinkling *bouzoúki* music? After all, isn't *bouzoúki* music the quintessence of all things Greek?

No. What most of the world believes is Greek music – urged on by record companies out to make big drachmas out of foreigners' ignorance – is really a Slavic-Turkish amalgam of insipid musical styles dressed up to become acceptable to the western ear and played on an instrument that itself has a Turkish name. The pear-shaped stringed instrument which is known as the *bouzoúki* takes its name from the Turkish word for "head." Its tinny tone is more suggestive of the steppes of Asia or the deserts of the Middle East than the bracing air and clear mountains of Greece.

Debunking the *bouzoúki*: The great *bouzoúki* myth was fanned to a flame by the *Zorba the Greek* fad in the mid-1960s, and has overshadowed the *real* Aegean music hidden away behind the false tavernas and blaring speakers. It has an altogether cleaner sound – gentler, nobler than the commercial pap being sold in Athens record shops and souvenir dens. The rhythms, often in unconventional time-signatures, are lilting and hypnotic. The melodies are exquisite, and the lyrics grapple with eternal human themes – the sea that took a loved one, the island mother who wonders if her sons will ever return from foreign lands, the precious days when the endless fishing can be laid aside and clean clothes can be donned for the festival of the Virgin Mary.

In the Ionian islands – Corfu, Zákynthos and Léfkas, for example – the Italian sound reigns. Its emphasis is on guitar and violin and western harmonic progressions, with somewhat Italianate orchestrating.

And then there's the music of the mountains – prouder and more heroic than the island variety. Again, this has nothing to do with commercialism. In mainland Greek folk music, clear notes of the clarinet dominate, its melody line whirling in incredible improvisation to the accompaniment of a plain guitar and a rudimentary drum.

As the catalogue continues, the great variety of Greek music becomes more apparent. Composers such as Yannis Markopoulos have successfully developed Greek folk themes into modern, orchestrated works of great emotional power. Mikis Theodorakis

is a name known to Europeans and Americans for more than 20 years, though his political activism has often let his artistic labours suffer. Manos Hadjidakis, the greatest modern Greek composer, forged an orchestral Greek sound that sells worldwide.

Greek music, of course, is as old as Greek history. The ancient music was monophonic – without harmonies – and its scales were apparently simple, probably much like an ecclesiastical chant line today. The scale of traditional Greek music is still five-tone, a system passed on to all the later peoples of the Middle East. The musician places notes not in the *do-re-mi* (C-D-E) order as western

Preceding pages: musicians on Kárpathos playing lyra and lute. **Left**, a music shop. **Right**, an island-hopping bouzoúki.

people do, but *do-do sharp-mi* (C-C sharp-E). It can be argued from this that Middle Eastern music, through the Byzantine Empire, is based on Greek models.

Over the centuries Greek became a crucible of musical influences. The wind of Africa blows in the relentless throb of the Cretan lyra. The gentle Aegean island songs have some of the tinkling Turkish *santdouri* (a zither-like instrument played with felt sticks) that brings out the echoing stretches of blue sea between the island mountains. Slavic ditties have long been the staple of the northern Greeks, while the Italian *cantate* brought the seven-tone scale into use.

Greece's lyrics were never divorced from

11/8 beats of Greek folk music today are the natural continuation – something western jazz musicians have only recently begun to appreciate and use in their music.

The Greek has always written music easily – although the term "written" hardly applies. He never had to sit down with pen and paper and worry about whether he wanted a 3/4 or 4/4, a major or a minor key, or whether he should drop a word because the bar could not hold another eighth note. He had it all ready in his soul, where there were no "bars" to confine what he felt. He was restless, so he pounded his feet on the floor, flung out his arms, tossed back his head.

Thus were born the laments out of which

the music, as they were in the West. From Homer onwards, both have been inseparable; instrumental music remains a relative rarity. While western theoreticians coldly dissected melody, harmony and rhythm and promulgated strict laws governing them, the untaught Greek felt no such restraint.

Western rhythm, for example, was boxed into a space measuring 3 by 4, out of which not even a Beethoven dared venture. The Greeks, on the other hand, adapted their music rhythms to the cadences of their speech. Homer's hexameter is the clearest indication of how ancient Greeks spoke in their inspired moments. The catchy 5/8, 7/8, 9/8 and even

modern Greek folk music springs. If this primitive dance-feeling came out as a regular 2/4 or 4/4, fine. If not, better still. The only rules were no rules.

The composer Mimis Plessas, a former jazzman who now accounts for a good portion of Greek movie soundtrack music says: "Imagine the field cry of the black man transported to Greece – that's what Greek music is."

Plessas relates an interesting account of a jam session with American jazz trumpeter Dizzy Gillespie in 1953. Being Greek, Plessas had no trouble fingering a nimble 7/8 folk rhythm on the piano – and promptly lost

Dizzy. "I can't do it – something's missing," said the great jazzman.

Rebétiko, rebétika: It is these odd rhythms that can be found even in *bouzoúki* music – the kind that is not too commercial and that accurately expresses the proletariat yearnings of the workers of Piraeus in the 1920s. This was the time of the *rebétika*, played in dead serious demeanour in smoke-filled basements where hashish and fast women were an evening's delights. The soundtrack of Costas Ferris's movie *Rebétiko* provides the clearest picture of *rebétika*, to be appreciated only by keeping in mind that it expresses the soul of just one small corner of Athens, and not Greece as a whole. One record album that

crescendo of pride, and one comes away purified as from an ancient Greek tragedy.

The Cretan Yannis Markopoulos brings an earthier tone into his themes. But, a dominant melodic line and pungent harmonies in just the right places give a power quite out of proportion to its component part.

Markopoulos's most celebrated work, *Periodia Proti*, is an album of instrumental music issued in 1978. Here, the magic of the Cretan lyra mixes with nostalgic melodies from the Asia Minor coast, an ancient homeland that the Greeks lost in 1922 and have never forgotten. Nostalgia, in fact, permeates the record. Markopoulos takes us to a purer, nobler Greece before the deafening

made Greek musical history is Manos Hadjidakis's *Gioconda's Smile* recorded in New York in 1964, a work that has not been equalled for sheer emotive power. While listening to it, one feel that this is indeed Greece: the Parthenon shining in the moonlight, the white sails in the breezy Saronic Gulf, the geraniums on the poor verandas, and a happy, hospitable people. No trace of Asiatic pessimism here, no tremulous halfnotes; but plenty of uniquely Greek timesignatures that clear the soul of its cobwebs. A breath of fresh air here, a tear there, a

Left, and **above**, a musical interlude on Zákynthos.

bouzoúki carried all before it.

But for a proper first contact with the roots of Greek music, one cannot do better than visit Athens's Dora Stratou folk dance theatre just behind the Acropolis. On warm summer evenings, as the cicadas buzz softly in the surrounding pine wood and the bustling city is out of sight and sound, the folk musicians appear to stroll out of another time. As the dancers whirl and leap, the traditional clarinet, guitars, lyra, *santdouri*, Thracian bagpipe and drum echo off the slopes. It is in such a place, rather than in the expensive *bouzoúki* tavernas and nightclubs, that one hears the authentic sound of Greece.

What *is* craft work and what isn't? Strictly speaking, it is something which is made individually or in small quantities out of local materials to serve some useful purpose, and so the definition covers textiles (including embroidery and weaving), lacemaking, pottery, wood work, basketry and some forms of stonemasonry and metal work. If the article is embellished so that the function of which it is technically capable becomes secondary, it becomes "folk art".

What neither definition covers is tacky souvenirs which materialise wherever tourists congregate in any numbers. As these are usually mass-produced, probably imported, completely impractical and only dubiously decorative, they fail on all counts.

Many of the craft pieces on display in Greek island homes are between 50 and 150 years old. Anything older would have required extraordinary care in order to survive under the rather spartan and at times extremely damp conditions which frequently exist in small stone-built island houses. A particularly fine piece of silk embroidery may have been handed down over several generations, but the same degree of attention is unlikely to have been extended to, say, a wooden utensil or basket. Really old objects of value are generally of a religious – rather than a secular – nature.

Vital clues: Greek island crafts are normally associated with, and identifiable as the work of, one or other of the island chains. A certain form of design and motif would be recognisably from the Cyclades, for example, and not elsewhere.

There are interesting exceptions to the rule, however: Páros, although geographically one of the Cyclades, has a dialect and crafts more closely related to the Sporades; while Skýros, which *is* one of the Sporades, has gone off on its own to become the odd man out in that chain.

Bed curtains, door lintels and wooden panels of the Cyclades use a standardised and repeated pattern of geometric motifs; Skýros,

Preceding pages: a summer evening in Corfu. **Left**, an 18th-century bed-curtain from Kos. **Right**, a carpet school in Santoríni.

on the other hand, has a preference for large birds, flowers and ships on wide-open backgrounds of white.

To enter a house in Skýros even today is to be taken aback by entire walls dripping in pottery, vases, plates, dishes – household articles in such numbers that there could not conceivably be a use for all or even half of them. It has always been so. As these collections represented a large measure of a family's wealth, security in troubled times in the form of pirates could be a problem. The

solution was to have a second home within the protective walls of the city fortress used exclusively for personal belongings.

It doesn't necessarily follow that these compulsive hoarders kept a large force of local craftsmen in full employment. Much of it might have come from abroad, or even from the pirates themselves. Nevertheless, Skýros did have its own craft industry, and an important one.

In the last century Greece tended to be a backwater. The islands were often cut off from one another by being subject to different political masters, isolated, and of necessity self-sufficient at a desperately low level of subsistence. The crafts flourished because what the islanders couldn't make for themselves they had to do without.

The economic changes of the present century, including the gradual move away from subsistence to a cash economy, made the islands more outward-looking, and there was a natural desire to acquire "prestigious" and costly foreign goods which made daily life less arduous.

As a result, fewer traditional objects were produced and those which already existed attained the value of relatively rare objects. A mother might therefore take embroidery which had been part of her dowry and cut it into pieces for daughters unable or not in-

clined to invest a similar amount of time and attention in their own marriage endowments.

The craft items most likely to be supplanted were things like embroideries and small wooden items for which there were cheap and more modern substitutes. Local production of large pots, for example, was prolonged because they were awkward to import and were needed in large numbers for carrying and storing water, cooking and a dozen other purposes. Eventually, however, even these considerations became immaterial, and within the past 50 years there has been little in the way of craft work which has not been overtaken by development.

There was always a very pronounced division of Greek crafts between those produced by men and by women. The latter went in for weaving, embroidery, lace and basket-making; the former for potting, wood and stone work. That in itself is not surprising, but some of the pragmatic implications may be less obvious.

The crafts practised by women tended to be more suited to being taken up for short periods and then laid aside at a moment's notice in order to attend to other pressing domestic duties.

On the whole, these crafts required no special equipment and could thus be carried out in or near the home. This fitted in well with the social conventions of traditional island society in which women were not as visible as men and, in particular, young girls of marriageable age were restricted in their contacts even within their own village.

In contrast, the men on the islands treated their work as a full-time job, performed it in premises reserved for the purpose, and relied on being able to call on colleagues to lend a hand whenever it was necessary.

Pride of place: Both men and women in their respective ways worked with local raw materials such as wool, clay and wood. If small quantities of silk, for example, had to be imported, it would be given pride of place in the finished article. They were producing goods only for themselves, or at most to fulfil a need within the immediate community.

The notion of producing a surplus for sale to other people was virtually unknown, although there were some famous exceptions to the rule: the itinerant Thrapsano potters of Crete, for instance, took just their skills from one island to another and worked with local clays. They were paid for their services in cash or goods.

It would be premature, however, to compose the final obituary for traditional island crafts; one needs only to travel to Skýros to see a thriving, albeit small industry. The dire necessity that put such a premium on the skills may have passed, but they are not yet dead. Production may be down to a trickle but the results, when the souvenirs are brushed aside, are still there to be seen.

<u>**Left**</u>, **many tourists choose textiles as souvenirs.**
<u>**Right**</u>, **women's crafts are done in short periods to allow for domestic duties.**

ZORBAS

PIZZA ZORBAS   390

SPAGHETTI BOLOGNESE   178

SPAGHETTI GARBONALA   250

SAGANAKIA   155

FRESH FISH (κιλο) per kg   1600

VILLAGE SALAD   146

POTATOE SALAD   77

The British popular press revelled in the case of a London grandmother who invested her £30,000 life savings in a restaurant on Rhodes and looked forward to a happy and prosperous retirement. Instead, she found herself locked up in a police cell with the prospect of spending the next five months there unless she bought off the sentence for the equivalent of £1,000.

The first lesson for any foreigner wishing to follow Mrs Molly Huddleston's example by starting a business on a Greek island is that the Greek legal process can all too easily begin rather than end with a spell in prison. Detailed prosecution, defence, litigation and so forth take place later, often much later. A knowledge of the law and the resolve to remain meticulously on the right side of it are therefore desirable starting points – although developing the knack of shadow boxing with an opponent of stupefying complexity is the ultimate triumph.

So where had Mrs Huddleston, 55, gone wrong? It was her belief that visitors to the island might occasionally enjoy "traditional British food" after so much Greek, and that is what she provided. Cucumbers and tomatoes are optional ingredients in a British salad, but she had forgotten (or perhaps had never known) that she was in Greece and that the contents of a salad are defined by law. Mrs Huddleston's salads were either light on the cucumbers and tomatoes or omitted them altogether, a serious matter.

Furthermore, while Mrs Huddleston was aware of the fixed price for a potato, she rashly assumed that she could charge a little more if she filled them with chilli sauce, a dish popular with her more discerning customers. That, too, went into the policeman's notebook.

Mrs Huddleston's misfortune was not a flash in the pan – the work, say, of a bad-tempered policeman with a grudge or a hangover. At the same time, at the other end of the Aegean, a young American chef had given up his job at a prestigious New York hotel to pursue the ambition of opening his own

Preceding pages: sausages for sale. **Left**, a taverna in Santoríni.

restaurant. He had never seen a Greek island, but the enthusiastic description by a Greek friend who knew the islands and of a restaurant that happened to be for sale on one of them made up his mind.

The friend was a lawyer, so Fat Ronnie, by nature a cautious fellow, avoided some of the pitfalls into which naïve foreign investors might plunge. The sale of bars and discos, in particular, is seldom cut and dried. The owner will probably open negotiations asking for a large lump sum for "goodwill", a percentage of turnover in perpetuity, and "rent". Buyers anxious to secure next year's place in paradise before this year's charter flight goes back should not be too eager to accept that all property transactions are concluded along such lines.

Legal advice may not be cut and dried either, however. On the smaller islands, there are probably no more than a couple of local lawyers (if any lawyers at all) and they will each act for one half of the population against the other. Being lawyers, they will respectively be at or near the top of ferociously polarised municipal politics and the make-or-break powers of patronage flowing from them. The foreign buyer ought to find out who the vendor's lawyer is (anyone would be able to tell them!) and proceed forthwith to the other one.

Lobster tale: Fat Ronnie had astutely, if unknowingly, overcome potential difficulties in that direction, but he was nevertheless faring no better, (and possibly rather worse) than Mrs Huddleston in Rhodes. Within a fortnight of opening, he had logged no fewer than 107 separate offences which, in addition to violation of the notoriously demanding cucumber legislation, included the extraordinary business of a consignment of lobsters which, although still alive and still kicking, were deemed by the inspectors to be "not fresh".

A bemused Ronnie tried to find out what it all meant. The 107 offences? Prison, undoubtedly, until and unless he bought off the sentence or, as Mrs Huddleston was proposing, appealed quickly to the European Court of Human Rights. The "not fresh" lobsters? If he couldn't produce a suitable receipt showing the precise date when he bought the lobsters, it was assumed that he had not bought them within the prescribed definition of "fresh" and therefore – presto! – his were not and the menu lied when it said they were. This was a compound offence, including a failure to meet the Greek equivalent of "truth in advertising".

The wisdom of business: The condemned lobsters were still alive when Ronnie had to destroy them under official supervision. At that point, Ronnie was seriously reconsidering the wisdom of starting his own business in Greece.

Foreigners who wish to pursue a career on an island writing books or poetry or painting

laws were drawn up by Greeks for Greeks. The fact that foreigners become entangled is nothing more than incidental.

The cucumber, tomato, fresh lobster regulations were designed specifically to give visitors a fair deal and to prevent profiteering. "The Greek government thinks all Greeks are crooks," a restaurateur – a Greek himself – explained. One of his colleagues, who was also a Greek, had been in court the previous year because he had charged more than the stipulated price of a fixed portion of chicken for what was a lovingly created authentic chicken curry with, in Greece, expensive extra ingredients.

The man in question was prominent in

– anything, in fact, which the islanders themselves would not normally be doing – will be made to feel tremendously welcome, and the island economies depend on the annual influx of foreign waitresses and barmaids. Greek men are fiercely protective of their own interests when it comes to filling well-paid summer jobs, but they will concede that it is sometimes necessary to employ women, and they would rather have foreign women in those menial positions than their own.

Potential competitors, however, are likely to feel the full weight of the Greek mountain of legislation. Before catatonic paranoia sets in they ought to remind themselves that the

local politics, and even the fact that his party was in power could not prevent the charges being taken through the courts.

Fat Ronnie had originally planned to serve French and Italian food, but the inspectors rejected his draft menu because, without special dispensation, restaurants must have a preponderance of Greek dishes on the menu in the interest of cultural integrity. The law was brought in commendably to inhibit the fast-food, sausages and chips blight that has ruined so many places pandering to the tastes of mass tourism.

A shrewd restaurateur might get round that problem by putting on the menu as much *moussaká* and other staple Greek food as the inspectors require and even keep a token supply in stock. The waiters, however, would delicately – and with great stealth – steer customers towards the specialities of the house. The government's good intentions in both respects, making sure that visitors are not overcharged and that the tourist areas are not reduced to anonymous cultural slag heaps, unfortunately have a tendency to backfire rather badly.

Learning the rules: In the wrong hands, moreover, the rules become lethal ammunition. Prospective foreign businessmen should divide their time between learning the rules and discovering acceptable ways of evading

bus owners and water-sport concessionaires is impregnable. Islanders have been warned by taxi drivers not to allow any passengers other than close members of family into their cars; bus drivers will remonstrate violently with anyone who offers a lift to a hitch-hiker; and it is not worth speculating about the continuing seaworthiness of an unauthorised boat accepting payment for sightseeing or waterskiing.

If this prospectus for foreign business on the islands is less than flattering, it could not truthfully be otherwise. The smaller islands have only a short period in which to earn the money that will sustain the population over the closed and unlucrative winter months, so

them. Their Greek neighbours would certainly approve!

The emphasis so far has been on restaurants, bars and discos because those are the businesses to which foreign investors gravitate. The action in other spheres is even rougher than in the entertainment field because it is not so much the law of the land which rules but that of the jungle no matter what the bureaucrats of Europe demand or try to legislate.

The protective self-interest of taxi drivers,

Left, having a coffee on Hydra; tile style. **Above**, Greek meals tend to be simply presented.

the competitive element to be found among entrepreneurs anywhere is telescoped accordingly. Mrs Huddleston chose Rhodes because she knew the island well, having thoroughly enjoyed many holidays there in the past.

There have been too many histories like Mrs Huddleston's sad case to pretend that they didn't happen. All the more merit, then, to the minority of foreigners who have had the dream of countless visitors lazing on a beach and who have been equal to pulling it off. Eventually, and in a curious, quintessentially Greek way, the islanders probably admire them as well.

MANAGING THE TOURISTS

Greece is a small place – just a jagged hump of rock, sand and grey-green vegetation that supports an indigenous population of 10 million. Yet every summer, that population nearly doubles with the influx of tourists. By the early 1990s, more than eight million tourists were descending on Greece and its islands and pumping more than $3 billion a year into the economy.

Apart from direct exports, tourism was the country's biggest foreign exchange earner during a period of severe balance of payments problems. Tourism had become, by all accounts, *the* national industry and in its honour Greece's first Ministry of Tourism was founded with Nikos Skoulas, a knowledgeable Greek-Canadian businessman, as first minister. Under his tutelage, a national consensus on tourism policy took shape. And none too soon: the future of Greek tourism into the 21st century depended on it.

Greece's limited resources and facilities had begun to be stretched to their limit. Every summer, the most popular island destinations – Corfu, Mýkonos, Rhodes, parts of Crete, Hydra, Aegina, Santoríni, Skiáthos – teemed with hundreds of thousands of visitors. From June until September, when tourist numbers swelled exponentially, streets that had been constructed for a donkey and one or two passers-by became a sea of slow-moving gawkers.

Natives with other business to conduct often lost their tempers – albeit in private. Hotels were booked up much ahead of time and some had to turn away foolhardy travellers who arrived without a reservation. Arid islands, to which water is supplied by tanker, had to ration water at certain hours of the day.

Beautiful island beaches were often packed with sun-worshippers lying only inches away from one another. Nude sunbathers, who were searching for the ultimate sybaritic experience, appeared more and more on family beaches. Native Greek islanders, whose pleasures and priorities centred around the church and the community, were not amused.

Sleeping under the stars: Still less popular

Preceding pages: sleeping rough by the harbour. **Left,** gearing up for a good time.

ISLAND HOPPING

Island-hopping may be the choice of the tourist, but ferryboats are for the convenience of the Greeks. This fact – conflicting, frustrating and woefully under-publicised – has been the undoing of many a holiday.

The pleasures of travelling from one island to another using the country's series of inter-linking routes are numerous. There is the never ceasing view – a bas relief pattern in blue of low, mysterious mountains. A chance to mingle with the Greeks themselves who pile on board with food, children, and as often as not, a *bouzoúki* or two. Plus, a unique opportunity to visit other islands not on the itinerary – 15 minutes in a port closely observed from the top deck can reveal much about a place and its people. A bustle of activity takes place within view – reunions, farewells, and the redistribution of a virtual warehouse of goods. Is that a piano being loaded on board? Is that crate of chickens really being exchanged for blankets?

Without advanced research, however, it's all too easy to fall prey to the worst aspects of island-hopping in the form of missed connections, being stranded, or – a particularly Greek pastime – sailing straight past a chosen island, and then having to make a two-day journey to reach it again. To travel wisely, it helps to be in possession of a few basic facts.

First, ferry journeys can be long. The trip from Piraeus to Crete can take anywhere up to 22 hours, an unenthusiastic prospect for anyone on a two-week holiday. Ferry journeys can be frustrating. Should a trip to one of the smaller islands terminate in the middle of the night, no one will bother to wake you even if you've paid for sleeping accommodation. Seasoned travellers always pack an alarm clock, just in case. However, this haste to disembark in darkness has resulted in more than one independent traveller finding himself on the wrong island altogether.

Less frequently, and with a commendable disregard for time, purpose, or duty, ferries have been known to lie banked on the water for hours on end, oblivious to the needs of fee-paying passengers. "The Captain wants to fish," was a first-mate's response to one agonised plea.

There are ways to circumvent these problems. One is to travel in the high season, when Greek transport is relatively organised and hydrofoils, caiques and the little known inter-island sub-routes are fully operative. A trip from Páros to Sífnos in the Cyclades, for example, will take about four hours in August (when ferries sail direct); and up to 20 hours in late September, when the only way to travel the minor distance between them is to return to Piraeus and head out again. Unfortunately, the high season is also the time when accommodation is at a premium.

Fortunately, there are a number of established ferry routes which provide satisfying island-hopping with a minimum of fuss for several months of the year. The best known are the central Cyclades route (Santoríni, Ios, Náxos, Páros and Mykonos) and the Saronic Gulf route (Aegina, Hydra and Póros). Another is by cruising the major Dodecanese; travelling between Rhodes, Kos, Kálymnos, Leros and Pátmos is easy.

Less well known, and therefore more satisfying, are the western Cyclades (Kythnos, Serifos, Sífnos and Mílos) and three of the four Sporades islands (Skiáthos, Skópelos and Alónissos). These chains depend on domestic – rather than tourist – travel and operate all year, albeit at a reduced level. Both Rhodes and Kos in the Dodecanese are hubs for several satellite islands which are easily reached in summer by tourist caiques and hydrofoils, and out of season by keeping a close eye on the cargo and passenger boats used by the locals.

Bookshops in Athens sell a monthly guide called the *Greek Travel Pages* which gives details of most sailings. A map is useful when studying it, for some islands are listed under the name of the island; some under the name of the port.

There is one final, vital rule: always leave plenty of time at the end of your holiday to travel back to Piraeus. Greek ferries may be cheap and cheerful, but international flights rarely linger.

One for the alarm clock, perhaps. ∎

were the thousands of young backpackers who arrived on the most crowded islands without a place to stay. They often had barely a drachma to their names, pushed up the island crime rate, and drove out quieter tourists. Many shelterless visitors were forced to sleep on rooftops or beaches with nothing but the stars for cover.

Ferryboats to several islands, acrid with the smell of churning humanity and petroleum fumes, were spilling over with Greek families, replete with bawling children and awkward bundles, and small cliques of impecunious tourists huddled against their backpacks. Seats on island-hopping airplanes were so hard to get they had to be booked two

neighbouring countries such as Turkey were attracting potential marina users away from Greece. It was an ironic twist – Greece's greatest tourist-related asset was its phenomenal 15,000 km (9,300 miles) of seashore – almost double that of Turkey – and it was barely being exploited.

Something had to give. Tourist arrivals and income were escalating annually. But international studies predicted an onslaught in the future of young, lower-income tourists as leisure time increased. In the 1990s, travel could become the largest industry in the world. By the year 2000, an estimated two billion travellers will tramp the globe in search of individualistic holidays.

months in advance, and Athenians with island homes found they had to reserve their seats in spring for the entire summer.

After a series of terrorist attacks in the 1980s, cruise ships berthed in foreign – rather than native – ports for a time. Marinas were congested with the huge yachts of moneyed Greeks and foreigners, the chartered yachts of temporary high-fliers, and the small pleasure craft of devoted boatmen and fishermen.

Many boats were turned away for lack of a berth and facilities were often minimal: marinas were little more than boat-garages, and

Above, 30 cruise ships serve the islands.

Government tourism officials decided to gear Greek tourism away from the mass market that brought in so many penniless backpackers, and to concentrate instead on specialised packages for the upmarket traveller. A programme had to be devised to put things right. This was done, but not without great difficulty.

The job fell to Mr Skoulas, first as General Secretary of the Greek National Tourist Organisation and later as Minister of Tourism, who used his managerial skills to coalesce disparate elements of the highly opinionated Greek tourism industry. Hoteliers, cruise ship owners, tourist agents and government officials eventually hammered out a national consensus: to develop selective (i.e. upper-income and specialised) tourism, and to build projects to support it.

Classical goals: The most immediate goals were to turn Greece into the first marine tourism country in the world, to build special programmes around Greece's Classical and Byzantine monuments and to develop a high level of professional services.

All this was in the name of building up quality tourism for the quality tourist. The emphasis would not be on quantity – in fact, controlling the number of incoming tourists would be a prime consideration. The idea was to avoid straining Greece's limited re-

sources and to increase tourism income by increasing *per capita* spending, i.e. by attracting the well-heeled.

One of the first measures taken was to forbid charter passengers to stay without an accompanying room reservation. This mainly affected the English, who numbered one in four arrivals. These roomless young travellers congregated on islands such as Corfu, sleeping in the open and spreading minor crime waves. The new measure put a stop to what Greek officials called "hooliganism" among young tourists.

National aims: The Greek government also put a halt to licensing accommodation cate-

gories on islands where there was an over-supply, in an effort to let supply shape the demand created by tourists.

Officials decided when permits would be granted based on available space, and prior availability of basics such as roads, water and sewers. At the same time, more permits were granted for the construction of four-star and five-star hotels.

"But beds alone cannot do it," as Mr Skoulas said. Officials pushed through a law giving up to 50 percent grants to build supplementary and entertainment facilities, especially in areas where no new beds were allowed. Such facilities included golf courses, marinas and tennis courts.

To corner the marine tourism market, a score of new full-service marinas were built and the existing ones improved and extended – all with the help of the European Union's Integrated Mediterranean Programmes.

Three schools of tourism management were established and advertising became a national affair, directed by the Ministry of Tourism and funded by both government and private tourist-sector money. The first campaign attempted was a $100 million three-year marketing programme – the largest ever attempted in Greece – which appealed to the upper-income tourist. Conservation programmes – to help save monk seals and sea turtles – have also been aimed at the tourist.

To the existing stock of 37 airports, which are mostly on islands, Olympic Airways have added 20-, 30- and 50-seater helicopters for "the people who can afford them". Luxury Greek cruise ships have increased to around 30, and harbours have grown bigger and more expensive.

Finally, the impact of terrorism within Greece has faded. Ironically, however, one recent crisis was provoked by reports of possible Kurdish violence in southern Turkey: this caused some German tour operators to switch their business to Greece with the result that, at one point, hotels on Rhodes threatened to be 70 percent overbooked in the peak holiday months of July and August.

Although, inevitably, the future of tourism in the Greek islands will not be all wine and roses, it will, as one tour operator put it, "be a heck of a lot better than it's ever been."

Left, young visitors contemplate Knossós. Right, tranquillity returns to the islands.

SEA, SUN, SAND AND SEX

"Where else," Air Chief Marshall Sir Christopher Foxley-Norris, GCB, DSO, RAF wanted to know, "would your bank manager offer to toss you double or quits when you want to cash a cheque?" He was also intrigued by the mice on the island, which on two successive nights robbed a trap and got away. On the third, he set the trap but forgot to bait it – and caught two mice at once. Sir Christopher was explaining what had persuaded him to buy a house on Skiáthos. The question always being put to people like him is whether in the first instance the appeal lay in island life generally, the Greek islands specifically, or in Skiáthos in particular. The answer is invariably "yes" to all parts of the question, but as the islands have changed greatly in recent years so, too, have the attractions which lure visitors.

An airport was built on Skiáthos in the mid-1970s and put the island within three or four hours of direct flight from northern Europe. The number of visitors multiplied many times over, and the queues waiting to cash cheques and change money at the bank would quickly have put an end to leisurely games of chance between Sir Christopher and his bank manager.

Skiáthos retains, against the odds, much of the charm that appealed to Sir Christopher, but it had to adapt to the mass market. The lexicon of modern tourism is four "Ss", the belief or hope that a beach in a hot country will produce the desired result: Sea plus Sun plus Sand equals Sex.

With probably the best beaches in Greece, 70 in all, Skiáthos was inevitably going to be the setting for many such expectations. The tourist industry boomed and gave the island a reputation as "the straight Mýkonos".

Until the construction of the airport, Skiáthos was typical of small, relatively inaccessible Aegean islands. The unmarried men on the island might have assumed that unattached women were old dears who shrouded themselves in black and hobbled about on sticks. If other types existed, they

were without exception under lock and key.

The Northerners disgorged from charter flights seemed to arrange matters differently. Many travelled as couples – but not enough, it was observed, to preclude a surprisingly healthy surplus of single women who, moreover, welcomed male company, not least local fishermen.

One of those early arrivals was a woman, now respectably middle-aged, who was to return year after year. Her annual pilgrimage began in Australia. What was it that made the immense journey worthwhile? "At home,"

she said, "I worked in an office and was one in a million. Here, everyone got to know me. I walked down the street and waved back to them, felt like a queen."

Was that the *only* reason? Australians are commendably candid straight forward: "No, I used to come for what all the single women were after: sex."

Traditional word, new meaning: The local response to this interesting turn of events was, if not a lexicon of their own, a password: "*kamák.*" To the older fishermen, it was simply what they called the trident used for spearing octopus. To the younger ones, the word retained some of the old meaning in

Preceding pages: foreign girl meets island boys. **Left**, idling on the beach at Paleóhora, Crete. **Above**, inspired by the view at Chaniá, Crete.

referring instead to the pursuit and conquest of foreign females.

Fumbling island novices couldn't believe their luck and probably interpreted it as a belated blessing from the notably randy deity on Mount Olympus. *Kamáki*, some decided, could be played as a divine game, in the way gods clocked up merit by doing good works. In the modern idiom, they played for points, as in bridge or billiards.

The rules of the game, with local variations, are supposed to be secret, and a request for details would normally be as productive as asking the mafia for their end-of-year profit and loss accounts. Lips can be loosened, however, by vanity (or perhaps a mis-

old Canadian girl who, the *kamáki* set were fascinated to learn, was a serving member of the Royal Canadian Mounted Police. The theoretical maximum of 10 points, which few expected ever to achieve, lay in the rarified realm of "North Korean and Eskimo" women.

Reversing the roles: While male-orientated hedonism in Thailand or the Philippines attracts criticism from certain quarters, *kamáki* reverses the roles and the female victims, if any, are willing. There are occasional casualties among the men, however, the result of hectic preparations for the opening of the *kamáki* season. Serious contestants will spend the spring energetically working on their

chievous sense of humour), so it is possible to reveal here that on Skiáthos points are awarded on a scale of one to 10.

An Englishwoman is worth just one point, while Germans and Norwegians are joint second-to-last and worth two. The criteria, *kamáki* contestants take pains to emphasise, are not concerned with individual or national performance. They reflect availability. The English are the single largest group of visitors to Skiáthos; Germans and Norwegians are roughly equal next in line.

At the time of this exclusive interview, the highest score possible on the island ("six, maybe seven") was invested in an 18-year-

physiques by lifting weights. The modern idea of Adonis, on the evidence of the past few years, is not only muscular but blond. Very blond.

The climax of spring training is the ritual anointing of heads with peroxide bleach, but stubbornly swarthy scalps may end up with an identity crisis which results in that sad *kamáki* casualty, the Greek piebald as the dark roots rapidly appear.

Frantic, untutored weight-lifting can also go horribly wrong. Like rabbits out of a hat, muscles can pop up where least expected, useless for all practical purposes and aesthetically very absurd.

On the whole, though, the results would seem to be satisfactory. "The boys are beautiful," said an American woman reminiscing about happy times spent on a number of Greek islands. "Personally, I've only been to bed with a couple of them, but I love looking at them. Women feel they're a long way from home, nobody would know, so… It helps if the boy can speak English but, if he can't that's okay too."

In response to a question based on inside information, she recalled that on the morning after the two occasions she remembered best, she was indeed asked for a photograph of herself.

If the nomination of the *Kamáki* King at

asked to read out loud, and conceivably then write a reply to, missives from their predecessors. The pressure was too great for one young woman who arrived on Skiáthos late in the summer with the intention of remaining over the winter. She wrote: "I arrived here carefree, honest and innocently trusting. It broke my heart when I had to acknowledge that you cannot trust 90 percent of what a Greek boy says to you, and that, however genuinely sensitive and warm he sounds, there are always ulterior motives behind the eulogy. It's sad, it's true, but then this is a Greek island."

A proposal of marriage: What the letter omitted was that she had received, and given

the end of the summer season is at all contentious, the collection of photographs could be introduced as evidence and influence the island jury. Failing photographs, letters (written on flights home with time to kill?) do almost as well.

While the majority of *kamáki* contestants have picked up basic conversational English over the years, their proficiency may not extend to reading or writing letters in return. Even the most stoical providers of *kamáki* points may feel slightly squeamish on being

Left, limited range of self-expression on Rhodes.
Above, the beginning of a brief encounter?

consideration to, a marriage proposal from a young fisherman who was the unchallenged *kamáki* champion of the season just then drawing to a close.

He had made it known, although not directly to her, that the intended marriage would last only until the following spring, when he would have to shed his conjugal entanglement in order to prepare for the defence of his *kamáki* title that summer. If that were not enough to demoralise the girl, she also discovered that at the end of the previous summer and on exactly the same principles, he had married – and subsequently divorced – someone else.

Having more than 50 inhabited islands, means having transport to serve them, and in shipping Greece has made its mark on the world business scene. Anyone who has experienced the airy ride over the blue Aegean waves, with the prows of the white ships rivalling the dazzling sun itself, knows the Greeks' affinity for their boats.

The golden days of the Onassis and Niarchos magnates, however, are over. With the death of Aristotle Onassis and, later, his daughter Christina, the dynasty which thrived on oil and the dubious utterances of gossip columnists has elected for a low profile. So, too, has Stavros Niarchos and his like. Greek shipping, in fact, is run from about one square kilometre of office blocks untidily clustered together in the port city of Piraeus, centring on the seafront Aktí Miaoúli, where international bankers in pinstriped suits rub shoulders with burly crewmen and dusky banana vendors.

There are fewer ships than before around Piraeus and the islands, too. It was in 1981 that the number of ships flying the blue and white Greek flag hit the 4,000 mark. But decline was swift and sudden. World trade slumped, the election of a socialist government in Athens frightened many business people, and Far Eastern countries grabbed a lot of business with their cut prices. By 1985 Greece's ships fell to about half the 1981 peak figures. Only recently has a slight rise been noted again.

Through it all, Greece's shipowners have shown themselves to be a resilient breed. Despite the frightening drop in the Greek-flag merchant fleet, very few of the 600-plus shipping firms jostling cheek-by-jowl in Piraeus actually went out of business. The reason was simple: they simply switched the flag on their ships. It takes just 6 hours of red tape to do this. Owners run down the blue and white and run up what are known as "flags of convenience". Countries such as Panama and Liberia, eager for new business, offer their flags plus minimal taxes. Shipowners in financial trouble grab this opportunity,

Preceding pages: a Mýkonos boat. Left, cruising in the Aegean.

thus saving thousands of dollars a day in operating costs.

The owners, too, remain emotionally, even mystically, committed to their businesses. Indeed, few satisfactions can equal that of gazing out of one's air-conditioned headquarters seven floors over the Aktí Miaoúli and watching one's ship come in, plying the waves among the myriad coastal and cruise vessels. It is this feeling of ranging, ocean-going freedom that has made Greek shipowners cling to their profession like barnacles on a hull.

"We sat here day and night watching the shipping crisis going from bad to worse," said shipowner Nikos Efthymiou. "We could do it because shipping is in our blood."

Shipwrecked: The same love affair has lasted a long time. When the first Greek tribes pushed down from the Balkan peninsula after 1900 BC, they found a highly developed shipping civilisation on the coasts and around the islands. Archaeologists believe thousands of ancient wrecks litter the floor of the Aegean Sea.

Two of the oldest wrecks in the Mediterranean have been located, dating back to perhaps 2500 BC, hundreds of years before the Greeks appeared on the scene and far too deep to be retrieved by presentday methods. Later wrecks are more common – and fortunately, accessible.

In the Roman era, between 150 BC and AD 300, hundreds of wooden ships criss-crossed the Aegean carrying Greece's chief exports: wine, olive oil and art. One work of art salvaged from a Roman wreck is a bronze likeness of Augustus Caesar, now being kept in an Athens museum.

Ancient traditions credited the ruler of the Minoan kingdom of Crete, usually termed King Minos, with building up the first real navy in the Aegean. Thucydides, Greece's greatest historian wrote: "He conquered the Cyclades, and was the first coloniser of most of them." Minos also cleared the sea of pirates, a recurring scourge.

Interestingly, when the Romans conquered Greece they remained quite fearful of the open sea and used Greek crews for their ships. The remains of the villas of Roman shipowners (*navicularii*) have been found on the once sacred island of Délos, just off Mýkonos. At the time of Christ, Délos had become a busy shipping centre, boasting colonies of rich shippers from as far away as Sicily and Palestine.

When the Roman Empire became the Byzantine, the powerful state required a powerful merchant fleet, which was why the Greeks, when they decided to throw off the Ottoman yoke in the 19th century, had redoubtable ships and seaman who effectively harassed the Turkish men of war.

After independence, the island of Sýros became young Greece's shipping and trading centre. Greece's oldest operating ship-

change: in 1833, four years after independence, it had a single church and a handful of houses, and all of 22 inhabitants. By the turn of the century, the once bare rocks and pebble strands had been transformed into a densely-packed city of 50,000 people, with belching smokestacks on the horizon and quaint Dreadnought battleships darting among the merchantmen with their masts swaying in the wind.

Piraeus had another, obvious advantage: it was far closer to the administrative and government centre of Athens, which wanted to control as much as possible the young nation's economic growth.

Cruising the waves: As far as the Greek

yard, Neórion, was founded on Sýros in 1861. At the time it was a revolutionary development, attracting British know-how and capital. The first Greek shipping bank, Archangelos, in 1879 published the first national shipping statistics: 3,025 sailing ships and 49 new steamships – about the same as in the year 1983.

Sýros didn't have much of a heyday, because Piraeus, the ancient shipping port of Athens, was being rebuilt. It had been a tiny backwater after the Roman general Sulla had razed it in 86 BC. But two illustrations of 1900, preserved in the Aegean Maritime Museum on Mýkonos, show the startling

islands are concerned, it is passenger – rather than cargo – shipping that is the big foreign-exchange earner. The jewels in the crown of Greek passenger shipping are the cruise liners, some with floating hotels, complete with swimming pools, boutiques, and a choice of restaurants and entertainment, which ply routes all over the world from the Aegean and other Mediterranean ports of call to Alaska and the Caribbean.

There are 30 Greek cruise ships plying the islands, operated by a dozen companies with offices in Piraeus. They are one-class ships, though accommodation ranges from economy to en-suite luxury. Itineraries vary from season to season, and stops en route may include mainland sites, such as Delphi, Olympia, Corinth, Meteora and Thessaloniki as well as the island groups.

Cruise liners and other passenger craft also touch at Turkish ports, mainly Kusadasi, contributing to a bridging of the eternal political and ethnic tension between the Greeks and the Turks. But here the Greeks plan to keep competing nations out of their lucrative Aegean trade.

The magic word is *cabotage*, an international law term meaning that any nation has a right to exclude others from carrying goods and passengers between its own ports. So far, Greece's passenger ships have served their

step towards claiming some sovereignty over the eastern Aegean Greek islands?

Conflict on the seas: This argument isn't as far-fetched as it might at first appear. Greece and Turkey have been glaring at, and occasionally fighting, each other over the Aegean for decades. Their last major clash was the Turkish invasion of Cyprus in 1974, which led to the permanent partitioning of the island. When not worrying about Macedonia, politicians in Athens are concerned about Turkey eyeing some of the easternmost Greek islands; Sámos, for example, is a shotgun-blast away from the Turkish coast. Turkey is the only major country that has not signed the 1958 Geneva Convention on the Law of

own island routes, connecting them with Piraeus. But now that Greece is a member of the European Union, the other European Union partners have been asking that Greece opens up its domestic ship routes to competition from other maritime nations – a demand that Greece has been strenuously resisting.

The argument in Athens is that, if the sea-lanes are opened up to ships of other countries, what will stop Turkish ships from grabbing the Aegean routes – possibly as a first

Left, and right, shipping and cruise liners are major foreign-exchange earners.

the Sea giving islands sovereign rights, even when off the coast of bigger countries.

Why the refusal? The Greeks answer that obviously, Turkey is "expansionist". And, regardless of how much pressure is exercised by the European Union or by other maritime nations, Greece intends to keep a firm hold of its Aegean. The delicate nature of the relationship surfaced recently when plans by Greece to extend its territorial waters in the Aegean rapidly generated rumours that Turkey was planning to mount an invasion of the Greek islands. One day soon, some feared, the rumours could all too easily turn into reality.

While the package holidaymaker and the ubiquitous backpacker are forced to rely on the ferries and their often impenetrable time-tables in order to travel among the islands, the yachtsman can enjoy a remarkable degree of independence without having to face excessive bureaucracy. But some paperwork, unfortunately, is unavoidable.

For those sailing into Greek waters in their own yacht, customs clearance in one of 28 designated entry ports (the list may be obtained from tourist boards or a country's national sailing authority) is necessary to obtain a Transit Log (yachts over 12 metres (39 ft) long) or a Temporary Duty-Free Admission booklet for yachts under 12 metres (39 ft) long. Usually, both these documents are valid for 6 months and enable a crew to sail freely throughout the country.

A visiting yacht should be officially registered in its country of origin and its skipper should make sure that each member of the crew has a valid passport. It is worth writing out a crew list with passport numbers so that any official check can be made easier.

Those who choose to charter a yacht in Greece will find the system simplified because all charter vessels must be sailing under the Greek flag, even if the person chartering the yacht has hired it from, say, a British-based company. Nevertheless, crew lists must be completed on arrival and charterers should not leave their holiday base until this has been completed. Some of these regulations may eventually be relaxed as Greece implements the European Union's myriad rules.

Sailing in the Dodecanese has the added problem of negotiating the Turkish/Greek border which weaves its way through a string of islands. The Turks insist that anyone sailing in their waters should clear customs at one of their ports of entry. The border is policed at sea and it is therefore unwise to zig-zag across this imaginary line unless you intend to enter Turkey officially.

Chartering, now a fundamental part of the sailing scene in Greece, began throughout the islands in the mid-1970s, and was the

Left, ship ahoy! **Above**, running repairs.

idea of an enterprising group of British boat owners who decided that they had had enough of miserable English summers and wanted to holiday in the sun.

This type of sailing is increasingly prevalent and has done much to encourage the development of marinas and improved facilities, for example the extensive provision of fresh drinking water. At the same time a flood of vessels in recent years has seen a spread of poorer quality boats.

Most chartering operates on a fairly so-

phisticated basis. All boats must be Greek-registered. Competition has enabled reputable charter companies to supply yachts which are renewed every 3 years or so. They are designed for holidays in the sun and equipped to a luxurious standard with deep freezes, deck showers, snorkelling equipment and even a pair of gardening gloves to handle the anchor chain.

It's important to match experience with the correct type of charter. Inexperienced sailors should select a flotilla holiday where 12 yachts cruise in company under the instructive eye of a lead boat crew. For the more experienced who have a basic knowledge of navigation and can handle a boat in stronger winds, a "burbot" aboard which the charterer becomes the skipper, provides a really independent holiday.

Finally, those who can afford a crewed charter can simply relax on deck and leave all the sailing, boat handling and even the cooking to paid hands.

Whether you are taking your own yacht to Greece or chartering, the choice of sailing areas is large and careful selection should take particular account of varying local wind characteristics.

The recognised sailing season is from April to October when the skies are clear, and temperatures rise into the 80s and 90s Fahr-

wards the Cyclades, predominantly from the north. More recently, the strong midsummer northerlies which blow down the Turkish coast have led some charter companies to grade this area, the Dodecanese, as the most difficult in which to sail.

Weather forecasts for yachtsmen are broadcast by Athens Radio in Greek with special warnings in English. Don't rely on the advice of local port captains when it comes to the weather.

For those looking for less lively sailing conditions, the Saronic Gulf and the Ionian islands offer the best prospects. This is because both are well protected by islands in close proximity to each other.

enheit (25°C to 35°C) in July and August.

Winds throughout the Greek sea area tend to be from the north and the most talked-about weather phenomenon is the *meltémi*, which affects the whole of the Aegean and can reach Beaufort Force 7 to 8 in midsummer. It is an unpredictable wind, can arrive without warning and blow for as little as one hour or for as long as one week.

Yachtsmen must take care not to be caught on a lee shore and they should be aware that the *meltémi* can cause an extremely uncomfortable steep, short sea.

In the northern Aegean the *meltémi* blows from the northeast and, further south to-

The Ionian is blessed with a wind called the *maéstros*, again from the north but nowhere near as strong as the *meltémi*. The *maéstros* tends only to blow in the afternoon when the heat of mainland Greece accelerates the wind off the sea. Occasionally a hot, southerly *sirócco* wind, often carrying red dust from North Africa, will blow hard in the Peloponnese but it doesn't last long.

Despite all these descriptions of local winds, Greece is often quite windless and yachtsmen should sometimes be prepared to motor. Whatever the conditions, the sun and the increased glare off the water – which can produce momentary blindness – should be guarded against at all times, particularly when out sailing.

The biggest concentration of marinas in Greece is on the coast of Attica near Athens and Piraeus; but because of the commercial shipping and general ship movements in and out of the capital – to say nothing of the conurbation's industrial waste – it is not an area of peace and beauty.

Zéa Marina, which is near Piraeus, is hot, noisy and smelly; Mikrolímano, the home of the Greek ocean racing fleet, is cleaner and prettier and Kalamáki, 5 miles away from central Athens, is large, new but featureless. The other major marinas among or near the Greek islands are at Thessaloniki, where

there is an excellent development at Kalamarias; Gouvia, near Corfu, is still far from finished and is polluted by a local sewer outfall; and the large Mandraki marina at Rhodes is more suited to larger yachts.

All these marinas make excellent "staging posts" for yachts which need to re-stock with food and water. There are, of course, charter bases in all these locations which normally means there are repair and chandlery facilities on hand.

But the greatest appeal of the Greek is-

Left, sailing the seas. **Above**, a passenger savours the sea breeze.

lands is the beauty and solitude offered by their remoteness. The green islands of the Ionian are, perhaps, the yachtsman's first choice for a number of reasons. As already explained, the Ionian offers safe cruising because of the shelter to the east of the islands, but if yachtsmen want more lively conditions, a sail to the west of the islands of Léfkas and Cephalonia will provide marvellous sailing. Easy anchorages and safe village moorings are within a few hours' sail of each other throughout the chain.

Spring sailing: Anyone cruising the area is likely to traverse the recently improved Léfkas (Lefkada) Canal and beat north for 48 km (30 miles) to Corfu. Apart from the already mentioned Gouvia marina (about an hour's sail from the city), Corfu boasts its own, more convenient marina, ideal for a city tour and for bunkering water and fuel but appallingly dirty, full of the city's rubbish and sewage. The time to sail the Ionian is definitely during spring and autumn months – mid-summer sees Italian yachtsmen pouring over from the heel of Italy, clogging up the numerous but small harbours.

The Saronic Gulf is a favourite haunt of cruising yachts because of the attractive towns which offer shelter on islands like Hydra, Spétsesand the much underrated coast of the mainland Peloponnese. In mid-season it might be difficult to find a berth close to one of the quayside tavernas where restaurateurs have developed their entrepreneurial skills to tempt crews to their quayside tables. Almost without exception, mooring is stern or bows to town quays and are close by to the best tavernas.

Moving east from the Saronic, the influence of the *meltémi* becomes stronger and it is not until one travels north of the Sporades, still affected by the northeast *meltémi*, that one finds more virgin cruising grounds among the great inlets and peninsulas to the east of the deep bay which has Thessalóniki at its head. There are fewer villages and towns along this coast and yachtsmen should be prepared to anchor, sometimes in water more than 30 metres (100 ft) deep.

Sailing a yacht is a rewarding way of exploring this country of islands. In many cases, it is the only way of reaching some remote corners. (For more information and useful addresses see the *Travel Tips* section at the end of the book).

It is only when the charter flights have finally returned to base that the real character of a small island, such as Sérifos or Pátmos, staggers out of its unseasonal hibernation. The larger islands are capable of absorbing a deluge of visitors without having to adopt when they arrive (and discard when they leave) a totally different identity. A visitor arriving in Crete in October would not discover, as could happen on a smaller island, that the police station had just closed and would not re-open until needed again late in the spring.

It is difficult to exaggerate the disfiguring impact when an island with a population measured in hundreds or the low thousands is swamped by 10 times the normal number all at the same time. How would Britain, say, with a population of 60 million, cope with 600 million visitors in one go? Residents of the United States wishing to imagine something on the same scale might like to consider the simultaneous arrival on their doorstep of the combined populations of China, India and the Soviet Union, plus a couple of European countries.

Quick change: Understandably dazed by the whole thing, the islanders have to find their feet again when everyone goes away. Superficially, the change into winter uniform is swift. Migrant waiters and kitchen staff pile on to departing ferries to look for winter jobs on the mainland. Awnings over pavement cafés are rolled up and stowed; the chairs and tables stacked and dragged away. Most of the shops are closed and padlocked.

Stray puppies sniff about, disconcerted by the interruption in the supply of unfinished *moussaká* handed down on visitors' plates. They learn cunning fast enough – both to eat and to escape the furtive culling necessary to keep their numbers down. Surplus cats are treated more leniently – except, perhaps, by fugitive dogs.

A good sign that the islanders are feeling themselves again after the grinding hours they have put in during the season is the resumption of the evening promenade, an

almost formal ritual in which small groups file from one end of the locally prescribed route to the other and back again. Overtaking is apparently not allowed. Among them are the elderly and handicapped who are seldom seen in public places during the season. Winter visitors who join the throng are bound to attract curious glances from the traffic going in the opposite direction. The process of recognition and acceptance as an honorary member of the community is a ritual in itself. First, perhaps, a half-cocked eyebrow; later, a nod; then ultimately, triumphantly, a stop for a chat.

The promenade is a chance to observe all kinds of island machinery in motion: frocked and hatted Orthodox priests, symbols of a former propriety that doesn't stand a chance against the summer heathens, reassert their magisterial presence among the faithful. Office-bearers and petitioners in the schismatic world of island politics fall into step alongside the mayor in order to hold a mobile conference.

A winter's tale: If the municipal elections are in sight, the plotting that goes on during the promenade will explode into campaigns which sound like the rumble of impending civil war. The party manifestos may commend or deplore, as the case may be, the state of the village drains, but the winner's powers of patronage are such that the outcome is regarded, not unrealistically, as a matter of economic life or death.

Visitors can skip politics, however, and still feel that they are part of local life. There are any number of processions through the streets, the mayor and priests conspicuously linked in secular-clerical solidarity at the head of an enthusiastic brass band. The religious festivals, notably Easter, usually include a pilgrimage to a monastery where – and this is not a literary invention – the fellow who falls over three times a week in the *ouzerié* may materialise as a solemn acolyte with a good voice for ceremonial chant. When the service is over, the grounds are turned into a picnic area for a party which may last until dawn.

Ouzeriés, basic drinking establishments where a request for a cocktail would draw a blank stare, stay open through the winter. Some of the tavernas and posher bars may keep their doors open too, although probably on an informal rota as if the owners were sharing the workload, or some may just open at weekends. Even a disco may re-open, but that could last for only a night or two and on the next it may just as inexplicably close down again.

The locals have to buy food and other supplies, so there is never any difficulty getting hold of provisions. The smaller islands are seldom self-sufficient, however, and if they have to rely on ferries which are not nearly so frequent during the winter – and are liable to be cancelled in bad weather

(travellers with deadlines please note) – there may be temporary shortages of most fresh produce.

Power failures which last more than a day cause a commotion because the bakeries can't function. The lesser kind go unnoticed, although not by wintering writers with electric typewriters or word processors. The latter may be found crying in the *ouzerié* after losing the contents of an electronic memory.

Fresh fish looks expensive next to frozen meat mostly imported from Italy. The fishermen sail at dusk and return at dawn but, for the rest of the male population, the longer nights are the cue to bring out packs of

playing cards. Officially, no money changes hands, but passers-by could not fail to notice scraps of paper and meticulous accounting. In reality, there is a massive and endless redistribution of the summer takings, although by the following spring most of the money is supposedly back where it started.

Landlords don't expect to earn any rent in winter, so when a visitor comes along out of season the negotiations are friendly and flexible. Prime accommodation on the sea may be worth a slight premium while the water is still at a tolerable temperature, although after September and before May there is hardly a beach in Greece which couldn't be annexed and occupied as private property.

If outdoor conditions are an important criterion, the southern islands are generally warmer. All over the Aegean, however, the winter wind will sometimes cut through to the bone, and houses that were not built specifically for the summer trade are more likely to have some form of heating. Tenants would, however, be expected to pay for the fuel they use.

It is worth asking about vacant farmhouses; these have the added advantage that neighbours are always popping around with eggs, a bottle and an extra glass. Today this wholly agreeable way of life could be had for a very reasonable rent per month, not excluding fairly lavish consumption of local drink and cigarettes.

The English novelist Simon Raven spent the winter of 1960 on Hydra looking into "what goes on when winter comes, when the last epicene giggle has hovered and died in the October air". He decided he was among a bunch of atavistic pirates who, happily preoccupied by making money during the summer, reverted in winter to the old distrust of strangers who used to come only to spy on their illicit booty.

Hydra, like other islands, has since become accustomed to having a few foreigners stay on after the rest leave and, on the assumption the islanders never saw what Raven wrote about them, he would probably feel more comfortable among them now. The one impression formed then which he most definitely would not wish to change now is that only in winter could his eye make out what the island was really like.

Left, a heater on Ikaría. **Right**, January on Hydra.

WRITING THE GREAT NOVEL

Bring a woman, Lawrence Durrell advised Henry Miller in 1938, promising that in other respects his Greek island was the perfect place to get a novel written. "We could sail and bathe in mornings, have a fine sunny lunch with wine, then a long afternoon siesta, bathe before tea and then four hours' work in a slow rich evening." At the time, Miller was keen to finish a book and might have wondered about the efficacy of Durrell's idea of a hard day at the office.

Miller did finish the book – it was *Tropic of Capricorn* – and, although the extent to which it materialised on Corfu is unknown, the achievement ought to stand as a benchmark for the permanent presence that has since imposed itself on nearly every Greek island: writers wrestling with great works. Most of them would have thrown a beach towel in with a typewriter and decamped to their island expressly to write a book; others might have arrived for other reasons but been inspired by the amount of writing going on around them.

One such, a taxi driver from the Channel Islands, had taken a year's sabbatical on a small, green island, intending to devote himself to nudism. Suddenly inspired, he would take willing listeners aside to reveal the names of the main characters in the novel he was going to write. There was a Greek named Dimitris and an Italian, Giovanni, although he had not yet decided on surnames. The novel would be set in Greece and Italy, which were the two foreign countries he had visited. He had run into a problem, however, and would be grateful for help. He had been unable, he said, to think up a plot.

Of the ideas tossed at him, a weave of sex and murder most appealed. Every morning thereafter, he would set off for the nudist beach with his new notebook in hand.

He reported back to say that the novel was progressing well and had reached the murder scene. He admired the Len Deighton school of thriller writing and was determined to get exactly right the technical details of the weapon used, in this case a hand gun. He had

__Preceding pages__: a typewriter and its distractions. __Left__, a literate man on Chíos.

heard a name which he felt had the authentic ring of menace. He would call the gun "a Howitzer".

It was one of at least four books actually being written by expatriates on that particular island that year – as opposed to those under discussion over long lunches. It could be any island today. One of them, a local history, had been in production for more than 20 years. It was by a clever Englishwoman who led a semi-reclusive existence in a primitive cottage high on a mountain. She would descend to the village once a week on a moped to do her shopping; otherwise nobody saw much of her. It was said that she'd come to the island to forget an unhappy love affair at Oxford.

The expatriate colony once published a little book about the island and in it was an article by her which demonstrated convincingly the rigour of a trained historian. The article is probably as much as anyone will ever know about a project which had occupied most of her adult life. That year, she destroyed the manuscript. Asked why, she shrugged and said nothing.

Conspiracy of distraction: During the tourist season, a conspiracy of distraction forever drives a wedge between writer and great work. Durrell's invitation to Miller sets out some of them: the weather is magnificent and the sea so congenial that there is always a plausible excuse to dive in and remain there for some time.

The temptation is to go swimming more and more as summer approaches, starting on one beach and coming ashore at another. Ostensibly, the goal is "to keep fit"; the parallel purpose is to keep an eye on the deliveries from heaven, manna arriving daily by chartered jet and, from the moment they stretch their long, lovely legs to apply sun tan oil, totally committed to the proverbial good time. Durrell's advice to Miller contains one anachronism: the women are here already.

Durrell's "fine sunny lunch with wine" is another of the yawning man-traps set for the island writer, especially the "with wine". By any criterion, expatriates who settle on islands are slightly odd. That makes them excellent company; it also means that, on the whole, they drink a bit. Nobody ever resolves to drink less on a Greek island for the sake of saving money.

Somewhere on the island there will be a wholesaler or a grocer who sells *ouzo* and brandy from the barrel – bring your own bottle. Short-term visitors are unlikely to have the time to find out who or where they are; expatriates, on the other hand, can find them blindfolded.

Credit is extended everywhere to resident writers. The trusting and hospitable Greeks revere Homer and are willing to regard anyone who can type with two fingers as a potential heir. The less flattering explanation is that in winter there is no way off most

Wine sold in huge bottles is commensurately cheap, and etiquette seems to require that once opened the bottle must be finished at one sitting.

One writer on the island discovered that, by reversing Durrell's timetable and applying himself in the mornings, he could turn out a slim volume of poetry per decade. Over lunch at his special table in a taverna below his house, he would discuss with another writer their respective great works. He was working on his third volume and was fairly confident that it would be ready by the turn of the millennium.

Lunches "with wine": These were definitely lunches "with wine", and he would mysteri-

islands except by boat, and creditors are more than likely to be lining the quay.

Either way, their generosity can be a lifesaver because even writers who are in a position to have their banks at home send them money are often caught short. The rumour, never proven, is that banks in Athens will not forward foreign currency transfers to their branches while there is still hope that, unnoticed, they can play the markets with it.

Anguished telexes to Athens will eventually achieve a sheepish surrender and the means to go out and pay a trifling sum for a litre of the strong stuff.

ously arrange the bottles in a straight line on what seemed to be a constant compass bearing. Greek waiters don't clear empty bottles; it is their way of keeping track of the ever-increasing numbers.

A visit to the poet's house revealed that the view from the terrace bore down directly on the taverna and, in particular, on to "his" table. Concerned that too grand a lunch on the Durell model might, the following morning, jeopardise work on volume three, the poet's wife had acquired a powerful pair of binoculars and turned the terrace into an observation post. His favourite retsina was sold only in small bottles which, together with the tendency of a great many friends and acquaintances to drop by for a chat, meant the number of bottles could proliferate at impressive speed. All of this was monitored through the binoculars, and if the situation appeared to be getting out of hand, the loyal wife would descend imperially either to speak on the virtues of moderation or, *in extremis*, to march him off by the ear.

The studied arrangement of the bottles, then, was a smokescreen. "He thinks that I can only see one," his wife admitted when he went off to fish a bottle out of the fridge. "In that belief he is mistaken."

Whatever cloud may have been hanging over the third volume of poems, the first two

nothing for the expatriate colony to do. It would be inconceivable, for example, to squander the need to call at the post office and at the bank by allowing both errands to occur on a single outing, even if post office and bank happened to be close neighbours. Shopping is sensibly stretched over a whole day: a loaf of bread and eggs in the morning, say, and the balance after lunch – a lunch with friends and, of course, "with wine".

Corfu cannot have had many visitors when Miller dropped in on Durrell in 1938, but Durrell's own literary output from his island base proves that it can be done, if only by observing the sanctity of those four hours, either in the slow rich evening or, for a

were accomplished facts. Moreover, they were on sale in the local bookshop, a vindication for any writer whose credentials are called into question. Very few island writers are in a position to dispel doubt so triumphantly. Very few, indeed, are on sale anywhere or, deep in their hearts, expect to be. It is enough merely to be writing a book, regardless of the outcome.

In the winter months, when all but one or two of the bars and tavernas are closed and the sea is too cold for swimming, there is

certain kind of poet, in the morning.

Less dedicated writers are more inclined to use the great novel as a filling for the vacuum, a cushion over atavistic Puritan misgivings about months of bone-idleness. It soothes the conscience and enhances the fun: after all, 150,000 completed words on paper are a better memento of an island visit than the stamps registered in one's passport before and afterwards.

All too often, of course, the great novel is never actually published – or indeed finished. But the possibility of its being completed provides the perfect excuse to return to the island for one more try.

Left, creating takes enormous concentration.
Above, nourishment for would-be writers.

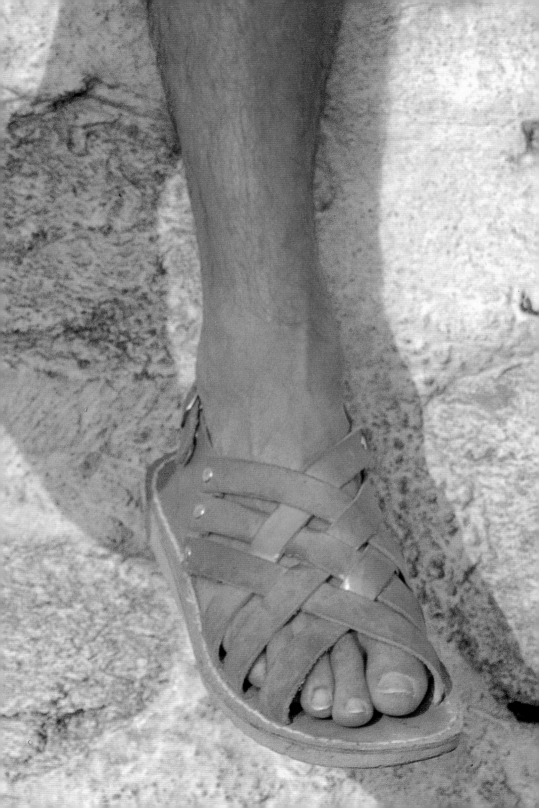

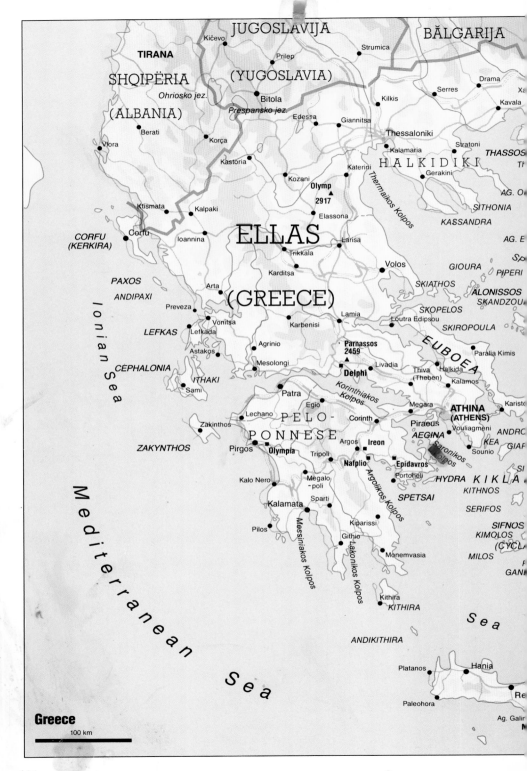

Greece

100 km

PLACES

"Greece rests on the sea," said the poet Odysseas Elytis, an observation few countries could claim with such authority. Some 25,000 sq. km (10,000 sq. miles) of the Aegean and the Ionian seas are covered by islands, the exact number of which has, in characteristic Greek fashion, been the topic of discussion and dispute. There may be 3,000 islands and islets, of which 167 are inhabited; there may be only 1,000, of which under 60 are inhabited.

The frame of reference, too, which defines a populated place is open to interpretation. Does a tiny outcrop, bare save for one shepherd and six goats, constitute an inhabited island? Can an island totally deserted except for pilgrimages made annually to a small chapel at its summit claim to be inhabited?

The reality matters much more to foreigners than to Greeks, who are interested in sea and sky rather than in facts and figures. What is indisputable, however, is the sheer variety of landscape and experience to be found lurking behind the obvious clichés.

It is this we attempt to show here, islands with an ancient past and a modern outlook, the complex choice and the pure simple pleasures.

In order to accommodate much of what is implied in the phrase "a Greek island" almost as much space has been devoted to little-known Aghios Efstrátios as to over-exposed Corfu, to the attractive islet Telendos at, perhaps, the expense of Mýkonos.

Those clichés you can read in other guidebooks. For now, welcome aboard the ferry.

Preceding pages: fisherman works on his boat; have backpack, will travel; footloose and waiting for the ferry.

ATHENS STOPOVER

The columns of the classical temples on the **Acropolis** used to be so clearly etched against the blue Attica sky that literary-minded tourists compared them to the strings of a harp. Now they are often blotted out by the haze of pollution that Athenians call the *néfos* – Greek for cloud.

But they remain as impressive as ever, looming into close-up as you clamber up the rocky hill. Stop for a moment while crossing the wooden walkway through the **Propylaea,** the monumental gateway that was designed to frame the Parthenon Temple from exactly the right three-quarter angle. Looking up to the left, you will be able to see part of the coffered marble ceiling of a top-quality 5th century BC building: they hardly ever survive.

To the right is the **Temple of Athena Nike**, completed around 420 BC, roped off on a bastion that recalls the hill's original use as a fortified citadel, long before Pericles decided to spend a fortune in taxpayers' money to make Athens the marvel of the age.

Soon after Greece won independence from Turkey, the archaeologists moved in to pull down a maze of ramshackle buildings around the temples and start excavating – a generation after Lord Elgin stripped most of the sculptures from the Parthenon. He was keeping up with a tradition of looting ancient Greek treasures that started when the 12-metre (39-ft) high gold-and-ivory statue of the Goddess Athena that stood inside the temple was taken off to Constantinople in late antiquity.

Parts of the **Parthenon**, completed in 432 BC in honour of the virgin goddess and patron of ancient Athens, are being dismantled in an ambitious restoration programme that may take 25 years to complete – seven years longer than it took to erect the structure originally. To avoid masking Athena's temple with scaffolding, a folding crane was placed inside on a specially laid floor. It lifted down the blocks in turn so that non-rusting titanium clamps could be inserted in place of the iron fixtures used by restorers in the early 1900s. The iron had corroded and expanded, threatening to split the marble.

The last remaining sculptures have been removed, their delicately carved details blackened and pockmarked by air pollution – sulphur fumes combine with rainwater to form a dilute acid that turns the marble surface into gypsum.

The **Erechtheum Temple**, built over the tomb of a legendary Athenian king, has already been restored so successfully that some experts complain too much was done by way of filling in the gaps with freshly-cut marble from the ancient quarries on Mount Pendeli, north of Athens, even though no attempt was made to decorate them. One has to imagine that the columns were once painted in red, blue and gold.

Four of the original Caryatid Maidens can be seen in the **Acropolis Museum,** looking battered but still dignified inside a nitrogen-filled case. And even the **Acropolis Hill** itself has been

Left, the Parthenon encased in scaffolding. **Right**, Athens as seen from the Acropolis.

COPING WITH PIRAEUS

There's no point in pretending that Piraeus is the kind of place anyone wants to spend much time in – unless that person happens to work in one of the air-conditioned shipping offices overlooking the harbour. But it is possible to idle away a few hours while waiting to catch a ferry, even if there are few echoes of *Never on a Sunday* these days. (Low life moved to Athens during the puritanical colonels' dictatorship. Since then, successive mayors have been elected on a "smarten up Piraeus" ticket.)

The basic rule about Piraeus ferries is to get there one hour before sailing time so that there is half an hour to find the right quay before the boarding deadline: unlike other kinds of transport in Greece, ships really do leave on time. But, unless it's high summer or a berth is required, don't worry about getting tickets in advance: these can be picked up from one of the dockside agencies.

An express bus now runs direct to Piraeus from both terminals at Athens airport and stops outside the Port Authority (OLP) passenger building on Akti Miaoúli Street – a useful place to know since bags can be left in the café upstairs free of charge between 6am and 7.30pm (the other passenger terminal on Provlis Tselepis Quay where the Mykonos boat comes in is more crowded and the staff there are less accommodating). Unencumbered, it's now easy to get equipped for the islands and take a look around Piraeus and its environs.

Drakopoulos' bookstore on Second Merarchia Street has a good selection of English paperbacks, maps, and island guides as well as useful items like toothpaste and stationery. For a quick meal, the Do-Nut shop nearby offers something for every stage of the day, from orange juice and breakfast to *patsás* (tripe soup) – a traditional late-night dish for those arriving back in Piraeus in the early morning hours and who are unable to find a taxi on the deserted streets.

Nuts and fresh fruit for the voyage are on sale at the stall next door. For something lighter, try the *ouzerié* round the corner on Filonos Street.

To enjoy the view over Piraeus or catch a breeze, take a taxi up to the Veiákeion open-air theatre at the top of Kastélla hill. Further along at Neo Faliro is the Palais des Sports (the Stadium of Peace and Friendship), the venue of rock concerts and political gatherings as well as sports events. If totally lethargic, one of the few patches of green grass to stretch out on is the park opposite the Town Hall on Akti Miaoúli.

The radical cosmopolitan atmosphere for which Piraeus was famous 2,500 years ago still flourishes – the port and its industrial suburbs are left-wing strongholds – but few remains survive. A stretch of elegant 4th-century BC wall runs beside the coast road beyond the Pasalimáni yacht harbour and an amphitheatre backs on to the archaeological museum on Philhellínon Street, which is well worth visiting if there's time before the ferry departs.

Its prize exhibits are two bronze statues found by workmen digging a drain in Piraeus: a magnificent *kouros*, (6th-century BC figure) of a young man, and a 4th-century helmeted Athena, looking oddly soulful for a warrior goddess. Both may have come from a shipment of loot overlooked by Greece's Roman conquerors in the 1st century BC.

Pasalimáni is crowded with medium-sized yachts – a floating campsite in summer – but towards the Flying Dolphin hydrofoil terminal huge, old-fashioned two and three-masters and sleek motor-yachts can be admired. Further round the headland are fishing dinghies moored in the rocky inlets beneath the ancient wall and the cafés and fish restaurants frequented by Piraeots which overlook the Saronic Gulf. The gulf is badly polluted but still manages to look a brilliant blue from only a short distance.

Back toward Athens – it's easier to take the yellow trolley or green bus – lies Tourkolímano (Mikrolimani), a small yacht basin surrounded by fish restaurants. This is the place for a leisurely lunch. Although tourism has given most establishments a glossy look, the Black Goat, close to the boatsheds beneath the Yacht Club, still has the atmosphere and rowdy ambience that old-time Aegean sailors remember. ∎

restored, strengthened, like a broken hip, with metal pins to hold the crumbling limestone together.

You could be forgiven for not bothering to hunt down the lesser monuments of Athens (in fact, to avoid the high season crush on the hilltop, it's perfectly possible to sit on the terrace of the Dionyssos Café opposite and enjoy a striking view of the Parthenon). But some are worth looking out for.

The grandiose **Herod Atticus Theatre** beneath the Acropolis, built by a Roman millionaire in the second century, is best seen from a seat in the front rows during the Athens Festival as the moon rises above the towering arches. Whether the show is classical drama or imported opera or ballet, the spectacle is what counts. (Performers also say it's unforgettable looking up at the steep tiers packed with people.)

While shopping in the **Plaka district** on the other side of the Acropolis, keep an eye out for the **Tower of the Winds**, a tall marble octagon dating from the first century BC. The winds are shown as relief figures flying amid swirling draperies. In Ottoman times, the building was the centre for a sect of whirling dervishes. Look out, too, for the 13th-century Byzantine **Church of St Katerina Sinai**, a few feet below street level in a palm-fringed courtyard near Hadrian's Arch.

For a restful hour or so, try the **Kerameikos Cemetery** in the ancient potters' district of Athens. The funerary monuments – sphinxes, a prancing bull, scenes of farewell – were erected by wealthy Athenian families of the fifth and fourth centuries BC. A stream trickles through the ruins and there are turtles in the undergrowth. The museum boasts a remarkable collection of pottery that illustrates Greek vase-painting over 500 years.

Further afield – a 20-minute taxi ride from the centre of town – is **Kaisariani**, a Byzantine monastery at the foot of Mount Hymettus, once famous for its honey. The domed church goes back to the year 1000 but the frescoes are much later, dating from the 17th century, with

A view fit for the gods.

pale faces gazing out from a blue-black ground. Next to a shady plane tree outside the gate, spring water from a fountain with a ram's head is still supposed to encourage pregnancy.

From the slopes above the monastery – a 10-minute walk up the road takes you to a ruined medieval watchtower – there is a wonderful panoramic view of Athens spreading down the shores of the Saronic Gulf.

On the other side of Athens – 40 minutes by car from the centre – next to the site of the summer wine festival stands **Daphni Monastery**, built in the 11th century. A Gothic porch was added later when it was taken over by French Cistercian Monks and it also became the burial place of the Frankish Dukes of Athens. Its 11th-century mosaics glisten high up in the dark interior, and a gloomy Christ Pantocrator looks down from the dome.

If you have an afternoon to spare, take a trip to **Cape Sounion** and **Poseidon's Temple**, still a landmark for sailors rounding the tip of the Attica Peninsula.

The organised tour is easiest, routed either down the coast road (its construction triggered the first Greek seaside property boom), or through the Mesogeion, the olive-and wine-growing heartland of ancient Attica.

The temple dates from the mid-fifth century BC and among the travellers' graffiti carved on the columns, you can find Byron's name. Sunset is the traditional time to be there.

Naturally, Athens is rich in museums: the **National Archaeological Museum** holds the world's largest collection of Greek art, much of it badly displayed and labelled. But it's still worth fighting your way past the crowds for a glimpse of some superb objects.

In the Mycenean room, head for the sheet-gold deathmask of a bearded man from one of the shaft graves. (The excavator, Heinrich Schliemann mistakenly thought he was King Agamemnon, leader of the Greek expedition against Troy.) Then seek out the two gold cups found at Vafeio near Sparta but probably made by a craftsman from Crete.

An Athenian pleasure: eating outdoors in Plaka.

120

Stride through the sculpture galleries until you stop short at the bronze figure of Zeus, tensed and ready to throw a thunderbolt. It dates from around 470 BC. In the same room is a remarkable marble relief of the fertility goddess Demeter handing an ear of corn to the Eleusinian prince, Triptolemos.

Further on comes the heavily restored bronze racehorse from the Hellenistic period, with an anxious-looking boy jockey perched on its back. And don't miss the frescoes from Santoríni (also known as Thíra and soon to be returned to the island), found in a prehistoric Pompeii beneath layers of volcanic lava that engulfed the city in the late Bronze Age. (The swallows-in-spring painting caught the imagination of film-set designers and features in more than one exotic epic set in the Himalayas.)

If you have time and inclination for just one museum, the **Benaki** is crammed with treasures from every period of Greek history (as well as some Asiatic collections). Between the basement filled with silk and gold embroidered folk costumes and the terrace café on the rooftop, the neo-classical mansion is filled with delights.

The museum was the lifelong hobby of Emmanuel Benakis, a wealthy Greek from Egypt and it reflects his eclectic taste for all things Greek and often Turkish, Persian and Arabic – not to speak of Coptic. There is a stunning roomful of jewellery from Mycenean times onward, two early works in the icon room by El Greco, who was born on Crete, and a vast collection of pictures, weapons and other memorabilia from the War of Independence period, including crockery used by Lord Byron.

Near the Benaki is another museum with a world-renowned private collection on display. The **Museum of Cycladic and Ancient Greek Art** features the prehistoric white marble figurines which were dismissed as barbaric by turn-of-the-century art critics but rated Picasso and Modigliani among their admirers. They come from graves in the Cycladic islands but scholars are still uncertain of their purpose.

Athens is a multi-faceted city.

THE IONIAN ISLANDS

CORFU, PAXOS, LÉFKAS, ITHAKI, CEPHALONIA, ZÁKYNTHOS, KYTHERA

The islands of the west coast are known in Greek as the *Eftánisa* – the seven isles. However, the seventh island, Kythera, lies off the southern tip of the Peloponnese and, although it is linked by history, culture or architecture, it remains quite isolated from the other six islands.

During the 8th and 7th centuries BC, wanderers from Corinth settled on the most northern of these islands, bringing with them a distinct culture. Two centuries later the secession of Corfu from Corinth brought about the beginning of the Peloponnesian War. Over the years the Ionians have had many warrior landlords, but it is the long period of Venetian rule that has left the most indelible mark on the islands.

Artists, craftsmen and poets were often sent to Venice for their education, bringing back to the islands a cosmopolitan and international perspective. Even today, thanks to good air and sea links with Italy, the islands have a distinctly Italian flavour; and that doesn't only apply to the many pizzerias that jostle for space with tavernas on many a harbour promenade.

It is the heavy rainfall which makes the Ionians among the greenest of Greek island chains. Olive groves and vineyards are reminders that agriculture, rather than the dubious riches of tourism, still claim a part in the economy. But it is this same unsettled weather that has ruined many a traveller's holiday; from mid-September until mid-May, rains can wash out any beach outing suddenly and without warning. Fortunately, escape is never far away. The Ionians' links with the mainland are very good, and several coaches daily at the height of the season make the journey from Athens to Corfu (allow at least 10 hours), via a connecting ferry service. It's also possible to reach Cephalonia or Zákynthos by bus from Athens.

Today the Ionians are threatened, not by invaders (other than tour companies), but by earthquakes. A series of quakes has at various times beset the islands, the most recent and serious being in 1953. Casualties were great and the beautiful Venetian-built capitals of Cephalonia and Zákynthos were flattened.

Reconstruction began almost immediately. The residents of Argostóli in Cephalonia put up makeshift buildings which still remain, in order to resume busy, industrious lives. Zakynthians, however, elected to recreate their Venetian city on a grand scale, using original plans and grids. These contrasting attitudes to tragedy tell an island tale.

Preceding pages: a trio of beach bums. Left, a Corfiot mask for sale.

CORFU

A torturous catalogue of bloody invasions and changing foreign rule chequers the history of Corfu (Kérkyra). Today, the Corfiots reap the benefits of all those battles. Left a rich inheritance of olive trees dating from Venetian rule, they prosper from agricultural wealth and a thriving tourist trade.

Tourist dodging can become a game in itself for the more adventurous visitor; there is a real thrill in finding an unspoiled spot. Alternatively, mixing with the masses can be fun. Sadly, package tourism has brought a sprinkling of modern-day Vandals with it, intent on thoughtlessly trampling on the culture, customs and kindness of the islanders.

Corfiot hospitality to strangers remains remarkably unscathed. The legendary friendliness of the islanders dates back to a tale told of Odysseus, who, shipwrecked and exhausted, was washed ashore and rescued by the beautiful Princess Nafsicaä, whose family offered him a fabulous welcome. The traveller today who is not running with the tourist pack will be showered with generosity, as if another naked Odysseus, washed ashore by the waves.

Corfu Town: The pretty, bustling town of Corfu is an unmissable starting point for a visit to the island. The people and the places are extravagantly cosmopolitan. Each turned corner reveals a new architectural delight, with a mass of different historical influences evoked.

It takes time to find ways round the different parts of the town and lap up its medley of moods. Directionless wandering is best enjoyed while dodging a colourful *monippo* (horse-drawn carriage) in the narrow streets of the **Old Town**, squeezed between two ancient forts. The sounds of a brass band rehearsing in the upstairs rooms of dilapidated Venetian houses competes absurdly with Greek piped music blaring from the tourist shops below. High up in the quieter alleyways, the week's washing flutters on lines strung across the streets, looking like bunting strung up for an impending carnival.

In the heart of this charming chaos looms the darkly tranquil church of **Aghios Spyrídou**, the island's most dearly loved saint. In a glittering chapel his mummified remains rest resplendent in a silver casket, ready to hear a hundred whispered prayers.

The ancient landmarks of the town's past are the two forts, the **Néo Froúrio** (New Fort) and the Old Fort, the **Palió Froúrio**. The Old Fort is now a crumbling monument to the centuries during which Corfu was the prize of contesting foreign powers. Ambling through the overgrown buildings, its history comes alive, as one happens upon a Byzantine inscription or the bizarre British-built church of **Aghios Yeórgios**.

Flanking the eastern side of the Old Town, the pavement cafés suddenly have a Parisian air, and it's not surprising to discover that the **Listón** façade, modelled on the Rue de Rivoli, was erected during the French occupation. *Tsitsi birra* (ginger beer), a remnant of the British influence, is the drink to sip in

eft, an egant assage in orfu Town.

Corfu

20 km

Saranda

Akr. Ag. Ekaterini

Peroulades
Karousades
Roda
Sidari
Kassiopi
ALBANIA
Pandokratoras
Afionas
▲ 906
Nisaki
Aspiotades
Skipera
Paleokastritsa

Ormos Krevatsouta

Gouvia
Potamos
Kerkira (Corfu)
Monastery
Pelekas
Kanoni

Corfu

Kerkira

Ag. Gordis
Pendati
Achillio
Benitses

Strongili

Ag. Mattheos
Mesongi
Klopos Lefkimmis

Akr. Lefkimmi

Agirádes
Lefkimmi

Ionian Sea

Monastery
Kavos

Akr. Ag. Asprokavos

Map/ Text
Ag. Matteos/ Ayiós Matthaéos
Argirades/ Aryirádes
Lefkimmi/ Lifkimmio
Mesongi/ Messongi
Strongili/ Strongylí

these culturally-confused cafés, where you can watch cricket being played on the **Spianáda** (esplanade).

The regency style **Palace of St Michael and St George** dominates the north side of the esplanade. It houses the splendid **Museum of Asian Art**, to add yet another dimension to the town's cultural diversity. To the south of the esplanade, the **archaeological museum** boasts the delightful Archaic Gorgon pediment. A stroll along the sweeping bay leads towards the chic area around **Mon Repos**.

North Coast: Taking the coast road north from Corfu Town, there are a series of naturally beautiful but very busy bays, monopolised by the package tour operators. By **Nisáki**, the scenery becomes more dramatic, the tourists more sedate and the sea a deep sapphire. Beyond this lies the magical stretch of coast made famous by Lawrence Durrell's *Prospero's Cell*. Dropping down to **Kalámi**, there's a tranquil taverna in the White House, where Durrell stayed. Little bays offer enticing views across the crystal water to Albania.

Seeking solitude is a question of timing in such places. The unlucky traveller's visit may coincide with an invasion of the holiday-making hordes on a pleasure-boat cruise, stopping to noisily spew onto the shores of your chosen spot to eat, drink and disrupt your tranquillity. The thronging masses are to be found making merry in the ancient harbour town of **Kassiópi**, which has gorged itself on tourism. One wonders what past visitors such as Nero, Cicero and Cato would make of the town today. Perhaps the amorous Casanova, another early tourist, would enjoy endless conquests at the swinging discos.

On the north coast, the scenery becomes standardised, the coastal resorts uniform. Tourism at **Róda**, **Astrakéri** and **Sidári** conspires to ruin what must have been a luscious stretch of sandy beaches. Throughout Corfu, the most interesting places are consistently off the main roads and often inland. Looking for unspoiled villages hugging the

Cricket is a popular sport, usually played on th[e] Esplanade.

languid northern beaches is pretty fruitless, with the exception of tumbled-down **Perouládes**, which secretly hides a little cove where the local children play in the waves, surrounded by majestic cliff formations which mock their poor relations.

With such a history of invasion, the vulnerable islanders tended to live away from the coast so that much of the real Corfu lies quietly hidden in the hills. Treading carefully, the traveller can still find these timeless villages amongst the lush vegetation and spectacular scenery in the northwest part of the island. After the northern coastal resorts, travelling inland is to find a corner of heaven in a nightmare of tourism.

West Coast: Going down the west coast, it's easy to appreciate why **Paleo-kastrítsa** has become such a popular resort, comprising a series of beautiful bays embraced by ancient jagged rocks and a backdrop of dramatic greenness. Away from the maddening masses, the enterprising can discover a cluster of secluded coves to hide away in, where the only sound is of the silky sea water licking the shores.

At Paleokastrítsa's gleaming hillside monastery, the bizarre mixes with the Byzantine. Periodically coachloads of tattooed tourists noisily dodge priests and goats on a two-minute tour of the church. The sacrilegious soon depart from the house of God and the monastery can be visited in temporary tranquillity, before the next air-conditioned onslaught make an appearance.

Although the mid-west coast is now being hit by property developers it still feels less frenetic compared to the east and northern shores. By **Pélekas**, the tourist combination is a strange mix of the package variety and summer hippies, who sleep out on the quieter beaches round **Myrtiótissa**.

The South: The southern part of Corfu is often neglected by visitors. The landscape becomes flatter and less interesting, but there is ample opportunity for discovering the undiscovered. A venture down the eastern coast road through the tourist tat of **Benítses** and **Messongí**

wo faces of orfu.

would lead most discerning travellers begging to differ, but as with the north, the inland roads open up another country. A visit to the **Achillion** invites you inland. Loved and hated, this strange folly was created by Empress Elisabeth of Austria in a kitsch attempt at neo-classical style. Taking the road high up to Aghios Déka, the journey south is best enjoyed meandering down along the road through **Strongylí**. The east coast then begs for reconsideration by the time **Arghyrádes** is reached. Coastal villages such as **Boúkaris** and **Petrití** feel a refreshing million miles away from the dismally over-subscribed resorts up the coast.

With a river cutting into its heart, the visitor will note the deep south feel of the heated, dusty town of **Lefkímmi**. The southerners seem to have a healthy contempt for the *en masse* holidaymakers, keeping them carefully herded in at the fish and chip resort of **Kávos**, a ghastly enclosure at the southern end of the island.

Continuing on the road south of Kávos, the polite conspiracy to keep tourists at bay seems to reach its epitome. The signposts are strangely concealed by overgrowth and the road becomes sufficiently rough to deter any girls from hobbling far in their holiday high heels. However, the conspiracy theory can be left behind on reaching the unspoiled villages of **Sparterá**, **Bastátika** and **Kritiká**, as explorers are congratulated for their effort with warm welcomes.

Pretty villages: The western coastal section going north towards **Aghios Yeórgios** boasts long stretches of sandy beaches, which have a windswept, barren appeal. The marshland surrounding **Lake Korissíon** indicates that it is not going to be as exotic as its name, but the long, flat stretches of land and still water are fairly atmospheric. North of the charming settlement of **Aghios Matthaéos**, the scenery again returns to hilly splendour and the beaches get busier. Picturesque roads wind through pretty villages across the slim waist of the island, and wind their way back to the centre of Corfu Town.

Swimming near Pondikónisi (Mouse Island).

WORKING THE LAND

The silver olive trees which grace the Ionian landscape play more than a picturesque part in island life. For thousands of years the olive and its rich, distinctive oil have formed a staple part of not only the Greek diet, but the Ionian economy as well. For most island farmers, however, agricultural produce is for domestic use only and traditional non-mechanised farming methods, due to Greece's hilly terrain, are in some respects preserving an agricultural system which is finally well on its way to extinction.

A typical farming community is a disorganised scatter of between 20 and 100 houses closely packed together with small yards where chickens and the occasional pig (being fattened for Christmas) might be found. Most of these remote villages now have road communications and at least one telephone, but running water can often be a problem, especially at the height of a busy summer.

A village on any Greek island which is farmed in the traditional way can usually be spotted by the irregular fields which form its territory. It is the system of splitting up the land to form inheritances and marriage dowries which has resulted in this unusual visual aspect of the rural landscape.

A remote village has probably three types of farmers. First, there's the large-scale goat-herder with 100 to 500 head of animals, who purchases food such as maize and prepared animal-feed cake. He concentrates on producing kids or lambs for the peak periods of Easter and the New Year. The second type is the small-scale farmer, often a man who, in his retirement, wants to keep his household supplied with bread, pulses (lentils, broad beans and chick peas – the staple diet of winter) and vegetables. Finally, the list includes single, elderly women working on their own.

An example of the latter is Voula, a 50-year-old spinster who farms on the mainland island of Euboea, but whose aged, bent figure can be seen throughout Greece. Voula's father was deaf and mute. Fearing that any children would suffer the same disability, no villager would marry her. She has two acres split into about 10 fields, on which she keeps four goats, all female. After the first gentle rains of autumn, most of Voula's fields are sown with crops. Ploughing is done by donkey or mule. The plough is bladed and controlled by means of a handle at the rear. Crops for Voula's goats include barley and oats; crops for herself might be wheat, lentils and broad beans.

Once the bitter winds of winter arrive, most small-scale farmers collect branches from wild bushes like the strawberry tree which they bring down from the hills by donkey for feed. In some remote villages the proportion of elderly people is quite high, and it is not unusual to see 80-year-olds scaling mulberry trees.

In spring, people like Voula take their animals to graze in fields away from the village, once the height of the crop reaches four or five inches. As the season progresses the ubiquitous vegetable gardens begin producing tomatoes, potatoes, beans, and aubergines. These crops supplement the diet well into the summer but involve the investment of much time, labour, and effort.

In June the work in the fields is back-breaking, for the harvest is reaped by hand with a sickle or scythe. The cut crop is laid out in the fields to dry, then (if grain) carried back to be threshed.

Threshing is now usually done by machine but in some islands, such as Kárpathos and Amorgós, it is still done by walking a team of hired mules or donkeys over the strewn crop to smash the husks with their hoofs. The crop is then winnowed, thrown into the breeze to free the straw and chaff, then sieved.

These traditional farming methods are quickly disappearing. The exodus of the youth from the villages to the towns or mainland to find work, plus the introduction of Greek farming into competition with other European Union countries have meant that methods must change. The large proportion of elderly people within many villages, plus the number of fields over-grown with scrub, bear witness to this fact. This difficult but picturesque way of life does still exist, however; it just needs a sharp eye to detect and the willingness to climb a few hills to witness. ∎

THE IONIAN ISLANDS

PAXOS: Modest Paxos (Paxi, Paxoi), a three-hour sail from Corfu, is often written up in glossy magazines as the ideal Greek island. Natural beauty consists of rugged cliffs, a number of littoral caves, and several fine beaches, all interspersed with groves of olive trees. The gnarled, twisted trunks of these trees and the leaves like handfuls of silver coins tossed to the breeze are landmarks of the island, one of only several reasons why some people return to Paxos season after season.

The pleasures of a stay on Paxos are simple. There is little in the way of organised entertainment, and although each year the island becomes more popular, the unpredictable Ionian weather means that ferries and smaller craft occasionally cannot land at all, unintentionally preserving a tranquil and low-key atmosphere.

Most accommodation is located in the main port of **Gáios**, where island life is played out around one square consisting of *kafeneía* and shops. Gáios is sheltered from the winds by the islet Aghios Nikólaos, a rocky outcrop known simply as "Kastro" on account of its 14th century fortress.

Paxos's main road begins and ends at the bus station, although tracks do criss-cross the olive groves to service the farming communities. The road leads to the northern village of **Lákka**, a picturesque second port containing a Byzantine church.

Best beaches, however, are to be found in the south on the lovely and insular islet **Antípaxos** (Andípaxoi), reached by caique from Gáios. Home to just 126 people, the eastern coast of Antípaxos is gentle and rolling; the west coast landscape is wilder and more dramatic. Uncluttered sandy beaches are to be found on either side of the harbour. A day spent in Antípaxos is made all the more tolerable by sampling the locally produced red or white wine.

LEFKAS: Connected to the coast of Akarnanía by a floating drawbridge, Léfkas (Lefkáda) feels much like an appendage to the mainland. Several buses daily deposit visitors from Athens in the thriving capital, also called **Léfkas**, which has a busy marina.

A good network of local buses plies the road which follows each coastline. The east coast is home to Léfkas's most attractive resorts. **Nidrí** is a fashionable spot increasingly popular with yachtsmen and package tours. The beach is fair, the ambience relaxed and the tavernas offer decent but expensive food.

Nidrí looks out over the wooded islets of **Spárti**, **Meganíssi**, **Madourí**, and **Skorpiós**. In the high season caiques make frequent runs from Nidrí to Meganíssi. Skorpiós is owned by the Onassis family and was once a private playground for Jackie Kennedy and her children.

Five kilometres (3 miles) beyond is **Vlychó**, less crowded and pleasing. Perhaps the most attractive of all is **Vassilikí**, 40 km (25 miles) south of Léfkas and situated at the mouth of a deep blue bay. The long beach and the usually land-

ward breeze is popular with windsurfers.

At the end of the long headland across the bay is the island's best-known landmark, the bare, rocky headland known as **Sappho's Leap** 72 metres (235 ft) above an angry sea. It was from these white cliffs that Sappho and others allegedly followed a local tradition. An ancient legend (immortalised by Byron) held that a cure for unrequited love might be sought by flinging oneself from these cliffs into the Ionian Sea far below. Frequent caiques round these cliffs to reach the beautifully located, but now often crowded, **Porto Katsiki** beach on the western coast.

ITHAKI: This island, also known as Ithaca, is commonly thought to be the home of Odysseus, the voyager in Homer's *The Odyssey*. In chapter nine the hero of the Trojan War reveals himself to King Alcinous: "I am Odysseus, Laertes' son. The whole world talks of my stratagems, and my fame has reached the heavens. My home is under the clear skies of Ithaca. Our landmark is the wooded peak of windswept Neriton. For neighbours we have many peopled isles with no great space between them, Dulichium and Same and wooded Zacynthus. But Ithaca, the farthest out to sea, lies slanting to the west, whereas the others face the dawn and rising sun. It is a rough land, but a fit nurse of men. And I, for one, know of no sweeter sight for man's eyes than his own country."

Some scholars have disputed Ithaki's claim to be the "precipitous isle" of the fable, but few visitors who make the 1-mile journey from Cephalonia, or disembark by ferry at the pretty wooded capital of Vathí would agree. The island is indeed a "rough land", heavily indented with navy blue bays and flower-studded mountains.

It is a peaceful, low-key place, and the people who visit either linger only a short time to savour the Homeric associations or keep to themselves. There is little to do on the island save to walk and talk and enjoy the tranquillity of this "island of goat-pastures", but the locals are exceedingly friendly and eager to converse with strangers.

Many of the men speak a curious

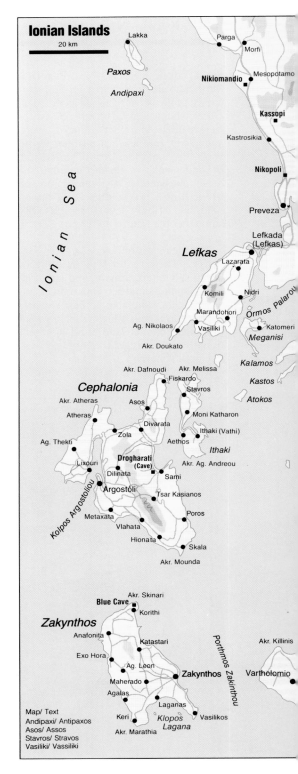

patois of Greek and English, having sailed the seas on merchant ships and then, like the local hero, returned home to their island again.

Ithaki is actually two peninsulas joined by an isthmus barely wide enough for the island's main road. For centuries there has been good-humoured rivalry between the inhabitants of each peninsula as to which can claim to be Odysseus's true home. Best contender would seem to be the prehistoric acropolis in the south of the island where archaeologists have unearthed significant finds of both the Classical and the Hellenistic eras.

Many of these relics are now being kept in the British Museum in London. Although all that remains of the acropolis today is one ruined tower and some ancient walls alongside, the structure has been optimistically named the **Castle of Odysseus.**

The town of Vathí is located at the end of a fjord-like finger of water off the Molos Gulf. The gulf, backed by silent green hills, is plunged into shadow much of the time so after a rather brooding ferry ride rounding the corner to sparkling white **Vathí** is a dazzling surprise. The houses ring a horse-shoe shaped bay, in the middle of which is an islet of pine trees off which Lord Byron is said to have gone swimming.

Buses leave from Vathí to the island's handful of villages. There is also a small **archaeological museum** containing vases from the 8th century BC. A short but energetic and hot 3-km (2-mile) walk leads to the **Cave of the Nymphs** where Odysseus is believed to have hidden the treasures bestowed on him by the Phaiakes.

Five kilometres (3 miles) south of Vathí is the spring of Perapigadi, which has been identified as Homer's **Fountain of Arethúsa.** The springs are said to have been named after a nymph of Artemis, who on hearing of her son's death wept so copiously that she turned into a fountain.

To appreciate fully the beautiful northern peninsula it is necessary to have transport (scooters and bicycles can be

hired in Vathí). However, the three principal villages can be reached by bus. These are the coastal resorts of **Frikés** and **Kióni** and the attractive town of **Stávros**, which is 16 km (10 miles) northwest of Vathí.

Stávros has only one main street but boasts a beautifully proportioned church. Within striking distance is ancient **Pólis**, the north's contender as the home of Odysseus's palace.

CEPHALONIA: The largest and most mountainous of the Ionians, Cephalonia (Kefaloniá) has long been popular with Greeks interested in rambling and exploring. Only in the past few years have foreign operators begun to exploit Cephalonia's potential and even now it isn't an island for everyone.

Distances are long, and public transport not only minimal but death-defying; the bus from the port of Sami to the capital, Argostóli, runs along a mountain road which is level with the tree tops in the ravine below. Mopeds and car hire can be expensive, even by Greek standards, but some form of transport is necessary to enjoy the island, for its appeal lies in the landscape – lush, green and rugged. **Mount Aínos** rises to a towering 1,628 metres (5,340 ft); its slopes are covered with the tree known, reasonably, as the "Cephalonia fir".

For some time the island has been of interest to geologists and students of animal behaviour. As well as providing a "bottomless" lake and a "rocking" stone, until 1963 no one was able to provide an explanation for the sea-water at Katavóthres, just outside Argostóli, which flows into two rifts by the shore. The mystery was solved by a team of Austrians and now the buildings around these "sea mills" (also known as swallow holes) with their big, gently rocking wheels, have been turned into a nightclub where plate smashing takes place on many a summer's evening.

Snakes and goats provide stories which have as much basis in science as in myth. The first story, to which locals swear, concerns the snakes at a small village in the southeast, **Markópoulo**. Apparently, during the hot summer month of August, small, harmless snakes

appear and, wiggling in a convoy, set out for the church heading for a silver icon of Our Lady.

Although some scientists believe the phenomenon has more to do with the migratory patterns of the snakes than religion, villagers regard "Our Lady's snakes" as a good omen and now catch the escaping reptiles in bottles to bring them to the church.

The "goats with silver teeth" to be found in the region of **Mount Aghía Dynámi** can also be explained by science; the soil on which the animals graze contains minerals which discolour the animals' teeth.

The village of **Fiskárdo**, 54km (34 miles) northeast of Argostóli and named after an 11th-century Norman ruler, is the only settlement on the island not to have been devastated by the earthquake of 1953. It is pretty and quaint, and its Venetian houses are clustered around an attractive harbour. Fiskárdo is popular with yachtsmen and, increasingly, foreign tourists, especially Italians.

Assos, well-known for panoramic

An elegant overview of Cephalonia.

views, a Venetian castle and a good, sandy beach, has the island's best nightlife, while the rather dreary port of **Sami** is best used for catching a ferry to Ithaki or Corfu or as a base for exploring two of the island's many caves.

Melissáni Cave, one mile north, contains an indoor lake which catches the sun's rays in some breath-taking configurations. **Drogarátis Cave** lies just west of Sami. Its main attraction is an enormous chamber filled with multi-coloured stalactites and stalagmites. During the summer months, concerts are occasionally held here under the illuminated ceiling – a dramatic setting.

The capital town of **Argostóli** has been rebuilt in a utilitarian, rather than a graceful style. Buildings are squat, square and unlovely, giving a vague impression of the frontier towns seen in a hundred cowboy films. Nevertheless, the town has a rough and ready charm centred around the main *plateía*. On Saturday night locals eat spaghetti outside one of the many tavernas and call out warnings to their teenaged children

who insist on revving the motors of their souped-up cars.

Sights to see include an **archaeological museum** and the **Korghialéneios Library** which contains a collection of Byzantine icons. **Platys Yialos** beach lies just outside town. Other sandy beaches on the island include **Myrtós, Makri Yalos, Plati Yalos**, and the shores around the resort of **Póros**.

ZÁKYNTHOS: Both Pliny and Homer found Zákynthos (Zante) appealing and there are understandable reasons why the island has been one of the more recent choices for international development. Its beaches are broad and sandy. An abundance of natural springs once earned the island the sobriquet "the Flower of the Levant" from the Venetians, and even now the twisting lanes and banks of wild flowers keep the land fragrant and fresh. For many years perfume has been made and sold locally from these flowers. The wine, a full bodied white or rosé, is perfectly palatable and very popular.

Zákynthians had, in the past, a rich

Panorama of the port of Zákynthos from Bóchali.

store of ethnic customs and a high cultural standing in the arts. Among a distinguished list of writers, artists and musicians two are outstanding: Dionýsios Solomós and Panayiótis Doxarás. Dionýsios Solomós was born in Zákynthos in 1798. At the age of 25 he wrote the poem *Hymn to Liberty*, which, when set to music, became the Greek national anthem. Panayiótis Doxarás and later, his son, became leading lights of the Zákynthos School of Painting. Fuelled with enthusiasm by a trip to Venice, Doxarás returned to revolutionise the existing concepts of Byzantine art; his influential icons can be seen in the church **Kyria ton Angélon** (Our Lady of the Angels).

Once the island airport began to accept international bookings, the construction of hotel complexes and tour companies was not far behind. Most of this development has been crammed onto the south coast, along the soft sands and clear shallow waters of **Laganás**. The unprecedented rise in tourism has in fact brought about a serious threat to the delicate ecology of Zákynthos and has provoked a debate which divided the islanders.

Other beach resorts popular with tourists are **Kerí** on the southwest coast, and **Alikés** on the bay of the same name. Beaches at **Vassilikós, Yeráki** and tiny **Pórto Róma** attract fewer people, especially out of season. Inland villages have up till now been spared the developer's axe, and Zákynthos's sweet-smelling terrain makes cycling to the beach a genuine pleasure.

Try the village of **Lithakiá**, 13 km (8 miles) south of Zákynthos Town, or in the north **Mariés, Orthoniés,** or **Volímes**; each claim important churches. From Volímes it is possible to take a boat trip to a well-known and interesting attraction, the **Blue Grotto**, where two sea caves interconnect. A 14th-century Venetian castle close to Volímes has fine views.

It was on the hill known as **Strandi**, just above Zákynthos Town, that Solomós was inspired to write the song which inspires a nation. His tomb occupies the ground floor of the **Dionýsios Solomós Museum** in the centre of town. Zákynthos Town itself is an admirable attempt to recreate the architectural splendour the town enjoyed before the earthquake of 1953.

When approached by sea at night, it does indeed rise up in magnificent splendour, its towers and tall elegant buildings illuminated by shafts of light. During the day, the effect diminishes as it becomes obvious that this is a "new" town. Nevertheless, the amenities are good, the restaurants are mostly above average and the boulevards remain pleasant and broad.

Paintings and icons from the Ionian School can be seen in the **Byzantine Museum** and in the previously mentioned Our Lady of the Angels church.

Other churches worth going to see are **St Nicholas of Molos, St Dionýsios**, with its relic of the island saint, and the **church of the Virgin Chrysopigi**, 3 km (2 miles) west in the garden suburb of **Bóchali**. Wonderful views of both sea and town can be had from the medieval walls of the ancient **Acropolis**.

The Venetians called Zákynthos the Flower of the Levant.

TURTLES

The loggerhead turtle (*Caretta caretta*) crawls out of the sea onto the moonlit beach of her birthplace, the island of Zákynthos. She has crossed the length of the Mediterranean to return, at last, to this spot. Summoning all her strength, the 90-kg (200-lb) reptile carefully selects a place in the sand where she digs a nest with her rear flippers. Satisfied with her cocoon, she lays 100 soft eggs, each the size of a ping-pong ball, covers them with soft sand and returns to the sea exhausted to rest in the shallows. Then she swims away, unaware that her maternal labouring may have been in vain. For here on Zákynthos, tourism is threatening these ancient creatures with extinction.

The survival of the loggerhead is endangered before she even reaches the beach. In the early evening, the shallow coastal waters are filled with female turtles resting after their long journey to the island. It has been estimated that nearly half these turtles are maimed or killed by the propellers of pedalos or speedboats taking out waterskiers and para-gliders. Carelessly discarded litter from the 30,000 tourists creates another hazard, as turtles suffocate trying to swallow plastic bags which they mistake for jellyfish, a favourite food of theirs.

For the female turtle, the hazards increase when she slips ashore. Disorientated by the glittering lights of hotels and the strange noises coming from the tourists and tavernas, she may scurry back to the seas, uncertain where to deposit her eggs, which are to ensure the continuation of a species that has lived on the earth for 90 million years.

Those mothers who try to continue their labours will suffer the indignity of ignorant spectators brandishing torches and flashing camera lights, frightening the turtles back into the sea where the eggs may be released never to hatch.

Those eggs laid in nests successfully are often doomed by motorcyclists, horse riders and car drivers who speed across the sand, packing it down so that it is impossible for the hatchlings to emerge. Beach umbrellas are unwittingly driven into nests, piercing the eggs. Tamarisk trees, planted in haste to shade the sunbathers, pose other problems as hatchlings become tangled up in the tree roots. Even the innocent sandcastle builder may create holes which become shallow graves for the young turtles.

Hatching takes place from early August to late September – at the time of year when most of the tourists arrive. Only one egg in 1,000 will reach puberty, even in normal circumstances. The 2½-inch (6-cm) hatchlings may emerge from their hazardous 50-day incubation and, instead of heading instinctively to the light on the horizon line at sea, frequently wander confused up the beach to the dazzling lights of the hotels and bars. This error brings death from exhaustion or from dehydration.

The natural struggle from nest to sea is of no small biological significance. Somehow, that short, arduous experience is imprinted on the hatchlings, as they return perhaps 30 years later to mate and for the females to lay their eggs in their own birthplace.

For thousands of years Zákynthos has boasted the greatest concentration of nesting turtles in the Mediterranean. The Langanás bay coastline was once a favourite spot for the nesting mothers. Confused by the combination of boats, buildings and noise the past few years of tourism have brought, the turtles have abandoned the busy sands. The majority now nest in the more secluded beaches of Sekánia and Dáphni, where there is barely room for the activities of the bewildered reptiles. Only 800 turtles now reproduce on Zákynthos, almost half the number to be found here 15 years ago.

Conservation efforts have led to the prohibition of construction near the nesting sites and now a marine park is being proposed. However, the islanders are divided on the ecology issue: the income available from tourism glitters with a profitability that outweighs very much interest in protecting the turtles. While this war continues, visitors to the island can all make a contribution to the survival of the turtles, by showing a little understanding of the loggerheads and helping them in their battle against extinction. ∎

THE SARONIC GULF ISLANDS

SALAMIS, AEGINA, PÓROS, HYDRA, SPÉTSES

The five islands of the Saronic Gulf might best be described as "commuter" islands. Lying only half an hour by ferry or hydrofoil from Piraeus, the temptation is to treat the islands as an extension of the mainland, or specifically, suburbs of Athens.

Merchants have been quick to exploit the proximity. The short cruise from Piraeus to Spétses which calls at three Saronic islands is a very popular attraction for tourists visiting Athens rivalled, perhaps, only by Delphi as the most enjoyable day spent out of town. When the cruise ships mingle with the hydrofoils, the ferry boats, and the regularly scheduled caiques, there is often a virtual traffic jam on the waves, and foreigners greatly outnumber Greeks at most Saronic ports.

In spite of all this, the islands are distinctive, rich in history and – behind the crowds and chi-chi boutiques – remarkably attractive. Salamis is renowned for the epoch-making naval battle in 480 BC which decided the outcome of the Persian Wars. Aegina is the site of the Temple of Apháios, one of the most important antiquities located on any Greek island.

Poros has been immortalised by Henry Miller in one of his books and Spétses by John Fowles in one of his novels. Not to be outdone, Hydra is the part-time home of the singer Leonard Cohen, who can occasionally be seen in the local cafés and bars.

Preceding pages and **left**, lunchtime on Hydra and Spétses.

THE SARONIC GULF ISLANDS

SALAMIS: This low, flat island (also called Salamína) is popular with Athenians but offers little interest to visitors. The most fun to be had might well be the half-hour journey from Piraeus; the tiny caique laden with commuters reading tabloid newspapers, threads its way between huge liners destined for more exotic locations.

Boats dock at **Selínia** on the east coast, an unimpressive port with a muddy beach and a few *pensions*. Most passengers take one of the larger ferries from **Pérama** on the mainland to the main harbour **Paloúkia**, a town with a strong naval presence and a couple of waterside tavernas.

The island's capital, **Salamína,** lies 3 km (2 miles) northwest, and hugs an expansive bay. The quayside teams with activity as much gossiping as well as shopping takes place at the open-air fish stalls directly in front of the harbour. At night, when the bay is lit by lights hung in the trees which separate the beach from the street, a much-needed touch of style is introduced.

Relics from the island's distinguished past can be found in the **archaeological museum**. Ancient sources have shown that not only did Salamína participate in the Trojan War, but it was also the site of a famous naval battle in 480 BC between the Greeks and the Persians. This skirmish was decisive for the outcome of the Persian Wars and Greek independence.

Aiánteio (also known as Moulíki) lies 7 km (4 miles) southwest of the capital. Aiánteio throbs to the sound of a disco beat and offers a sweeping view of the southern peninsula. It is the best place to eat seafood, preferably at sunset when the bay a beautiful turns golden red colour.

The only site worth visiting by the surprisingly good bus network is the **Panaghia Convent**, 8 km (5 miles) northwest of Salamína. Situated among pine trees, the chapel dates from the 11th century. Walls are decorated with handsome frescos and more than 3,000 figures are painted in detail.

AEGINA: The island's close proximity to Athens and a strategic position in the Mediterranean trading waters has meant that, since ancient times, this sophisticated community has enjoyed an outlook more urban than Greek island. The first settlements on the island date from around 3000 BC. In 650 BC European coinage was minted here, and in 1828, the year Aegina became the capital of free Greece, drachmas were made in a local foundry. John Capodistrias, the first president of independent Greece, ordered the building of fine mansions, many of which still line the streets of the modern capital today.

Unfortunately, the same qualities which produced this worldly aspect are responsible for Aegina's present-day disadvantages. Passengers from the 30-minute hydrofoil journey and the one-day cruises from Athens flood in by the thousands and the merchants are quick to cash in. Souvenir shops and tacky stalls selling (admittedly very fresh)

Saronic Gulf Islands

25 km

pistachio nuts clutter the landscape and the island's masterpiece, the magnificent Temple of Aphaías, can barely be appreciated above the babble of multilingual tour guides.

There are a few compensations. Roads are good, beaches are maintained and easily reached by bus, and most people speak English. Fortunately, the trippers tend to congregate in only two towns, **Aghía Marína**, a resort on the east coast boasting a sandy beach backed by pine trees, and the island capital 14 km (9 miles) to the west, which is also called Aegina.

Aegina is a handsome town, with its wide marina dominating the seafront and its well-proportioned 19th-century buildings providing a dignified aspect. The cathedral, where Capodistrias was sworn into power, dates from 1806. Above the crescent-shaped harbour lies the most ancient part of town, the **Hill of Korona**, where one column of a **Temple to Apollo** can still be seen.

This is a place to seek out relative tranquillity until the daily boats depart and life resumes at a more pleasing pace. Twilight in the capital is played out against a backdrop of strolling tourists and locals, plentiful seafood restaurants and the clip-clop of hooves from the horses which pull brightly decorated carriages.

The **Temple of Aphaías** (Aféas) was constructed on a hill 12 km (7 miles) east of Aegina, above the resort town of Aghía Marína.

The temple is one of the most important in antiquity and one of the finest ruins to be found on any Greek island. Dedicated to the goddess of wisdom and light, the temple was built between 510 and 480 BC and commands a stunning view of the sea and the island – the best time to go and see it is at sunset, it really is a sight to behold.

Of the original 32 columns, 24 have been preserved, as well as the foundation of an altar and the remains of a priests' chamber. The magnificent sculptured pediments depicting scenes from the Trojan War were, sadly, removed by Prince Ludwig of Bavaria in 1813 and

The Temple of Aphaías, one of the finest ancient ruins to be found on the islands.

are now housed in Munich, in Germany although lesser finds from the temple are on display in the **archaeological museum** in Aegina.

Palaiochora is a spooky Byzantine hill town riddled with churches and ruins, worth a dedicated ramble if stout walking shoes are to hand. Islanders sought refuge here from pirates in the ninth and 10th centuries and the site was a flourishing community right up until 1800, when the population drifted slowly back to the sea ports.

Perdika, 9 km (6 miles) southeast of Aegina with its many fish tavernas along the small harbour is a marvellous place for lunch or dinner. Excursions by boat from Perdika can be made to the neighbouring islet **Moni** for a swim in the clear blue waters there.

PÓROS: Sailing through the straits of Póros is so impressive that ferry captains often call out to the passengers to hasten deck-side so as not to miss the magnificent view. Henry Miller, writing in *The Colossus of Maroussi,* describes it this way: "To sail slowly through the streets of Póros is to recapture the joy of passing through the neck of the womb. It is a joy almost too deep to be remembered."

Miller's "streets" are actually 400 metres (1,300 ft) of water which separate Póros from the mainland and from which the island takes its name. (The word *Póros* means "passage".) Sailing them today might not be quite as joyous as Miller's interpretation, but certainly it is disconcerting, not least, one assumes, to the Porians who must contend with boat-loads of foreigners peering through their windows.

The mainland plays an economic as well as a scenic part in the lives of the islanders. Some of them farm the land on the other side of the straits and "commute" between Póros and their farms on the mainland.

Póros is actually two islands, united by a causeway. The northern section is verdant and green, at least 10 times the size of the volcanic islet on which most of the population lives. Although midway between Aegina and Hydra, this

he greenery nd pistachio roves of egina.

industrious island lacks the glamour of its near neighbours and as a result is much less frenzied.

In the last few years, the wooded bays of the north have become the destination for many British package holiday companies, an influence which is also felt in the town of **Póros**.

Póros is built around several hills, one hill crowned with a blue and white clock tower. The climb to the tower is revealing – melons, grapes and flowers overhang domestic verandas. Staircases which begin with promise are apt to end in a villa-owner's market garden. This disregard for tourism is also evident along the harbour, where pride of place is given to a busy, even smelly, meat market.

On the northern side of town stands the **Naval Training School.** The buildings, completed in 1849, were Greece's main naval base until 1878. A stroll through this part of Póros can be quite refreshing on a hot summer afternoon, due to a series of fine family mansions surrounded by their well-tended gardens.

The **Monastery of Zoödóchou Pighís** lies 20 minutes by bus from Póros next to a hillside spring. This 18th-century whitewashed building is dedicated to the Virgin of the Life-Giving Spring. Although it is common practice for Greeks to be buried behind the sacred walls of a monastery, Zoödóchou Pighís is exceptional in that it contains the graves of three foreigners – one English, one Russian and one Italian.

The first two were victims of the War of Independence in 1821. The latter was the daughter of the noted painter Raffaelo Ceccoli, who helped to create, among other things, the Athens School of Fine Arts. Ceccoli and his family were living on the island when his daughter fell ill and died at the age of 21. Ceccoli painted the portrait of the Virgin (the Life-Giving Force) inside the monastery near the altar and as a memorial to her, embellished the painting with the features of his daughter.

HYDRA: Although mentioned by Herodotus in the 5th century BC it was not until the 17th century that Hydra

The "Flying Dolphin" hydrofoil calls regularly at Póros.

148

(Ydra) came to prominence. Shipbuilding brought a welcome and lucrative income and by the next century Hydriots dominated the seas, sailing as far afield as America and bringing back goods of distinction and beauty. Captains built huge mansions in the port to house their booty and the island's experienced seamen made a substantial contribution to the War of Independence.

In an act of remarkable charity, the people of Hydra offered to shelter the population of nearby Spétses, an island which suffered greatly in the conflict. Although the offer wasn't taken up, it was a commendable gesture for a people known more for inter-island rivalry than solidarity.

In the 1960s, artists, attracted by the port's symmetry and clear, bright light, took up residence which in turn attracted well-heeled hippies. Hydra became a minor jet-set destination and even today, the movie stars and artists having, for the most part decamped to other resorts, the island is a fashionable, expensive place more akin to Athens' Plaka

or Mýkonos than her nearer Saronic neighbours.

Chic boutiques line the quayside (US dollars are accepted) and cocktail bars overflow with poseurs sporting the best hair-dos to be found in Greece. Cruise passengers and daytrippers add to the general parade and although the atmosphere is far from restful, this onslaught of visitors does not erode the island's charm at all.

Many of Hydra's *archontiká* (Italian-style mansions) have been refurbished in their original style, grey stone on the outside, tastefully furnished on the inside. A branch of the Athens School of Fine Arts is housed in the Tombázis villa; the Merchant Navy Academy in the Tsambadósa mansion.

The streets behind the harbour are prettily cobbled, narrow, and twisting. White-washed walls give way to elegant doors (lion's-head brass door knockers are much in evidence) and small squares provide refuge from the worst of the crowds.

Better still for peace and tranquillity

A 19th-century bridge at Mlychós, Hydra.

is the rest of the island. The only real town is the capital and port and as cars are banned, the trippers and the trendies rarely venture farther afield than a far-flung café.

An hour's walk upwards and inland leads to the **Convent of Aghía Efpraxia** and the **Monastery of Profítis Ilias**, while the Zoúrvas Monastery is to be found in the extreme east. Island beaches, however, are less impressive. One of the few sandy beaches can be found at **Mandráki** just east of the town.

SPETSES: Just 22 sq km (8 sq miles) in area, Spétses (Spetsai) is the birthplace of a national heroine. During the 1821 revolution, Laskarína Bouboulína, as the story is told, was on Spétses when a Turkish fleet approached. Bouboulína organised for all the hats available on the island to be gathered together (and there were many, as all Turkish subjects were required to wear a fez) which she then placed on towering plants which grew along the shore.

From the sea the fezzes looked like a platoon of soldiers crouched in the grasses ready to do battle with invaders. The Turks fled, the women rejoiced, and the island was saved from invaders. Laskarína, who became a captain on her husband's ship after he was murdered, went on to inspire many poets and writers. The historian Filimonas said of this brave Spetsiot: "She put cowards to shame and brave men made way for her." A rather flattering portrait of Ms Bouboulína can be found on the present-day 50-drachma note.

The 1821 revolution constitutes the most glorious chapter in the island's history. Spétses was one of the first islands to raise the flag of rebellion in the War of Independence and its notable fleet fought with dignity. In the centre of the harbour town, the Dápia, cannons protect the harbour.

Today the **Dápia** is the hub of island life, ringed by tavernas and cafés. Tiny red and white water taxis buzz between the port and the mainland with scenic regularity; there is a slight touch of Venice in the carefree atmosphere. Many of the narrow, cobbled alleyways threading through the town are inlaid with pebble mosaics, primarily of mythical marine figures. These back streets contain several fine *archontiká,* most of which are owned by wealthy Athenians and used as summer homes.

The former Chadziyannis Mexis mansion is the **island museum** where Bouboulína's bones now reside. Her house, too, has been preserved, but is not always open to the public. Just outside the town is a curious phenomenon: a Greek impression of an English public school called the **Anarghyrios and Korghialenios College**. The novelist John Fowles taught here and used the island as a setting for his book, *The Magus.*

Boats depart regularly from the Dapia, calling in at several coves sheltered by trees. **Bekíris's** cave on the west coast was used as a hiding place by islanders during the war. Further south, at the very tip of Spétses, looms the hilly terrain of **Spetsopóula.** This well-tended, well-guarded islet is owned by the wealthy Greek shipping magnate, Stavros Niarchos.

The sophistication of the Saronic Gulf islands is mirrored in Spétses.

PLUMBING

A scribbled note behind the bathroom door warned: "Greek loos are dodgy. Throw your paper in the bin provided." Another notice, in another place, was more to the point: "Don't put anything down the toilet you haven't consumed first." It's a sobering thought after *kalamária* and a few ouzos.

In Greece, all things lavatorial are a snare and a delusion. Greek plumbing is the eighth wonder of the world. You wonder how it works at all. Everyone has a plumbing experience to relate.

Seasoned Grecophiles know all about the no-paper rule, thus avoiding clogging, flood and hysterics from landladies. They also know that it's a good idea to carry tissues or *hartopetsétes* (napkins) nabbed from taverna tables, just in case. Cramped cubicles at the back of Kostas's, Yorgos's or Charis's seldom bear close inspection with overflowing bins, floors awash and no loo roll. *In extremis* the brand-name cry of "Softex" is a nationally recognised distress signal.

Squat-over loos are common, especially if they are public conveniences. You might even come across a hole in the floor over the sea for instant and natural flushing. Brace yourself: some toilets can be grim. For reasons known only to themselves – fear of lavatory seats? Aids scares? – some Greeks prefer to ignore the pan altogether and use the floor instead. And that's just in the Ladies.

In the main, toilet facilities in most tavernas and restaurants are adequate with soap, towels and the ever-present bottle of *chloríni*. But perhaps the biggest mystery of all is why the Greeks go in for bathroom fittings which are straight out of *Homes and Gardens*.

Visit the remotest of islands, the poorest of village rooms and you can be sure that the *tó loutró* (bathroom) will be sumptuously equipped and decorated. Colours outmoded in more sophisticated countries, like avocado, rose pink or even deep, hard-to-clean maroon, are all the rage. Patterned tiles, the more garish the better, are a must, as are the bidet, shower with backless chair but no curtain, fancy taps and mirror-fronted bathroom cabinet.

The fact that there's rarely a shower tray, just a hole in the uneven floor down which water refuses to drain (you have to urge it along with your loo brush) or that the door won't shut because it's been warped by all this water and the posh fittings have also gone rusty is neither here nor there. Sometimes even running water seems optional. But the matching suite is essential, especially if your lodgings are eventually to become a dowry for a lucky daughter.

"Can we drink the water?" is a normal tourist question. "Where can we find the water?" is a specifically Greek inquiry. Lack of fresh water is a giant problem for many islands so you may have to get by with bottled, and wait patiently for the waterboat to arrive.

When the boat comes in there's usually a mad scramble with hosepipes as families fill up their wells, jugs, and containers. You may find you have to make daily trips to the pump or village tap as well. Most countries take good old H_2O for granted, but in arid Greece in high summer water is a precious commodity and conservation is the key.

"Save water: shower with a friend," one taverna sticker advised. In the Dodecanese a yachtie almost got lynched by furious villagers for doing his washing at the communal fresh-water tap. So be warned, and pursue cleanliness accordingly.

Some islands like Chálki, in the Dodecanese, have Heath Robinson water systems relying on pumps, fittings, and a spaghetti junction of bewildering pipework. The natural water supply is brackish but every now and then it can be switched over to fresh for a virtual feast of salt-free washing.

Pondering over pressure, bores, cisterns, pumps and ball-cocks one visitor asked a Greek plumber why he couldn't put paper down the pan. What was the secret of Hellenic plumbing?

The workman scratched his head, sipped his coffee and eventually revealed: "The pipes. She is different size from the rest of Europe. *Ti na kánoume*?" (What can we do?) He wandered off, wrench in hand. ∎

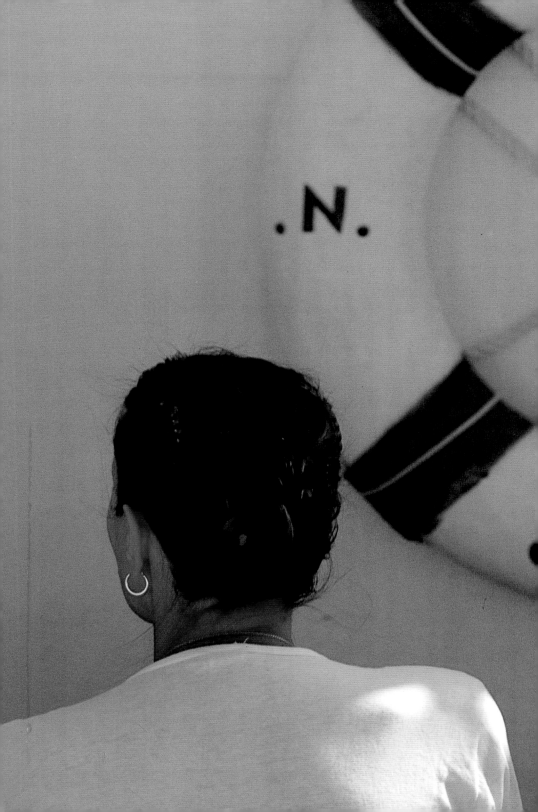

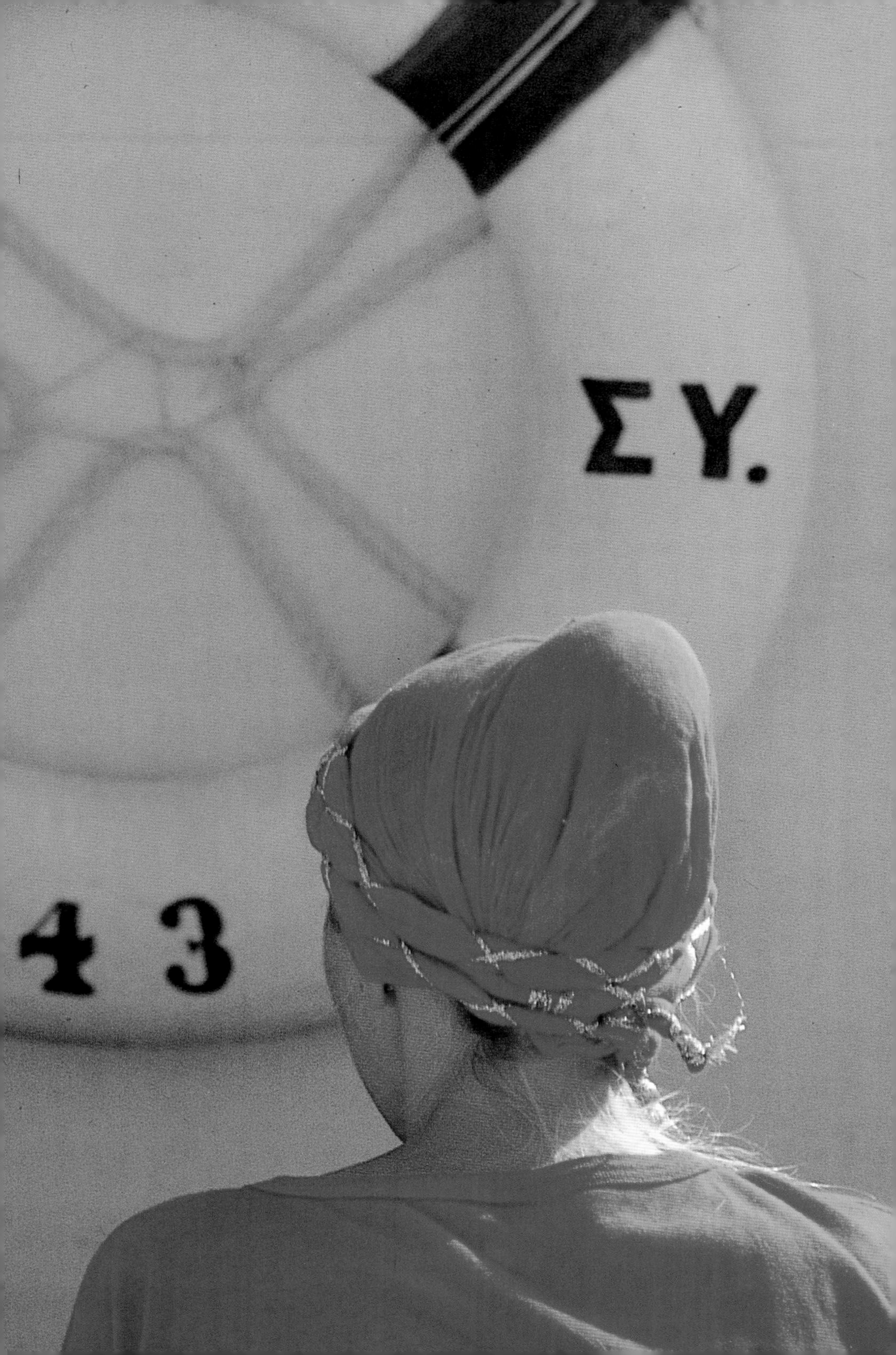
ΣΥ.
43

THE CYCLADES ISLANDS

SANTORÍNI, ANÁFI, FOLÉGANDROS, SIKINOS, IOS, NÁXOS, PÁROS, ANTIPÁROS, MÝKONOS, SYROS, TÍNOS, ANDROS, MÍLOS, KÍMOLOS, SÍFNOS, SERIFOS, KÝTHNOS, KÉA

The Cyclades are travel brochure islands. Every cliché, every memory, every dream of a sun-drenched beach can be realised here. The white cubed houses are justifiably famous, inspiring the work of many modern architects, Le Corbusier among them. The beaches are good, the food fresh, fellow travellers companionable, and the ferry connections so organised it is easy to sail to more than one "paradise" while on a relatively short holiday. It is not surprising, then, that for many people the Cyclades *are* Greece; other island chains merely aberrations in national character.

There are 56 Cycladic islands in all, 24 of them inhabited. Their spiritual centre might well be Santoríni, for although flung to the south geographically, it is to this dramatic, volcano-created island that most people gravitate before venturing further.

The eastern and central islands fan upwards from Santoríni in a loose chain which includes the Náxos/Páros/Mýkonos back-packers' beat, takes in little discovered islets like Donoussa and Iraklia, before concluding rather grandly in the rich red soil which is the island of Andros.

The western Cyclades form a different chain, a spine of islands self-contained in their unity, sharing a common culture linked by history and ferryboat connections. Odd man out is Kéa, popular with Athenians and Archaic stone lions, little known outside the tavernas around the Acropolis.

The Cyclades were inhabited as early as 6000 BC. The end of the fourth millennium and throughout the third saw an advanced civilisation, with many inroads made in art, craft and commerce. A high standard of living was enjoyed, as anyone who visits the Goulandris Museum of Cycladic Art in Athens, on Neofytou Douka Street, will appreciate. The museum is the world's first to be devoted exclusively to Cycladic art, exemplified by its long, linear, bright-white sculpture.

This vast backdrop of culture and history might not be evident amidst the gaudy cafés or hedonistic merry-makers of Mýkonos, but it is never very far away. One sunset over the Vale of Klíma, the valley in Mílos where the Louvre's Venus de Milo was discovered, is all that's needed.

Preceding pages: keeping close to the lifebelt; the dovecotes of Tínos. **Left,** Mýkonos.

SANTORÍNI

On the approach, Santoríni (Thíra) looks like something out of a science fiction movie: an impossibility. Broken pieces of a volcano's rim form a dark circle around a wide expanse of sea. Santoríni is the longest, easternmost piece of the rim, a crescent of land whose precipitous inner curve is formed of petrified lava, which at sunset seems to reflect a fire from the underworld.

Firá (Thíra), the capital, sits high on the rim, its white houses protruding from the edge like ancient teeth from an old man's mouth.

To the east, the land smoothes out into a fertile apron. A few bare hills push up again in the southeast. One of them is the setting of **Ancient Thíra**, a stupendous ruin of a city founded by Dorians in the 9th century BC. It last supported 5,000 Romans, but was emptied by one of many eruptions that racked the island, aggravated by the clashing of two of the earth's plates which meet beneath it. Further south, **Akrotíri** is an ongoing, multi-tiered excavation of a large Minoan settlement built over a Cycladic period town. This "live" excavation is much more interesting than the usual piles of rubble left after finds have been dispatched to a museum. (If you plan to visit either site, Firá's Archaeological Museum is highly recommended.)

Today, Santoríni is as famous for the rock 'n' roll atmosphere of the main town as for its geography and excavations. Although packed with the jewellers, boutiques, and cave-like discos that are the stock and trade of the more tourist-conscious islands, its beauty hasn't been dampened.

The blazing whiteness and sensual lines of Cycladic architecture are doubly disarming against the smoky purple banks of old lava, and from every portside passage there is a sombre, fantastic view to be seen of the ocean-bound volcano with "Burnt Islands" at its centre. Lights twinkle across the strait on the islet of **Thirassía**, sparse in vegetation and inhabitants, as though from some lost planet.

Most people stay in Firá. Consequently, it's relatively easy to find quiet accommodation almost anywhere else. At the island's northernmost tip, **Oía** (Ia) is a fishing community reachable by bus. For those with time and no cumbersome luggage, the hike along the caldera's edge from Imerovígli (on the bus route north) to Oía brings the cruel reds and purples of the petrified lava and the island's tempestuous geography into sharp focus. The volcano is only dormant, not extinct; earthquakes are always a disturbing possibility.

Oía is a town of beautifully restored houses. In 1956, a severe earthquake sent the uppermost layer of settled lava catapulting down over the houses. Afterward, people dug their way back inside their homes. A steep walk down twisting stone steps from the western end of town ends at Amoudí beach, which is overhung by deserted houses. Each year, there are more places available to stay in Oía.

Kamári and **Périssa** are busy resorts

on the east coast. Périssa has the main campground; both have roasting hot black "pebble" beaches.

However, they make a good starting point from which to climb to Ancient Thíra and then **Mount Profítis Elías**, the next hill inland. The museum in Profítis Elías Monastery exhibits tools and even complete workshops of the various crafts practised here by the monks since time immemorial. Homemade wine and liqueur are still set out for guests. Be sure to check whether the monastery is open, though, before setting out on the climb. The hours Profítis Elías is open to the public tend to be erratic.

It is also possible to walk to the monastery from **Pírgos**, an island village on the central plain which characterises the island's untouched interior. Yellow wheatsheaves, grapevines twisted into wreaths Santoríni-style, tiny tomatoes, and riots of spring wild flowers – all growing out of angry-looking pumice soil – make up the island's gentler side. Small caves used as tool sheds, barns, and sometimes even as homes, occasionally yawn up from wide stretches of grassy fields.

The town closest to the airport, **Monólithos** (a 45-minute walk from Firá), consists of one grass-roofed taverna furrowed into a hillside on the ocean, plus two houses. The taverna's owners, a sweet older couple who have, sadly, outlived their four children, keep an assortment of dogs. The last stretch of road before Monólithos is lined with hollowed out sandstone formations that emit eerie piping noises when the wind rushes through them. There's quite a good beach here too.

Bus transportation on the island is good, augmented by excursion buses to places like Akrotíri. Near Akrotíri on the sea is a taverna set in caves where sweet, lava-nurtured Santoríni wines are served in dented tin jugs.

Some boats put in below Firá at **Skála Firá**, accessible via a stone stairway, donkey, or funicular. But most put in at **Athiniós**, 10 km (6 miles) further south.

Right, the church domes of Oía.

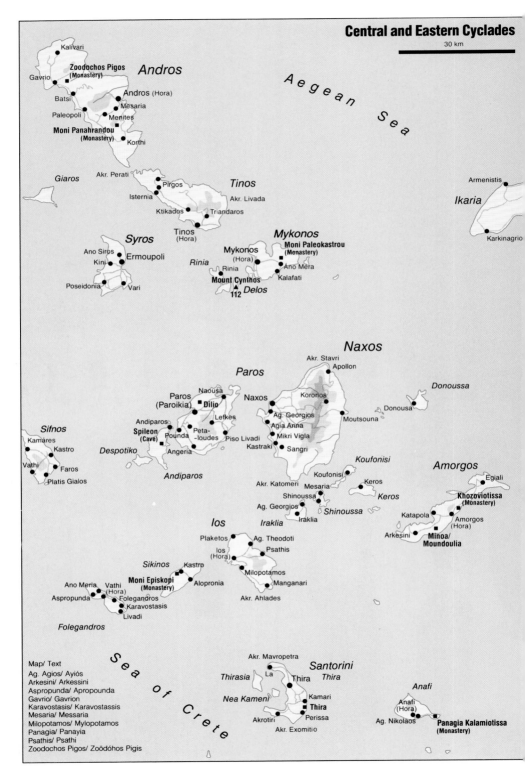

CENTRAL AND EASTERN CYCLADES

ANAFI: In legend, Apollo conjured up Anáfi to shelter Jason and the Argonauts when the seas grew rough and they risked losing the Golden Fleece; Apollo's shrine was built here in thanksgiving. Divine intervention has never again been reliable. Earthquakes originating at Santoríni usually shivered through Anáfi, causing tidal waves and maelstroms of volcanic detritus.

Anáfi's appearance has probably not altered much in the interceding years: it still looks like a rough boulder heaved up out of the sea and kept in place only by the goodness of a tenacious god. However, a different god is involved now: the **Zoödóchou Pighís** monastery was erected over the old shrine in the island's southeast corner. Extensive courses of marble masonry in its walls are believed to be remnants of the old temple. Above Zoödóchou Pighís looms the improbably set smaller monastery of Panaghía Kalamiátissa, high atop a pinnacle that is Anáfi's most distinctive feature.

Under 300 people live on Anáfi today, surviving mainly by fishing and subsistence farming. Mostly German, mid-summer tourism has not provided much of a boost to the economy, nor has the island made many concessions. There is a twice-weekly caique from Santoríni; ferries from Piraeus.

The south-facing harbour, **Aghios Nikólaos**, is directly below the **Chóra**, (also known as Anáfi, or Chorió), and has rooms available in summer. Continue up to the Chóra by bus or half-hour walkway for a wider choice and finer setting – the remains of a medieval *kástro* looms over it, and life in the quiet streets has so far been unaltered by the presence of tourists. Feast days on Anáfi – 10 days after Easter, and September 8 – are an occasion for all-out dancing.

Hikes eastward lead first to the beach at **Klisídi** (with seasonal taverna) and then to half a dozen more, all superb, before reaching the two monasteries. The interior is virtually empty, except for the rubble of another Venetian castle above central Roúkounas beach. Goat paths amble aimlessly, as you may feel like doing… above all, Anáfi remains a supreme place to be alone.

FOLEGANDROS: The vaulting steepness of Folégandros's coast has served as a natural deterrent to outside invasion over the centuries and lent security to those who remained within. Despite its tininess – 32 sq. km (12 sq. miles) populated by barely 500 people – its role in very recent history has not been insignificant: many Greeks were exiled here during the country's 1967–74 military rule. Its ancient and early Christian ties with Crete were strong, and many paintings of the Cretan school can be found in its churches today. In myth, a son of King Minos founded the island.

Folégandros abounds with bays, wild herbs, and grapes. **Karavostássis**, the port, **Angáli**, at the waist of the island on the west shore, and **Aghios Nikólaos** above it are the little-developed beaches. With the recent spate of construction, it is unlikely you'll run into a "no rooms"

ght, a cat in Cyclades.

situation in high summer; if this happens there is camping at **Livádi** in the south. There are buses to the Chóra, a magnificently sited, medieval town with an inner *kástro* high above the sea. The second village, **Ano Meriá**, comprises stone houses and farms; the surrounding hills are dotted with chapels to which islanders make their way to pray. Historically, Folegandran supplications were for rain, and still are, for on no other Cycladic island is the well and rain cistern so closely watched.

Chryssospiliá, the "golden" cave near the Chóra, gapes over the sea. It is rich with stalagmites and stalactites; excavations show this was a place of long-term refuge into the Middle Ages. Enquire in Chóra about caiques to the cave, though be aware that only technical climbers can gain access.

SIKINOS: Even with its respectable quantity of harbourside lodging, for all tastes, Sikinos, ever-visible from the west shore of Ios, couldn't be less like its neighbouring island. Although connected to Piraeus and other Cyclades twice or thrice weekly by ferry, and by caique to Ios and Folégandros in summer, the island so far seems to have given tourism a big shrug. It also escapes mention in the history books for long periods of time, but there are antiquities – and as always, churches – to be seen here. The three beaches, Aloprónia (also the port), Aghios Nikólaos and Aghios Yeórgios to the north face Ios.

From Aloprónia harbour it is an hour's hike (or regular bus ride) to the twinned settlement of Chóra/Kástro, with its wonderful defensively arranged square. The abandoned convent of Zoödóchou Pighís sits above the town. Perhaps even barer than Ios, it is a solitudinous island with few obvious diversions. One site of note, the **Heroön**, stands on what was once thought to have been a temple to Apollo; this is now reckoned an elaborate Roman tomb, incorporated into a church during medieval times.

Sikinos' old Greek name, Oenoe, testifies to the fact that the island once produced a celebrated wine, but not any longer. The name Sikinos is mythologi-

Sikinos through the ruined doorway of an 18th-century *kástro*.

cal: when the banished Limnian, Thoas, was set adrift in a sea-chest by his daughter to save him from death, he washed up here and was taken in by a nymph. Their child was called Sikinos.

Ios: The centre of Ios nightlife shifts constantly. In order to ensure his corner of the market, the owner of the Ios By Night club cooks up a Miss Ios contest each Friday. The prize is 5,000 drachmas and a bottle of champagne. Mr. Ios contests are held only by default, when no girls can be persuaded to participate. In this case, the ringleader shouts: "OK. I guess there are no sexy girls on Ios." No one budges. The men are ready.

Ios has ethos; it is a state of mind. A tiny island with few historic attractions, it has drawn the bandanna-headed hordes in regularly since the 1960s. The current lot, mainly under 25 and a weak echo of their hippie forbears (who encamped the year round), flock here to live cheaply, drink and dry out in the blistering sun.

People still sleep on the beach at **Mylopótas**, although this is now less common. Boutique shopping is minimal. But one thing people are sure to spend money on while here is drinking. Nightclubs stud the hill above Ios harbour, with another large cluster of bars in the Chóra. Homemade music strummed on well-travelled guitars, and drugs, former stock items on Ios, aren't much in evidence anymore. After the sun sets, Ios resembles a downmarket, younger Mýkonos. At around 11pm, the still of the streets is broken by beach stragglers ready for night-time revels (a bus runs regularly between the beach and harbour via Chóra). Once ensconced inside a bar, they could be anywhere in the western world, for there is not a Greek in sight.

The permanent effects of the tourist invasion have been twofold: Ios is no longer poor, and traditional life has virtually disappeared. Chóra is the only town; there are no smaller villages to keep up the old ways. As one elderly resident recounts, weddings were once a week-long feast in which everyone participated. Now, unless they are held

pause in
e fast pace
f Ios.

in the dead of winter, they last a scant half a day, as everyone is too busy tending tourist-related enterprises. Island women even try to avoid summer pregnancies.

Ios is not devoid of natural beauty or charm; even the bleary-eyed can see it. The hilltop Chóra, capped by a windmill, blazes with the blue domes of two Byzantine churches. Its layout and the palm trees that flank it give an almost Levantine look to the location. Buses are frequent, and there is a marble stair path from the port. The flat plain north of the harbour is filling up with new houses, and at least one villa complex has been constructed on the main road. Ios has many good swimming beaches, including the nude beaches north of the harbour. There are summer caiques to **Manganári bay** in the south and **Psáthi** in the east.

A half day's walk east ends at **Aghía Theodóti**, with beach and seasonal camping. A traditional *panayíri* is held at Theodoti Church on 8 September, the only festival in which the entire island still participates. Beyond the church are the remains of **Paleokastro**, an elevated fortress containing the marble ruins of what was once the medieval capital of Ios. At a lonely spot toward the northern tip, in back of the cove at **Plakotós**, is a series of prehistoric graves, one of which the islanders fiercely believe belongs to Homer, who is said to have died en route from Sámos to Athens.

Kritikakis Travel in Chóra, with another office on the port, is one of the most helpful agencies one could hope to find; they also change money.

AMORGOS: The spine of mountains – the tallest in the northeast is Krikelas, 900 metres (3,000 ft) – precludes expansive views unless you're atop them. The southwesterly harbour town of **Katápola** occupies a small coastal plain. Trees overhang the quayside, and at the back of the town is a thick fringe of orchards. Unfortunately, new development is encroaching on the older Cycladic structures as Amorgós gets more tourist traffic each year, especially in the summer.

A man and his puppets on Amorgós.

Three important ancient cities once thrived here. At **Minoa** (just above Katápola) are very scant ruins of a gymnasium, stadium, and temple to Apollo. **Arkessíni**, in the far southwest, comprises a burial site and a well-preserved Hellenistic fortress, Aigiáli, above Amorgós's second northeastern harbour, was also an ancient colony; now only the ruined fortress is visible.

The elevated Chóra, accessible by a regular bus service, centres around a 13th-century Venetian castle. Forty churches and chapels nestle inside it, including one that holds only two people. The island's two most famous churches are outside Chóra: Aghios Yeórgios tou Valsamíti, 4 km (2 miles) southwest, is on a sacred spring once believed to cure lepers and now watering someone's market garden. Spilling from a jagged cliff like milk from a jug half an hour east of Chóra, the white-washed Byzantine monastery of the **Panaghía tis Chozoviótissas** is home to a revered icon of the Virgin from Palestine. Its sacristy holds myriad religious items. For the miraculous story of the chisel, linked with the vision that inspired the church's building, take a copy of the church pamphlet.

Below the monastery, Aghía Anna beach beckons. To the southwest lie empty, secluded coves for bathing and sunning; a line of windmills edges the ridge above. The coastal ledges are covered with wild thyme and oregano, which release their pungent bouquet when crushed underfoot.

The island's southernmost point, below Arkessíni, is marked by a Hellenistic watch tower looking toward Anáfi. High-perched villages characterise the north, excepting **Aigiáli**, a small anchorage with accommodation and good beaches nearby. Some ferry boats, plus caiques from elsewhere on Amorgós, put in here. Beyond it is **Tholária**, surrounded by Roman tomb sites.

Sheer rockfaces notwithstanding, Amorgós is riddled with tiny, hidden beaches. Locally produced maps name them all and provide valuable information, couched in comic English and German translations, about places like the former "valley of the old useless, doomed donkeys".

THE "BACK ISLANDS": Nicknamed the "Back Islands" because they represent the Cycladic back beyond, **Donoússa**, **Iráklia**, **Schoinoússa**, and **Koufonissiá** were once thickly populated. Now, there are only 100 to 200 inhabitants on each island. **Kéros**, virtually empty of contemporary human habitation, was excavated to reveal multi-levelled burial sites, scores of votive offerings of marble and clay, and jewellery.

A stay on any of the "Back Islands" means accommodation with local families and a very low-key existence. Water is a scarce commodity on all of them. Hilly Donoússa – with only one town (Donoússa) and two to four reliable ferry connections per week – is covered with vineyards; views from the harbour take in the barren **Makáres** islands, and beyond, the grand profile of Náxos. Iráklia has two settlements; the harbour, **Aghios Geórgios**, and Chóra above, just over an hour's hike up. Schinoússa's hilltop Chóra has a medieval fortress at

Khozoviótissa Monastery spills down the cliff like milk from a jug.

its back ("Chóra" is a generic term for "main village.") **Messariá** is a tiny beach settlement on Schinoússa's north coast. Koufoníssia (its neighbour, **Káto Koufonísi**, belongs mainly to the goats) has an actual hotel, and an east coast beach with a seasonal taverna. For Iráklia, Schoinoússa, and Koufoníssia there's a twice to thrice weekly ferry that plies between Náxos and Amorgós. Also, boats bound for the Dodecanese may pick up the "Back Islands" on their summer schedules. Páros is the best correspondence point; Donoússa has ferry connections four times a week, and is served by caiques from Náxos, Páros, and Santoríni in summer. There are no regular services to Kéros.

NÁXOS: Náxos is a dark horse amongst its showier Cycladic neighbours. It's the largest of the Cyclades, and yet very little is accessible by public transport. It is an extraordinarily mountainous and fertile island, with long beaches easily lending themselves to camping and relaxing. Chóra is a labyrinthine chaos of old homes complemented by churches, ruins, and an international bookstore. Hemmed in by the highest mountains in the Cyclades – **Zas**, the tallest, is over 1,000 metres (3,000 ft) – the interior is a country unto itself, as shut in and sequestered as some of the more forbidding parts of the Peloponnese.

To the north of the ferry dock in Chóra, a colossal free-standing marble frame marks the entrance to the **Temple of Delian Apollo** – which was never completed. Fully constructed, it would have been the largest temple ever to be erected in ancient Greece.

Náxos's size, natural resources, and the bravery of its warriors have given the island status throughout the centuries. The Venetian Duchy of the Archipelago, which began in 1207 and ended in 1566 with the Ottoman invasion under Selim II, was centred in Náxos. Marco Sanudo, the first Duke of Náxos, began a tradition of allotting surrounding islands as rewards to Venetian nobleman with whom he wanted to curry favour. Náxos also has a long, strong tradition of poets and sculptors. At Delos,

The evocative service at Easter in a church on Náxos.

the Naxians erected many examples of their culture, such as the House of the Naxians and the famous lions.

In myth, Minos's daughter Ariadne helped Theseus find his way out of the Minotaur's labyrinth on Crete. He left Crete together with Ariadne and they called at Náxos on the return to Theseus's home, Athens. There he left the sleeping Ariadne behind even though she had saved his life. Perhaps his ship was blown out to sea and couldn't get back to pick her up. Dionýsos consoled Ariadne on Náxos. Meanwhile, Theseus forgot to raise his ship's white sail when rounding Cape Sounion. Seeing the black sails against the sea, his father, King Aegeus, assumed Theseus was dead and pitched himself off the cliffs. The Aegean Sea has borne his name ever since. Theseus later married Ariadne's sister.

The Chóra is divided into sections, place names reflecting the port's long occupation by the Venetians. The **Metropolitan cathedral** at the back (east) of the town demarcates the Fontana section. The residential Borgo quarter behind the main *plateía* has a splendidly Cycladic aspect. Higher up, surrounding the **Kástro**, is an enclave of Naxian Catholics whose ancestors were Venetian overlords. Look for their coats of arms over the doorways. The former Jesuit Monastery now houses the **archaeological museum**. Just north of Chóra is an area known as the Grotta, with the remains of an Early Cycladic settlement.

On the northern shore of Náxos is the town of **Apollon**, a one-time hippie enclave. A huge *kouros* representing Apollo lies supine on the hillside above it, abandoned there when the marble from which it was wrought cracked. (Another *kouros* suffering a similar fate lies 10 km/6 miles east of Náxos near the road to **Kourochóri**.) If you hear the sound of jazz floating out of a window in the evening, it's probably one of the hundreds of recordings owned by Dimitrios Kariotos, an Athenian guitarist who turned his uncle's house here into a *pension*. There is a daily bus from

traditional aster fare: soureki.

Chóra, but beware of Sundays, when the Apollon bus goes only to **Kóronos**, 12 km (7 miles) short of Apollon.

The rest of the island is a sumptuous wilderness, ripe for exploration by anyone with the time and stamina (or hired means of transport) to do it justice. The rural villages of Náxos are numerous and unpredictable, with reception to foreigners varying enormously from one to another. Olive and fruit trees grow densely around them, concealing Byzantine churches and crumbling Venetian manors. As for the choice of beaches, **Aghios Yeórgios** south of the port is serviceable, although the further south you move, the lovelier are the beaches. **Aghía Anna** is a good beach for rooms; **Mikrí Vígla** beyond it has a fine taverna, and **Kastráki**, the furthest along, offers the most sand and solitude.

PÁROS: This island's open-air cinema has an amazingly good bill of fare. Townspeople, tourists, and laid-over boat passengers sit gazing at a screen under the stars, and somehow the experience feels supremely Greek. Reading Greek subtitles is actually a good way to pick up a few handy phrases – more so at least than in the bars and crêpe restaurants of **Paroikía**, Páros's main town. If you arrive at this heavily trafficked island in August, however, expect to sleep under those very same stars – rooms can be scarce.

Paroikía is as pretty as Mýkonos, but not so labyrinthine. The two main things to see in Paroikía are the **Ekatontapyliani church** (Our Lady of a Hundred Portals), and the **Archaelogical Museum**, both can be found inland past the post office on the road starting at the quayside windmill.

Páros is loaded with beaches. Chrysí Aktí or Golden Shore, on the east coast just north of Dryós (which also has a good beach), is a perennial favourite. At Píso Livádi a fold of rich Aegean blue separates Páros from the high, dark crags of Náxos. This island plays a close second to Mýkonos in popularity.

Léfkes is the largest inland village. There are several 17th- century churches, the two most prominent edged with an

The church is reflected by contemporary island life.

opaline-blue wash. It is also a good base for walking excursions, as the area is full of monasteries. One of the best walks is over an old cobbled road leading to the east coast and Píso Livádi. The sunwashed, church-pocked landscape yields little else in abundance but the brilliant marble for which Páros has always been famous.

Náoussa is a small, beautiful port on the north coast where the boats in their moorings seem to nudge up right against the fishermen's houses. Now it's overrun with hotels and villas, although the east side of the bay is still tranquil.

The island's southwestern shore has many Athenian-owned villas and is also the site of **Poúnta**, the small ferry terminal servicing the island Antíparos. Near **Angairiá** is a convent of nuns whose special craft is weaving. In the west is the touted "Valley of the Butterflies", or **Petaloúdes**, a verdant area of fruit and olive tree orchards which flutter with pumping butterfly wings in early summer. It's accessible via coach or by foot over paved roads.

Páros is an invaluable travel correspondence point. Boats connect with Athens (Piraeus, Rafína), the other Cyclades, the Dodecanese, Ikaría, and Sámos. The island has an airport, too, though the planes from here are the Olympic Airways 18-seaters, and so get full quickly.

ANTIPÁROS: This small, pretty island was once joined to Páros. The two are now separated by a narrow channel, plied by frequent car ferries bringing tourists to see the **Spílio** (cave). The French Marquis de Nointel made the Antiparian cave famous when he led a Christmas Mass inside it in 1673. Cement steps make exploration less of an adventure, but cannot subtract from the cave's primordial beauty; echoes bounce like crazy around the stalagmites and stalactites. Upon entering the cavern, which is adjoined by the Church of St John of the Cave, you will descend over 90 metres (300 ft) before coming to the vaulted chamber where Mass was held. Yes, Lord Byron was here, too.

Buses run from **Antíparos town** to

The bright, white arches of Paroikía, Páros.

the cave; it is a two-hour walk. Most daytrippers bypass the village for the cave, so it is relatively easy to find rooms here outside of July and August (the newer houses belong to Athenians). There is a beachside campground on **Diapóri** bay; it looks out over a snaketail of rocks trailing back toward Páros. Excavations completed in 1964 on one of these islets, **Saliagos**, revealed evidence of Neolithic habitation on the island.

Good beaches and bars have given Antíparos some of Páros's former business. **Sóros** is an east coast beach with a taverna; Aghios Yeórgios, on the south coast, has a taverna, too, and faces the islet of **Despotikó**. Antíparos is only 11 km by 5 km (7 miles by 3 miles), so there are no impossible distances. South of the cave the **Faneromeni chapel** stands alone on a southeastern cape.

MÝKONOS: If it weren't for Mýkonos's twisting dazzles of architecture, its plentiful beaches and chapels, and foremost, its reputation, this small blue and white island would be a dreary place. It's rocky, treeless, and there are no ancient sites. Yet people are irresistibly drawn here by the thousands. Why?

Mýkonos has glamour appeal. While the other islands share a rugged kind of beauty, Mýkonos has smoothed down and refined its natural features and moulded them into a tourist-pleasing package which works – making it more expensive than any other Greek island.

Mýkonos has its legends, however, which cover and include the beaches, bars, transvestite shows, fur and jewellery shops, and restaurants serving dishes like Lobster Thermidor. The most innocent looking *yia-yia* (grandmother) can be a hustler, charmingly unburdening a load of grapes on you and then demanding twice the going price. But even the smoothest of the locals is not truly in form until haggling begins for the fishermen's catch, for which they have to contend with Petros the Pelican. Later in the day, it's back to the tourists again. Luxury liners shimmer on the horizon, turning slowly around their anchor leads while passengers are shipped ashore for

Little Venice Mýkonos.

172

PELICAN POWER

Anyone who visits Mýkonos, either regularly or even for an hour, returns with clear-cut memories. The string of windmills on the horizon? The sun-bleached cubic houses? The beaches, the bodies, the bars? Perhaps. But for many one of the most enduring memories of Mýkonos is Petros the Pelican. How did the island come to have such a high profile mascot?

To unravel this mystery is to come up against two quintessential Greek conundrums: conflicting stories and inter-island rivalry. Mýkoniots questioned on the subject of Petros would concur on only two points. First, the original Petros is dead and the bird who now sticks his formidable beak under the elbows of the fishmongers is Petros Two. Second, Petros One went missing one year, and kidnapping was suspected by the islanders of nearby Tínos.

As for the rest of the Petros story, rumours run rife – and foul. Petros One is said to have died at least three different ways. He caught pneumonia and was taken (flown) to a Thessaloníki doctor, who put him down. Or someone strangled him. Or someone tried to bed the poor bird.

The record has now been set straight, and the man to do it, Bo Patrick, sits quietly each afternoon in his Little Venice photo gallery, and almost as quietly behind his bar (Bo's) near the town hall at night. He has a superb moustache, and squints deeply and thoughtfully at anything beyond the range of the doorway.

Born on Lésvos, Patrick spent much of his childhood and working life (mainly in television production) in America. He returned to Greece in the early 1970s. This time he came to Mýkonos, settling into his dual role as photographer/barkeeper. Bo has been happy here, but if it weren't for his dog Phillip, his cat, and other pesky possessions, he'd be off taking photos in India by now, preferably for the rest of his life.

Bo's skills and the fact that he got to know Petros One very well over the years have resulted in a book. It is dedicated to the "young at heart"

and told like a child's story. Yet the book is greatly detailed, the tale gleaned from older islanders and then sieved for the facts, not an easy task when dealing with any kind of Greek myth, ancient or otherwise. *Whitewash and Pink Feathers* also has a picture log, and will probably keep the story of the Petros dynasty from sinking deeper into the murk. For seekers of the truth, and for anyone who has admired this proud, handsome bird and wondered about his origins, here is the result of Patrick's research into the story. Four pelicans left their home near the Black Sea and were travelling to their winter home in Egypt. A storm drove them off course and grounded them on Mýkonos. Three of the birds perished, but Petros survived and was adopted by a local fisherman, Theódoros. He lived on the quayside and appeared to bask in the attention, drawing visitors to the then yet-to-be-discovered island. Mýkonos's fame grew. Jackie Onassis even sent two American pelicans to replace the ones that died. But they suffered on the journey and didn't live long after their introduction to the territorially-minded Petros.

One day, Petros followed a boatload of Mýkoniot schoolchildren to Tínos. A malevolent Tiniot fisherman clipped Petros's flight feathers, which turned the bird from a visitor into a hostage. The Tiniot refuted Mýkonos's claim to the bird, saying he was theirs. One day, Theódoros came over to the island and the bird leapt to his shoulders. Ownership was established, a deal was struck and Petros went home to Mýkonos again, to much joyous celebration. Today, Tínos has its own pelican, friendly but not as famous.

Female pelicans were introduced, too. Iríni Two (an earlier, French Iríni lasted but briefly) and Petros, though they never mated, strutted around together, until 1985, when Petros was hit by a car. Irini is still alive, but after Petros died she withdrew from the quayside to spend her days sleeping on a shaded square. In 1986, Petros Two arrived from Munich, donated by a German travel baron and dedicated to the lovers of Mýkonos.

All is now well, as pink feathers litter the quayside once again. ∎

ANCIENT DELOS

Minuscule Delos, southwest of Mykonos, is nirvana for archaeologists. Extensive Greco-Roman ruins occupying much of the island's 4 sq. km (1½ sq. miles) make Delos the equal of Delphi and Olympia.

Sufferers of *mal de mer* should remember, before setting forth, that the island is "windy and waste and battered by the sea". The voyage may be only 45 minutes but, as the caique heaves and shudders, it can seem 10 times that long. Dedicated travellers are advised to forego breakfast as an empty stomach is a good way to make the journey less painful; another tip is to take along a sweater or to dress in layers as the sea breeze is very stiff. Having accomplished these preliminaries it's then best to forget the physical and concentrate your mind on the metaphysical.

It was on Delos that Leto, pregnant by Zeus, gave birth to the twins Apollo and Artemis. (Artemis was actually born on the adjacent island of Rhenia, nine days after Apollo – surely a most difficult delivery!) Delos, at that time a floating rock, was rewarded when four diamond pillars stretched up and anchored it in the heart of the Cyclades.

On arriving at Delos, you should orient yourself to avoid getting lost among the ruins. Most of these occupy the two arms of a right angle which immediately faces you. Ahead (southern arm) are the theatre and mainly domestic buildings. To the left is the sanctuary to which pilgrims from all over the Mediterranean came with votive offerings and sacrificial animals.

For nearly 1,000 years, this sanctuary was the political and religious centre of the Aegean and host to the Delian Festival held every four years. This, until the 4th century BC, was Greece's greatest festival. The Romans turned it into a grand trade fair and made Delos a free port. It also became Greece's slave market where as many as 10,000 slaves were said to be sold on any one day.

By the start of the Christian era, the power and glory that was Delos was waning and soon afterwards the island fell into disuse. During the next two millennia the Mute Stones were silent; then, with the arrival of French archaeologists in the 1870s they began to speak.

Unfortunately, now it is Delos's snakes rather than its stones which are deaf – be sure to stamp your feet loudly when walking through little-trafficked areas, for they can nip at the ankles.

Follow the pilgrim route to a ruined monumental gateway leading into the Sanctuary of Apollo. Within are three temples dedicated to Apollo – there is also a temple dedicated to Artemis – and parts of a colossal marble statue of Apollo which was destroyed when a massive bronze palm tree fell on it. Close by is the Sanctuary of Dionysos with several phalli standing on pedestals and Dionysic friezes. Upstanding is a marble phallic bird symbolising the body's immortality.

Continue to the stunning Lion Terrace where five anorexic, archaic lions squat, apparently ready to pounce. Below this is the Sacred Lake and the palm tree which marks the spot of Apollo's birth.

Most visitors delight in that part of Delos which was occupied by artisans rather than gods. Their houses, close to the port, are a regular warren separated by narrow lanes lined by drains from 2,000 years ago and with niches for oil lamps which illuminated the streets. The main road leads to the theatre which seated 5,500. It is unimpressive but there are superb views from the uppermost of its 43 rows. Close to the theatre are grander houses surrounded by columns and with exquisite mosaics, to which they owe their eponymous names, on the floor.

From here a gentle stroll leads to the summit of Mount Kynthos (110 metres/368 ft), from which the views of the ruins and the Cyclades are memorable. Descend by first passing the grotto of Hercules and then stopping at the Sanctuaries to the Foreign Gods.

Remember, Delos was a free port and in Classical times practically the entire Levant traded – and probably banked – here under the tutelage of shrines erected to their divinities. All were welcome – as evidenced by the ruined synagogue, erected by the Phoenicians, in the northwest corner of the island.

For the return to Mýkonos, forget the rough waves and dwell on Kazantzákis: "Happy is the man who, before dying, has the good fortune to sail the Aegean Sea. Nowhere else can one pass so easily and serenely from reality to dream." ■

shopping sprees, then horn-blasted reluctantly back, laden with sheepskins and jewellery.

It's possible to eschew all this and still enjoy Mýkonos. There is **Delos**, the sacred island which is the centre of the Cyclades. The **Folklore Museum** and the **Archaelogical Museum** are at different ends of Mýkonos's quay. Little Venice, a row of buildings hanging over the sea behind the Town Hall, is the least frenetic part of town. Or one can strike inland to **Áno Merá**, the only real village, which houses Tourliani monastery, and toward Panormos bay, the 12th-century Paleokastro convent (indefinitely shut because of a collapsed roof).

Áno Merá, which is a trunk point for Mýkonos's quieter beaches such as **Kalafáti**, has an airiness and lightness unusual for a hill village. As often happens on Mýkonos, a British camera crew was here not long ago. They were filming a comedy about an English-Mykoniot marriage. As the wedding scene assembled, the church's courtyard filled with men in balloon-sleeved blousons and black vests and breeches while the women were veiled in gauzy pink gowns, their headpieces encircled by wreaths of tiny roses. Without the presence of cameras, this scene would be unlikely. Then again, traditional events like Greek weddings are not why most people come to Mýkonos.

SYROS: The *braggadocio* in Syros's tourist literature must be forgiven: when Syros ceased to be Greece's premier port in the late 1800s, it lost a lot of status, too. The island remains the administrative and cultural capital of the Cyclades but when Piraeus sapped its steam as a trade centre, Sýros was cut off and left, as one Greek guide says, "a grand but old-fashioned lady who lives on her memories of the good old days and on her half forgotten glories." This is a shame for with its excellent inter-island ferry links and low-key but useful facilities (launderettes and dry cleaners), Sýros can be a pleasant and rewarding place to stay.

Its modern port area, **Ermoúpolis**, is dominated by shipyards. Sýros calls it-

stormy day ⌐ Syros.

self the "Manchester of Greece", which doesn't help its resort image, either. Yet it does show how proud Syriani are of their industrial importance. Although little seems immediately appealing about Ermoúpolis, the scent of roasting octopus and the lights of the quayside tavernas give it a festive air at night. Behind the harbour itself a few grace-notes appear: the area called **Ta Vapória** ("the ships") is where you'll find old mansions (a few doubling as cheap hotels) uphill from the handier shopping streets. The main square, Plateía Miaoúlis, is lined with the dignified, neo-classical buildings that attest, a little fadedly, to the grandeur Sýros once possessed. In fact, as you poke around the back streets, Ermoúpolis reveals itself as the most elegant neo-Classical town in Greece. The Apollon Theatre adjacent to the Town Hall, modelled after La Scala in Milan, is still a point of pride, having benefited recently from a comprehensive renovation. Aghios Nikólaos church houses the **Monument to the Unknown Soldier**.

A hilly prominence at the north end of the town, **Vrontádo**, is capped by the Greek Orthodox Church of the Resurrection (Anástasis); on the other hill and higher up is **Ano Sýros**, the medieval Catholic quarter, dominated by Aghios Yeórgios church and Capuchin monastery (adjacent is a British World War I cemetery). Around late October a joyous *paniyíri* (saint's festival) is celebrated here.

The name Sýros may be derived from the name Osiris, a widely worshipped, originally Egyptian god of corn, the harvest, and the floods; scant remains of a temple to his wife Isis, lie just outside of Ermoúpolis, which was named, by the Chiote refugees who founded it, in honour of the god of commerce (Hermes). **Phoínikas**, a beachside town in the southwest, is named for the Phoenicians, who were probably Sýros's first inhabitants.

The island's south is softer and greener than the north and has more beaches, namely **Poseidonía**, **Phoínikas**, and **Vári**. At Poseidonía (also known as Delagráza) there is a series of churches.

Pythagoras's teacher, Pherekydes, inventor of the sundial, was from here; several caves bear his name. Up the west coast, **Galissás** and **Kíni** are emerging beach resorts. The north of the island is thinly inhabited.

Between 1967–74, political prisoners were interned on Yiáros, the empty island to the north.

TÍNOS: A penchant for neon crosses and a quirky power supply make Chóra on Tínos an eerie spectacle at night. When the electricity is restored after a power cut, everyone hoots and cheers as the neon crosses flicker noisily back on as though some crank evangelist had staged a sound and light show for their sole benefit.

Tínos's holy days are on 25 March and 15 August. Greeks from all walks of life pour off ferryboats to worship an icon of the Virgin within Chóra's massive **Panaghía Evangelístria** cathedral. In 1823, the icon, which a nun dreamt of, was unearthed at the site where the church complex now stands. The marble steps leading to it are carpeted to

The doorwa[y] and dovecotes o[f] Tínos.

176

accommodate those who go on their knees, and even sleep here.

Religion is a cottage industry; antiquity has fallen by the wayside. The site of **Poseidon's temple** at Kiónia beach, one of the few ancient sites, is neglected. The Tiniots' aesthetic sense has not been totally obscured, however. There is still one non-Christian figure to be found among the clutter of icons, man-sized candles, and plastic holy water bottles for sale in the cathedral quarter: a beatifically stark rendering of the nymph Amphitrite, special to Tiniots in ancient times. Amidst the religious paraphernalia are also locally-produced jewellery and marble sculptures by Tínos's artistic community, a cut above the factory-made tourist junk.

Tínos's other hallmark is the dovecote. Hundreds of them are inland, a tradition started by the Venetians. The pattern of triangular windows in the birdhouses is echoed over doorways and in fences and window-shapes, as it is on Mýkonos, Andros, Serifos, and Sífnos. It is a pliant symbol which seems to represent anything from the shape of a sail to, certainly in Tínos's case, the Trinity. A bus ride across the island will also reveal some weird, mushroom-shaped, wind-sculpted rocks, especially above Vólakas village, famed for its basket weaving, and a proliferation of chapels, many newly constructed.

Pyrgos, the marbleworkers' village, has a tiny art museum. It is the place to see Tiniot artists at work or hanging out in cafés. Of the several monasteries to see, **Katopolianí**, near **Istérnia**, is exceptional. Abandoned by monks, it's inhabited by a shy farm family who will heave the old door away from the chapel's entrance for the infrequent visitor. Kardianí, the next village south of Istérnia, is the island's most attractive and spectacularly set village.

The south (west) coast bay of **Isterníon** is a fabulous hike from Istérnia. Take the marble steps to a dirt path which, after 10 minutes of dust and goat blockades, leads to a marble-cobbled path down to the sea. Belying its reputation for more sombre attractions,

Ilgrims
urney from
l over
reece to
orship on
nos.

Tínos doesn't lack for beaches; **Kolimbíthra** in the north is one of the best. Pórto Aghios Sóstis on the south shore is a long decent stretch of beach, too, lightly commercialised.

ANDROS: The red Andros soil makes everything glow sienna at sunset, especially on its bare northern heights. Settled centuries ago by Orthodox Albanians who still speak their ancestral tongue, the stone huts of the north contrast with the whitewash and red tile of the other villages. Solitary eagles and long-haired goats may be spotted here, too. Farmland is divided by painstakingly built stone walls, unique for the pattern of triangular slates incorporated into them. From **Kalyvári**, the northernmost hamlet, roads appear as no more than chalk marks, and a diaphanous blue haze unfolds in the late afternoon to wipe out the distinction between sky and sea.

The main resort is **Batsí**, on a bay 6 km (4 miles) south of **Gávrion**, the port. Batsí's "Glari" tourist office arranges rooms, as much of the island's accommodation is pre-booked by package operators. There are also rooms in Chóra and Gávrion. A mix of faded buildings encroached upon by villa developments, Batsí's bland tranquillity is no measure of the rugged grandeur that characterises the rest of Andros.

Still on the west coast, on the **Zagora** promontory, is the site of an ancient walled city-state that flourished between the 6th and 8th centuries BC, the time of Homer. Much remains to be excavated.

On the east coast, Andros's Chóra, with cliffside promenades and neo-Classical buildings, looks more Ionian than Cycladic. Its surprise is the Modern Art Museum, a few steps north of the main square. Works by modern Greek sculptors and artists as well as European Modernists are featured. Entrance is free, and the sculpture garden, tiny and exquisite, is imbued with a modernist sense of play. The prize exhibit in the **Archaeological Museum**, indeed one of the prize exhibits in all Greece, is the famous statue *Hermes of Andros*.

Between Batsí and **Andros Town** (Chóra) runs a long, deep valley. Ter-

Ploughing the red earth in Mesa Vounio, Andros.

races run all the way up its sides toward the island's highest mountain range, culminating at **Petalóka**, 1,000 metres (3,000 ft). Sycamores, mulberries, and fruit trees grow in turn with acres of pine. Feeding all this verdure are a series of springs whirling down from the mountaintops, most notably at **Ménites**, where Panayia tis Koumulous is sited. The spring is considered sacred; possibly there was a major temple to Dionýsos here. According to a pan-Cycladic legend, the water turned to wine each year on Dionýsos's feast day.

The Monastery of Zoödóchou Pighís, however, also claims to be on the most sacred spot. Situated in the hills northeast of Batsí, the monastery is looked after by a diminishing order of nuns guarding a library of precious sacred manuscripts. Adjacent is a fountain straddling the Zöodóchou Pighís (life-giving spring).

To the northwest is the village of **Aghios Pétros**, remarkable for its intact Hellenic *pyrgos* (tower). To get to it a series of goat-tracks have to be negoti-

ated first. Or, it can be reached from Gávrion in just over an hour's walk; turn off the main road at the "Camping Andros" signs south of the port, then follow the Aghios Pétros road.

South of the Palaiópoli-Chóra road is the most spectacular of Andros's 13 Byzantine monasteries, **Panachrándou**, just past its 1,000th birthday, which still retains ties with Constantinople. The round trip on foot lasts about 3 hours (2 hours by donkey) from **Messariá**, a valley town with the Byzantine Taxiarchis church; in summer a weekly coach excursion leaves from Batsí.

Palaiópolis, the ancient capital, doesn't give much hint of its past; but the Hermes statue in the archaeological museum was discovered here. Kórthi is the only sizeable village in the south.

There are beaches all over the island, but the easiest to get to are Nimbórion just south of the port, the string of lovely beaches between Gávrion and Batsí, Kórthi and Yialia (near **Stenies**) – plus a number of lovely remote coves like Aghios Péllos.

sh.

THE WESTERN CYCLADES

MÍLOS: Most of the island's coastline was formed when streams of lava dribbled from the now dormant volcano. The lava dripped into caves and overhung as it hit the sea, thrusting up weird rock formations that take on animal shapes when caught in the purple shadows of the setting sun. The island has always been extensively mined, once for obsidian, now for bentonite, perlite, barite, and china clay. Evidence is provided by the gaping quarries peppering much of the island.

Mílos has graciously adapted to the thin stream of tourism it receives, concentrated in **Adámas**, the port, and **Pollónia**, a fishing village in the northeast. On the map, Mílos resembles a bat in flight; the island's total population is 4,500 but the western wing is nearly deserted.

One way to kill time while waiting for a boat in Adámas is to take a hot springs bath, if they are open. The entrance to the spa is a tiny door in the concrete wall near where the boats dock. Inside the Aghía Triáda church in Adámas, Cretan-style icons dominate; links have always been strong between Mílos and "the great island," most recently in 1835 when Mílos became the largest enclave of Cretan refugees.

The island's capital, **Pláka**, has both an archaeological and a folklore museum. The latter, set in an old house, is packed with artefacts from rock specimens and goat horns, to samples of native weaving. A hike to the chapel atop Pláka (follow signs for "Anna's Art Dresses") and the old Kástro walls gives a splendid views of the bay-bound Mílos and, on clear days, as far as Páros and Náxos. Southwest of Pláka lies **Ancient Mílos**, source of the island's far-famed statue, the *Venus de Milo*, now in the Louvre.

Mílos was long famous for producing superb statuary, wrought by succeeding generations of a family called Grophon. Their beloved Venus was probably from the 1st century BC. Mílos never quarried its own marble, yet always produced marblework of the highest standard. The marble itself was probably Naxian or Parian. Examples of Miliot sculpting include a (copied) bust of Asclepius in the British Museum, and a Hermes in the Berlin Museum. More examples can be found in the National and Archaeological Museums in Athens.

Particularly interesting are an ancient theatre and early Christian catacombs. This seaside slope, the **Vale of Klíma**, is littered with ruins from just below Pláka to the hamlet of **Klíma** by the sea; and excavations undertaken by the British school in Athens in the late 1800s uncovered a Dionýsian altar and remains of an ancient gymnasium. The marble tablet marks the spot where, in 1820, a farmer discovered the Venus statue (to the Greeks she was Aphrodite, goddess of beauty). Entrusted to the French consul to keep her safe from Turks, she has been a major draw at the Louvre ever since; it is no wonder the Greeks have been unable to reclaim her.

Follow the catacombs signs, detour-

ing onto the track to the theatre (sign in Greek only). The Dorian theatre is well preserved, probably because of its Roman renovation. Below the theatre lies one of the island's prettiest villages, Klíma. From the sea, it looks like a minute Venice, with brightly painted boathouses lining the shore. However, things weren't always so bucolic in the Vale of Klíma. When Miliots refused to submit to Athenian rule during the Peloponnesian wars, most of the male inhabitants were slaughtered. **Trypití**, meaning "serrated" or "perforated", probably was so named because it was just above the ancient burial ground, honeycombed with victims' graves. Those who had escaped returned to resettle the island.

Off the paved Trypití-Klíma road below the theatre turn-off are located the elaborate **catacombs**. Although cheerily lit by tiny electric lanterns, the frescoes and religious graffiti are hard to discern, and only the initial 50 metres (350 ft) are open to the public.

Pollónia, a restful base in the northeast, is a good starting point for several short walks that give the full measure of Mílos's eerie beauty. A short distance west along the coast (follow the town beach), four volcanic boulders do a ring dance atop a crest of sandstone; the feeling of movement is undeniable, though the rocks were cast and petrified here centuries ago.

A half hour's walk away on the Adamás road is **Fylakopí**, the extensive rubble remains of a 4000 to 800 BC city whose frescoes are in the National Museum in Athens. Just south of "modern" Fylokopí – a settlement of a few houses – is a narrow arm of water lined with widemouthed tunnels and caves. Two tiny sand spits would make the site a fantastic beach encampment, if they weren't in use as garbage tips.

Modern Miliots are possessed of a quiet sophistication and worldliness. (They boast of the first known school for women in the Aegean, no longer extant; no one, however, seems to know its founding date.) As skilled miners, many have travelled widely in pursuit of work, going to live as far afield as

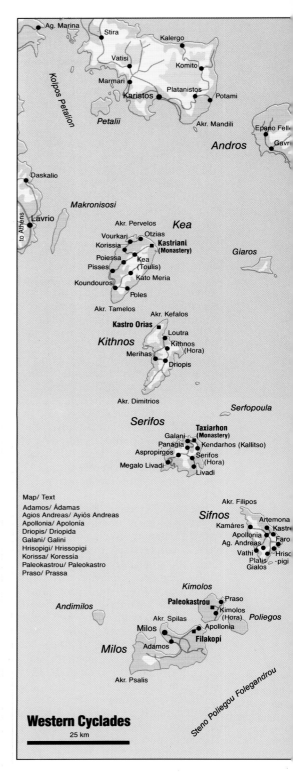

Australia, South Africa, and North America as obsidian became a less sought after commodity. But many Miliots come back. Greek Street in London is named for the Miliot ghetto in Soho, populated by refugees from both Mílos and Sámos in the 17th century.

KIMOLOS: This island is an alluring presence for anyone who has been staying in Pollónia on Mílos; the distance between the two is just under a nautical mile. Kímolos is a tiny isle – 35 sq. km (14 sq. miles), with a population of 800 whose chalky cliffs, mined for Fuller's earth, turn a velvety rose at sunset and then seem to disappear in the evening haze. It takes only 30 minutes to ply the narrow channel between Kímolos and Mílos by caique; landings are at Psáthi. The Chóra is a 15-minute walk inland. Ferryboats stop en route to and from neighbouring Mílos.

Kímolos was once known as a pirates' hideout and today it provides refuge from the more crowded islands. Although blessedly undeveloped, it has several beaches at **Alykí**, **Klíma**, **Prássa**, **Bonátsi**, and **Ellinikó**, and all sites are within easy walking distance. Offshore from Ellinikó is **Aghios Andréas**, a now detached piece of Kimolos that has been excavated, revealing a significant and fascinating Mycenean settlement. Prássa has a reasonable shingle beach plus some rooms to rent. The main population centre of the island is Chóra, where the Venetian *kástro*, sadly in an advanced state of decay, is of particular interest. There are also some churches here, including the honey-coloured Christos Church just outside the fortress; it is the oldest church on the island, dating from the early 17th century.

SÍFNOS: Resplendent with olive trees, bougainvillaea, and wind-bent juniper, Sífnos may well be the greenest of the Cyclades; it is touted as being so, far and wide. The island's villages are flawlessly pretty, and the valleys surrounding them are filled with dovecotes and monasteries. Indeed, even the harbour, **Kamáres**, has a pleasant aspect. Its mouth is narrow, formed by opposing mountain ridges that look like two dusty-

Mílos, with the islet Antímilos in the background.

flanked dinosaurs backing toward each other unaware.

Sífnos's central range of mountains softens as it meanders south; toward the empty north, it spreads into sand-coloured pyramids. The main road strikes through a steep, deep valley from Kamáres to sleepy **Apollonía**, the capital. Countless terraces cascade from the mountaintops; the pale soil makes it look as though a golden pudding was poured down over them, cooling in ridges along the way.

There is a tradition of pottery-making on Sífnos; potters still set out long racks of earthenware to dry in the sun. Weaving and jewellery-making are the other crafts, the jewellery-making harkening back to times when Sífnos was rich in gold and silver. According to legend, the Sifniots once gave a hollow rather than solid gold egg to Apollo at Delphi. Apollo avenged this slight by submerging their mines under the sea; from this new paucity Sífnos gets its odd name, which means "emptiness".

Near Apollonía is **Artemónas** (the towns are named for the divine twins Apollo and Artemis), a handsome inland village set on a low escarpment; it is the island's most populous village. The oldest community is **Kástro**, the former capital perched 100 metres (300 ft) above the sea and 3 km (nearly 2 miles) east of Apollonía. Kástro's layout of concentric streets set it apart from other settlements. Catalans and Venetians once ruled the town; the walls they built are still in evidence, as are some remains of an ancient acropolis.

Sífnos's south shore settlements make tranquil beachside bases, but it is easy to find rooms in the inland villages, too. **Fáros**, on a clover-shaped bay, abounds with pottery and churches. Sífnos's most important church, within **Chrysopighí Monastery**, is marooned on an islet set off by the narrowest of canals and spanned by a footbridge, the whole ensemble is most photogenic. No longer in monastic use, basic rooms are let here in summer. Several of the island's ancient watchtowers flank the bay, one of which was a *fáros* (lighthouse). For explanatory literature in English on the subject of Chrysopighí's "miraculous" icon and Sífnos's patron saint seek out the bookstore in Apollonía.

Platýs Yialós is a beach settlement with a winter population of less than 30 and – besides Kamáres – the place backpackers feel most at home. Camping on the beach – the longest on the island – may not be welcomed forever, though, as there is now a rather grim campground inland plus a number of pensions and small hotels. Public notices primly advise that nude bathing is prohibited and that "cleanliness is the key to civilisation". Many glorious walks into the island's interior begin around this area.

A paint-blazed footpath leads from Kataváti just south of Apollonía to **Vathí**, a coastal hamlet provided with a road only in 1993. Caiques make the trip from Kamáres in the summer, and there are tavernas and private rooms on the beach. Its sandy-floored bay is edged by a number of small coves, yet it is a man-made feature which makes Vathí so visually stunning: **Taxiárchis Monas-**

Space beach...

184

tery, poised as though ready to set sail.

SERIFOS: A long tail of land slashes out to enclose the harbour of Serifos. Consisting of perhaps half a dozen each of tavernas, hotels, discos and shops, **Livádi** is a pleasant place to stay, with better beaches found at either side. **Chóra** clings closely to the mountain above and has a precipitous beauty emphasized by the starker, taller mountains that lead from it into the island's interior.

The most frequent bus service is between Livádi and Chóra, with once-daily departures to villages beyond. The road is paved as far as the fortified Byzantine **Taxiárchon Monastery** at the extreme north end of the island. The resident monk, Makários, here since 1958, will show you the ornate *témplon* and such rare treasures as lamps from Egypt and Russia and an ivory inlaid bishop's throne. Makários somehow finds time to fish and raise livestock in addition to his duties as one of the island's two parish priests.

Another more scenic and walkable route to the monastery is via a footpath from Chóra. It begins from the square in upper Chóra, beside the **Káfeneíon I Mýli**, and consists of a wide, intermittently fieldstoned and walled path that winds northeast. Numerous small bays headed by tiny, empty beaches lie below. Habitation is sparse, and there are just a few small farms along the way.

After a good hour's walk, the village of **Kállitso**, or Kéndarchos, as it is locally known, appears at the far side of a steep valley. Marigolds and palm trees grow between the older houses; some abandoned stone huts straddle the palisade of rock overlooking the sea. There are no tavernas, but there is a fresh water fountain along the main cement path. The paved road cuts westward from here, leading to Taxiarchón in about half an hour; the monastery sits directly on the roadside, opposite a small chapel and cemetery.

Galáni, **Pýrgos**, and **Panaghía** are the rustic villages of the magnificent valley beyond Taxiarchón. You can cross this valley by one of two footpaths

.and space
ouse,
ífnos.

around the hill that bisects it, or stick to the road. The original, 10th-century Panaghía church, dedicated to the Virgin, is infamous for its 16 August feast-day *(Ksilopanaghía)*. Bachelors and maidens used to rush in pairs to be the first to dance around the church's olive tree, for the first couple on that day to complete the dance would be allowed to marry during the year. The element of choice caused jealousy and feuding, and when the island's youth started beating off unwanted competition with switches, a priest put a stop to the fighting but not to the custom: now the priest is always first to circle the tree.

Serifos abounds with beaches, all accessible only on foot, and all fantastically unspoiled. **Megálo Livádi** in the southwest is the island's second port (buses cross to it in the summer only).

KYTHNOS: After iron mining operations ceased, Kýthnos lost its prime source of income, one which has not been supplemented by tourism from abroad. There is, however, a fair-sized influx of Athenians to the island each summer.

Kythnioí (or Kýthniots) are mainly dairy and livestock farmers. Elderly residents and visitors frequent the thermal baths at **Loutrá**, on the northeast coast; therefore Kýthnos is a supremely quiet island. It is also quite barren. Bowers of blossoms cultivated in family gardens provide the only colour against the dun-coloured, flat landscape.

Mérichas has most of the accommodation on Kýthnos, at least for the moment. In summer, a "taxi-boat" runs from Mérichas to Episkopí, Apókrisi, and Kolóna beaches.

Kýthnos's landlocked **Chóra** 6 km (4 miles) northeast of Mérichas, is exquisite. Whereas most Cycladic towns crawl spiderlike over the area, this Chóra is on a rectangular plan. Wood-beamed arches span across narrow streets to join two sides of the same house. In the passages underneath, the rock pavements are playfully decorated with whitewash fish, stylized ships, or flowers. There is a small, sweet-smelling oleander-filled main square. The fields at the back of the town rise gently away from the ra-

Taxiárchis chapel on the trail between Chóra and Dryopída, Kýthnos.

vine south of the town, dotted with farmhouses and tile-roofed chapels.

Just east of Chóra is a "Wind Park," which helps supply the island's power (along with the "Solar Park" on the road to Loutrá), and rarely a day passes when its rotors aren't spinning and pinging away furiously. A walk to Loutrá (5 km/ 3 miles from Chóra) goes through the rural central plain. Cows sedately cross the road, udders swinging, and long-haired sheep cluster under the rare tree. Above Loutrá, at **Maroúla**, excavations revealed the earliest known settlement in the Cyclades.

Byrókastro (Ancient Kýthnos), is a seaside ruin where the foundations of the old town are visible. It is a two-hour walk from Chóra but obtain directions locally. A nearby islet fortress, glowering in the direction of Hydra and the Peloponnese, has also been excavated. The presence of so many graves on this islet points to a local belief that ghosts do not cross water. Sillika, the medieval capital, now called **Dryopída**, is split by a stream bed and has a chambered cave (Katafiki) linked in legend with the nereids. The town itself presents an appealing red-roofed spectacle, especially when seen from above.

KÉA: The island's main town, **Ioulís** (Chóra), rides a rounded ridge overlooking the island's northern reach; it was a spot chosen precisely for its inaccessibility from foreign and mainland marauders. Proximity to Attica signalled constant, if not always happy, relations with Athens. Kéa (locally known as Tziá) is now a popular holiday spot with beach-loving Athenians, but its present inaccessibility from the rest of the Western Cyclades makes it a cumbersome destination for the dedicated island-hopper. As a result, foreigners are welcomed for their novelty value.

Kéa-bound boats leave from the mainland port of Lávrion, some 50 km (30 miles) from Athens, and land at **Korissía**, locally called **Livádi**. The jagged west coast has many sandy spits, several impossible to reach. **Písses** and **Koúndouros** are just two of the established resorts which have sprung up to accommodate the Athenian overspill.

Close to Koríssía is the bayside village of **Vourkári**, with Aghía Iríni church, a Minoan excavation, and an ancient road. A short distance to the north, Cape Kephala is the site of the oldest Neolithic settlement in the Cyclades. The Lion of Kéa, about 15 minute walk northeast of Chóra, is a renowned statue carved out of stone, which may or may not date from the Archaic period; opinion is varied. The object of many local legends, the lion is almost 6 metres (20 ft) long and wears a smile.

Almost all Keans live in Chóra. The rest of Kéa is made up of resorts rather than villages. **Otziás**, in the north, the busiest resort, has the pick of beaches. Each 15 August, pilgrims make their way to the islands treasured **Panaghía Kastrianí Monastery** to the northeast.

The remains of four former Ionian cities – Koressía, Ioulis, Karthea, and Poiessa – testify to Kéa's one-time political importance. The first two are near their modern namesakes. Poiessa is near Písses and Karthea is near **Póles**, south of Káto Meriá.

Islanders are torn between the forces of tradition and modernity.

THE SPORADES ISLANDS

SKIÁTHOS, SKÓPELOS, ALÓNISSOS, SKÝROS

The Sporades – in English, "sporadic" or "scattered" – are a group of four islands in the northwest Aegean.

Skýros, the largest and in many ways the most interesting, is detached from the others, and while hopping among Skiáthos, Skópelos and Alónissos is very easy, Skýros involves a longer trip; but they all are connected now by hydrofoil. Skiáthos alone among them has an international airport with several (charter) flights daily in summer, mainly from England, Germany and Scandinavia, and domestic connections. Skýros has an airport but other than a feeder service from Athens it is reserved for the Greek Air Force. Ferries and hydrofoils run from Volos and Aghios Konstantínos.

Mainlanders have long recognised Skiáthos's beaches as the best in the Aegean and made an annual pilgrimage. They are now outnumbered by foreigners, and the fact that there are shops which sell nothing but expensive fur coats (a little something that in summer one might have forgotten to bring along?) and will accept any conceivable credit card is a forecast of what to expect. In spite of a rich history, Alónissos is the least developed in terms of tourism while Skópelos, more recently and self-consciously the senior partner among the trio, is a compromise. Skýros is like a scaled-down version of Crete. It has an independent spirit and a deeply entrenched local culture impervious to the events which are constantly swirling around it.

The islands are what's left of a mountain range which snapped away from the mainland in a geological convulsion and "sank". They lie within a narrow band where prevailing winds and other factors produce reliable rainfall and lush vegetation, notably pine forests. The rains do not intrude in summer. Instead, the *meltémi*, a northerly wind, helps to hold temperatures down a little.

The traditional trade route between the Mediterranean and the Black Sea via the Bosphorus passes the Sporades. Since antiquity, bad weather has brought unexpected and often unwanted callers, including distressed invasion fleets (for example, Xerxes) and pirates. Yet major archaeological sites are surprisingly few.

World War I produced a postscript to the strategic location: it was on a convoy heading for Gallipoli that the poet Rupert Brooke died. Skýros rose into sight, and it was here that they stopped to bury him.

Preceding pages: a somewhat ancient ruin; stretched out in the sun. **Left**, empty cafés are an uncommon sight.

THE SPORADES ISLANDS

SKIÁTHOS: The scythe of Koukounariés is used as evidence on thousands of postcards that the Aegean can produce the kind of beach normally associated with the Caribbean. Propriety would prevent as many postcards from featuring **Krassí** (colloquially "Banana Beach") because it caters for nudists. The fact that no one cares whether bathers at Banana Beach strip off or not is typical of the easygoing, relaxed nature of the people of Skiáthos as a whole.

The island has beaches for all occasions, not least because some will always be sheltered wherever the wind is coming from. **Koukounariés** and **Banana** are near neighbours at the end of the twisting 18-km (11-mile) coast road from the town; there are dozens along it, many with a taverna or at least a kiosk selling drinks and sandwiches. A path leading down from the road usually promises a beach at the end, possibly the kind of secluded cove which is the stuff of holiday fable.

Round-the-island boat trips pass the rocky and otherwise inaccessible northern shoreline and in particular **Kástro**, the abandoned medieval capital which for centuries was a haven from predators. The boats stop for swimming and lunch at other beaches. A moped or hired car – or perhaps a mule and infinite patience – would be necessary to follow the unpaved roads looping through the mountains. They provide stunning views as well as the chance to pop into monasteries which, with Kástro, are more or less the only buildings of historic interest.

The bluff above the under-used beach at the end of the very busy airport runway has produced fragments suggesting a pre-historic settlement, but neither it nor the rest of the island has ever been properly excavated.

The port village is lively at night, probably the most important consideration after the beaches for the type of visitor which Skiáthos attracts in intimidating numbers in August. The preferences of the fast-living set change constantly, but it is not difficult to spot which places are in vogue at any particular time.

The bright lights are to be found along **Papadiamántis**, the road which bisects the two hills on which the town stands, and along the *paralía* or waterfront. The cobbled alleys above the port provide more of the same as well as some quieter places to explore.

Expect restaurants rather than tavernas and be prepared to pay accordingly. Plate-smashing and other forms of sociable anarchy are at a safe distance out of town; to the fury of taxi drivers and the regular bus operators, the tavernas concerned lay on special transport from the ferry terminal.

The permanent population of 5,100 includes an expatriate colony in lovely houses on the **Kanapítsa peninsula**. The fact that they want nothing done to improve the deplorable state of the access road says something, as do doubts about the new – and larger – airport terminal building.

eft, the *lear*, clean *aters* of the *egean*. *elow*, a *heel* of *rtune*.

The island hardly needs to be able to admit more visitors than already arrive between mid-July and mid-September. Skiáthos has many devotees who return year after year – they know better and adjust their timing to suit.

SKÓPELOS: An enduring image of Skópelos, for anyone who has been there in August, is the way in which the famous local plum is picked, examined, wiped and, before being popped into the mouth, given a final polish with the thumb. And who, on sailing or driving along the coast between Glóssa and Skópelos town and knowing a local tale, would not be on the look-out for the spot which best fitted the dénouement?

It seems that a rampaging dragon had proved itself to be invulnerable to conventional weapons. The local priest, one Reginos, was implored to direct a sermon at the beast, the islanders having heard enough of them to think that it might do the trick. Finding itself as bored as they had been, the dragon reared away and fled until it could go no further. The pious Reginos followed dog-

gedly and, on cornering his quarry on a clifftop, prepared to deliver another one. Despairing at the prospect, the dragon dived off, and the impact on landing created one of the indentations which are characteristic of the deeply rugged coastline.

Visitors waiting in Volos rather than Aghios Konstantínos for the ferry to Skópelos (the alternative is to fly to Skiáthos and catch a ferry from there) could usefully call at the **archaeological museum** to look at the contents of a grave discovered on the island fairly recently. The gold crown and ornate weapons almost certainly belonged to Stafylos, a Minoan who colonised the island and then went on to be crowned its king.

The island's distinguished past is not so much demonstrated by prominent historical sites as by the exceptionally fine houses in **Skópelos Town**, a handsome amphitheatre around a harbour lined with bars and tavernas under mulberry trees.

Glóssa, the island's other town, is

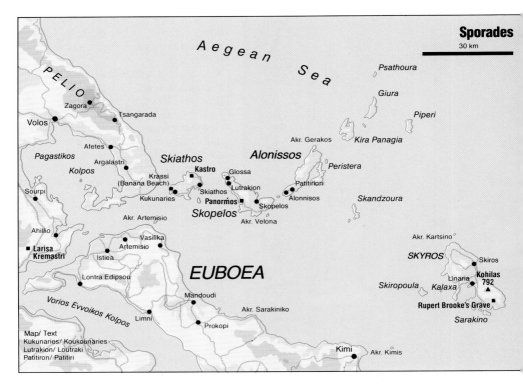

something of an oddity in that the people who live there have a pronounced dialect which, together with houses whose features are not like other island architecture, suggests that at some time they immigrated from Thessal. They seem to have made themselves welcome; other islanders refer approvingly to their "exaggerated hospitality".

The main road on the island runs between the port of **Loutráki**, where Glóssa used to stand before it moved up the mountain for safety's sake, and Skópelos Town. It is an attractive run which includes a number of hamlets and **Panórmou Bay**, where there are a few remains of a city which probably existed in 500 BC. The wise money is on the dragon having made its desperate departing leap somewhere around Panórmou Bay.

ALÓNISSOS: This island is full of ghosts whispering what might have been. On the hill above **Patitíri**, the port where the ferries from the other islands land, is the Chóra (also called **Alónissos**), the former capital destroyed by an earth-

quake in 1965. This compounded the blow the islanders had already suffered when all their grapevines withered and died from phylloxera only a few years earlier.

Alónissos seems to have been ever thus: the previous capital, Ikos, the name by which the island as a whole was known in Classical times, literally disappeared when the ground on which it stood toppled into the sea.

The submerged remains of the capital, off Kokkinókastro beach, are an important part of a "marine conservation park" which may be explored with a snorkel but not with scuba tanks (this is a general rule in the Aegean to prevent pilfering and damage).

Of the famous wines which were once shipped all over ancient Greece in urns stamped "Ikion", there is no longer any trace. Yet in 1970, paleolithic evidence was found which could mean that Alónissos was singled out for habitation before any other island in the Aegean, perhaps as early as 100,000 BC, and it was considered a prize over

THE FALTAITS MUSEUM

The Faltaits Museum is located near the northeastern edge of Skyros, high on a ridge atop massive stone fortifications built thousands of years before the founding of Rome. It is housed in a mansion built as the Faltaits family home in the late 1800s near to the original site of a temple to the goddess Astarte (Ashtar).

It seems only fitting that it is here that the oldest of the old *megála stráta* (upper class families), on an island even Homer and Plutarch referred to as "ancient", should have collected innumerable artefacts which eloquently present the history, tradition, and mythology of Skyros.

Manos Faltaits founded the museum in 1964. A well-known sociologist, painter, poet, writer, and peace activist, he has written several pamphlets and a fascinating book about the island. Manos has also conducted seminars about future community life based on traditional life, and his family home has become a base and a working monument to these ideals.

"Huddled on the northern tip of the island," one visitor noted in the 19th century, "the inhabitants think only of how best to safeguard themselves against their [Turkish] masters' greed and against piracy, which is hereditary to the Greeks." The solution was to have a second house within the city fortress used "for storing personal belongings... whole rooms filled to capacity with copper and earthenware".

The rooms of the Faltaits Museum are laid out in a similar fashion, the size and design resembling that used by Skyrians today. Fine porcelain plates decorate shelves and hang on walls, but the most distinctive features in the museum's first room are the tiny wooden tables surrounded by miniature, intricately carved wooden chairs. Skyrians were, and still are, craftsmen of renown. Walk down any village street today and, through lace curtains, one can glimpse household items carved with immaculate skill.

Some of the older, better pieces have been collected and are scattered throughout the mu-

seum. One superb example is found in the next room, the kitchen and above that, the sleeping area, both of which are framed by carved wood. Traditional clothing, normally stored in chests, is displayed on the walls here: the silken garb of upper class men, baggy pantaloons still worn by Skyrian shepherds, and the richly embroidered wedding and bridesmaid dresses with cuffs and hemlines sewn in golden threads.

Skyrian embroideries are distinctive and respected throughout Greece. A glass case in the central room shows them at their finest – at once colourful, imaginative, fanciful and serious. Designs are deeply symbolic: the pomegranate, representing fertility because of its many seeds; or intertwined snakes, which symbolise the protection because they are so universally feared.

The tree of life, the church, the fountain of immortality, the ship, the nymph, and the wedding couple are others, each carrying powerful messages of Skyrian history, legend, mythology, religion, or superstition. Other glass cases contain carved wooden spindles and spoons and bread stamps, or lavish jewellery fit for royalty.

The last room records in photographs and paintings the Skyrian goat dance, part of the three-week festival which takes place in the marketplace and back streets of the capital. The room's most important feature is a collection of rare books, the oldest dated 1503, about 50 years after movable type was first used.

A professor of Greek archaeology at Cambridge who visited the Faltaits Museum called it a "splendid collection", and another from Oxford referred to it as "most intriguing, truly superb". But the real voice of authority is the museum itself, one of the finest small folklore museums in Greece. The workshop produces hand-painted plates depicting designs of the Skyrian embroideries as well as pillowcases and tablecloths with these designs on them.

Visitors can sit and chat with Manos Faltaits and his elegant wife Anastasia on the terrace which overlooks the clear and still clean Aegean. Ask Manos about *Daismos* – an ancient way of community living – and an intellectually challenging dialogue is sure to develop. ∎

which Philip of Macedon and the Athenians fought bitterly.

The way the island has adjusted to its unrealised potential and bad luck is something for which many visitors should be grateful. It is the least developed of the Sporades, a much quieter island surrounded by an interesting collection of islets.

One of them, **Youra**, is home to a unique breed of wild goat and also has a cave that is full of stalactites and stalagmites which it pleases the islanders to believe was once occupied by a protective cyclops.

The fishing is excellent too, and many of the swordfish which provide some of the best eating in the Sporades are taken in the waters around Alónissos. In the absence of proper roads, apart from the one to Stení Vála, which is the centre for research and protection of the Mediterranean monk seal, caiques are the most practical form of transport. The terrain is rugged and walking accordingly quite demanding.

The path from Patitíri up to the site of the 1965 earthquake looks and is steep, but the old town is fast coming back to life, thanks largely to the efforts of foreign visitors, and there are several bars and taverna commanding stunning views as well as providing restorative drinks and food.

SKYROS: The main character in Skýros's Carnival goat dance, staged just before Lent, is a *yéros* (old man) who wears a mask made out of goat skin and by shaking his hips rings the many sheep bells hanging from his waist. The second figure is a young man dressed up and behaving as a woman.

Foreign visitors enjoying the spectacle ought to know that the third figure, a buffoon who has a large bell strapped to his back and blows into a sea shell, represents, well, a foreigner. Islanders might politely point out, however, that he is specifically a western European of the 17th century.

Visitors should not take the mockery to heart. Skýros does not have to put up with so many of them that their presence becomes intrusive, and in many ways

the island goes on in its own sweet way as it has always done.

Although the presence of the Greek Air Force doesn't intrude on the visitor, Skyrians have been adamantly against the military being on their island. But demonstrations in the square and petitions passed round local gathering have failed to stop the presence becoming a fact. In **Aspoús**, a village of about 30 people, three ship owners went on strike for two hours recently and put up signs saying that they did so to protest against what they saw as the increasing militarisation of their homeland.

Skýros has a unique breed of miniature horse, smaller than the Shetland pony, which is thought to have existed for 17 million years. They used to roam wild except when they were needed to help with the threshing after the harvest. This was the signal for a battle of wits with nominal owners who first had to find them and then rope them in. These tiny animals are thought to be the same breed as the horses depicted on the Parthenon frieze.

Older islanders will still wear traditional clothes as a matter of course, and behind their characteristic pebbled entrances the cubist houses contain amazing collections of craft work and other prized objects, many of them originally piratical booty. Carved wooden furniture passed down though the generations is often, like the horses, rather too small to be practical, which the islanders themselves seem to acknowledge by hanging a lot of it on the walls.

The ancient Greeks knew Skýros well, and it has a walk-on part in mythology as the place where Theseus was thrown to his death – off the rock which is the landmark of **Skýros Town** – and the baby Achilles was brought up disguised as a girl. He did not carry off the role very well, giving himself away when offered, while in the company of female playmates, the choice between jewellery and a sword.

Skýros was probably two islands originally, the halves joining near where there is now a road linking **Linariá**, the port, with Skýros Town. The southern sector of the island is barren, and visitors are unlikely to venture to that part unless they are in search of a quiet, secluded beach or unless they wish to see the English poet **Rupert Brooke's grave** at **Treís Boúkes**. Daytrips to Brooke's grave, the grottoes, and the south island beaches can be arranged from the capital.

Life in the town is played out on what is effectively a stage, a raised square where there is the option of joining the promenade or finding a table, ordering a drink, and watching it. This takes place within the shadow of the Gibraltarian rock which was Theseus's undoing. As an obvious stronghold, it was adopted for use by whomever ruled Skýros, and the evidence of their presence lies like layers of a cake.

The ruins are inanimate, however, while the little horses, the crafts and even the fun still to be derived from an absurd 17th-century western European at a carnival all show the extent to which Skýros's strong sense of its own identity has so far, at least, resisted any foreign blandishments.

Left, and Right, characters from the **Skýros carnival.**

ΚΥΡΙΕ ΙΗCΟΥ ΧΡΙCΤΕ
ΕΛΕΗCΟΝ ΜΕ

THE NORTHEAST AEGEAN ISLANDS

THÁSSOS, SAMOTHRÁKI, LÍMNOS, AGHIOS EFSTRÁTIOS, LÉSVOS, PSARÁ, CHÍOS, IKARÍA, SÁMOS

The islands of the northeast Aegean are grouped together for geographical convenience. The islands to the north, Thássos, Samothráki, and Límnos, bear scant resemblance to their grander neighbours to the east, and have little in common with each other either. Thássos belongs to the Prefecture of Kavala on the mainland, Samothráki to that of Evros, and Límnos to that of Lésvos. These islands for the most part look to mainland Greece for culture, history and now, food or supplies.

The eastern islands of Sámos, Chíos, and Lésvos at one time played a leading role on the world's stage, providing much-needed links between Asia Minor and western civilisation. Sámos and Chíos were in fact, once joined to the coast of Asia Minor and even today only a light craft is need to sail between Greece and Turkey. Politically, however, the waters are deep and it is best to tread warily if wishing to visit both countries within a short time span.

The eastern islanders were superb sailors and merchants, establishing trading stations throughout the Mediterranean. The arts and sciences flourished. Sappho of Lésvos and Pythagoras of Sámos are only two who achieved world-wide prominence.

Today it is transport rather than culture which divides the islands. Límnos, Samothráki, Chíos, and remote Ikaría are served by few ferries; as a result, they are comparatively free of tourists. Sámos, on the other hand, could be classed as an honorary Dodecanese island due to its popular caique service to and from the holy – and very much visited – island of Pátmos. As air links with the rest of Europe become more commonplace; so too will the islands with well-placed international airports. Lésvos already is a favourite with discerning package tour companies although it is fairly safe to say that the islands of the northeast – scattered, far-flung, and fiercely independent – will remain free from all but the more adventurous tourists for some time to come.

Preceding pages: last resting place in a monastery on Chíos; tomatoes strung up to dry in Pýrgi, Chíos. **Left,** an old woman meditates on her past.

THE NORTHEAST AEGEAN ISLANDS

THÁSSOS: The ancient claim to fame of the small, green island of Thássos is the "black" wine that disabled brutish Cyclops, allowing Odysseus to escape him. Gold, silver, and even amethyst and opal were once mined here. Marble, which is still actively excavated, and honey, are the island's other notable resources. The island also claims to be the birthplace of Demeter, goddess of the harvest.

Thássos, technically part of (East) Macedonia, was once a centre of panhellenistic worship, evidenced by a string of ruins adjoining the modern **Thássos Town** (Liménas). Signposts point the way first to the Hellenistic theatre (ancient dramas every Saturday in summer), on to a Genoese fort and hilltop sanctuaries to Apollo, Athena, and Pan; "secret stairs" snake back down to Heracles and Dionýsos's temples, and the Agora.

Further along are a shrine to Artemis and a Roman road. The relics are in Thássos's **Archaeological Museum**.

Thássos is popular with (German) caravan tourists, but they congregate mainly in a small west coast area, leaving ample stretches of the island peaceful and wild. In the north, olive trees spread across the lower valleys, beehives humming beneath them, while the mountain slopes are grasshopper-green with pine trees.

Travel around the island is inevitably clockwise or counter-clockwise, since only one road rings it. The first town clockwise from Thássos, **Panaghía**, is filled with fountains carved from plane trees, and rests above a long, gold stripe of **Chyrssí Ammoudiá beach**.

The riot of conifers and fruit trees then fades because, in 1986, southern Thássos's forest land was destroyed by fire. Some think it was maliciously started by hotel developers looking for cheap land clearance. The villages and a thin fringe of vegetation around them were saved.

Alykí, a fisherman's cove with a small neck of beach, encompasses an ancient marble quarry and shrine. Down the coast is the startlingly modern **Monastery Archangelou**. Both **Potós** and **Limenária,** where a factory was built by a German mining company around 1900, are large new towns given over to tourism. Macedonian **Theológos** and **Mariés** in the mountains, laden with flowers and grapes, are dominated by scallop-cut slate roofs.

Theológos was the medieval capital (and home to the island's liberation leader, Hadzigiórgis), for inland towns were safer from pirates than coastal villages. The collective memory of invasion is so potent that villagers still affix bars to their windows for extra protection. The burnt areas shimmer with strange green insects with opal wings which love to sun on the rocks.

Thássos's edges are unevenly fluted with beaches, and dolphins play off the east coast. Divers may want to check out the claim that Thássos harbour's floor is sheer marble. Thássos is accessible only by boat from Kavála, Néa Péramos and Keramotí, on the mainland.

SAMOTHRAKI: Also known as Samothrace, this is the island from which Poseidon is said to have watched the Peloponnesian War. The forest has since receded from the top of **Mount Fengári**, Poseidon's watchpoint, leaving a bald, craggy pate exposed to the rough winds that dance up its north face. Yet the steep ascent up Fengári (1,650 metres/ 5,400 ft), from Thérma is largely sheltered by plane and fruit trees, and supplied with water from the cataracts that spin down its sides. The summit view – if the haze isn't too thick – extends to Athos and the Ida mountains of Turkey.

From Alexandroúpolis on the mainland there is a regular ferry service which stops at **Kamariótissa**, a stepping stone to the older Chóra (Samothraki) 5 km (3 miles) to the east. The houses are densely packed, but many of them are occupied by pigs and goats. Shaped roughly like an aspen leaf, the island is sparsely inhabited; only the western half has a paved road.

The northwest is most heavily populated; the road fades at the **Thérma** turn-off, a spa town shaded by a thick web of planes.

Among the permanent residents are several Russian-born Greeks who arrived in the 1920s ethnic exchanges; the women wear a distinctive black wimple. The coast beyond Thérma is flat and wooded, making it prime camping turf for young Greeks in souped-up Volkswagen buses, many of them artists and musicians.

Just west of Thérma is **Palaiópoli** (which means old city), site of the Great Sanctuary of the Gods and source of the celebrated statue Nike, the *Winged Victory of Samothrace*. The statue resides at the Louvre, but there is a reproduction in the site's museum (closed Tuesdays). The sanctuary yielded a trove of archaeological finds charting early Greek religious practices. Its excellent condition – the oldest artefacts date to 700 BC – shows evidence of earlier Roman refurbishment.

The villages of the south coast rarely see visitors. Olives, onions, and grapes are cultivated under the rocky glare of

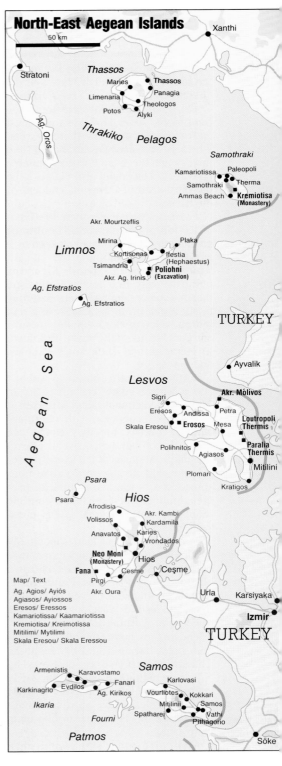

North-East Aegean Islands

50 km

Fengári. The trunks of some of the older olive trees have turned spongy and hollow, and it's not uncommon to see four or five sheep grazing with their heads stuck inside them. A haul over the dirt extension passing these villages ends at an idyllic beach, **Pachiá Ammos**.

There is no settlement here; only caves, and a taverna which is sometimes open. However, Samothrakians make an occasional pilgrimage (five hours by foot from the nearest town, a rough 90 minutes by car or motorbike) to give thanks at nearby **Kremniótissa**, a modern chapel perched on a high rock shelf. A series of smaller hills spans the distance between it and Pachiá Ammos, and it's possible to climb to the church in about two hours.

LÍMNOS: Except for the alluvial plains of Thessaly, Límnos may be one of the flattest patches of Greece to be found. A few craggy volcanic hills hug the bays around **Mýrina**, the main town; otherwise, Límnos is full of military posts and grain fields – wheat, tobacco and cotton grow here.

On a tour of the island, it's impossible to miss the garish scarecrows, dressed like medieval knights or Hell's Angels, totems of Limnian agriculture. Typical of the Hellespont region (the Dardanelles), the island gets a great deal of wind and cloud – but not much rain. Shellfish – especially from mussels nurseries – ouzo, and merchant shipping are sources of income.

There is little of substance to hold tourists' interest, despite Límnos's rich history. Jason and the Argonauts stopped here and their sojourn is intertwined with island lore. Just before their arrival, as a punishment for forgetting Aphrodite, the women were cursed with an odour so repulsive the men planned to seek new wives. The outraged females slaughtered their male relatives, but Hypsipyle hid her father, and was castigated for it. She alone welcomed the Argonauts, and later bore Jason's son, Euenos, the island's future king.

Maroúla was a local heroine in the uprising against the Turks in 1475; her statue is at **Kótsinas**. The excavation on

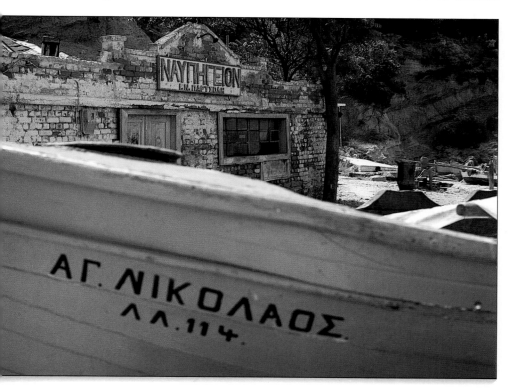

the east coast shows evidence of Limnian life as early as 4000 BC. Italian excavations continue, so the site is guarded. A remote temple dedicated to Hephaestus, god of the forge fire, sits near his namesake town, Iphaisteía, in the northeast.

Límnos also worshipped the Kabíroi, obscure demigods believed to protect sailors. Hephaestus's Kabireíon is claimed as Greece's oldest sanctuary. Mýrina's recently well renovated **archaeological museum** displays all the local discoveries.

Mýrina's bustling market street leads around the base of the mostly Byzantine **fortress**, where the Genoese finally surrendered to the Ottomans in the 15th century. The town, its cobbles and houses both making good use of local volcanic stone, is one of the most appealing in the North Aegean.

At **Romaïkós Yialós** ornate facades preside over beachside cafés, while just north lies the **Aktí Mýrina** complex, which is one of Greece's most expensive island resorts. More and better beaches can be found southeast of Mýrina, below the tiered hillside villages of Platý and Thános.

AGHIOS EFSTRATIOS: Límnos is the source of vital supplies to this lonely wedge of land in an unsettled reach of the Aegean. Everything from diesel fuel to fresh melons is imported on Aghios Efstrátios.

The island is really just a single village which comprises 200 residents, 10 soldiers, two cars, and a few cafes and tavernas. In 1968, a severe earthquake shook the island, killing half the population and levelling many buildings; hence the uncharacteristic rows of identical housing, provided as emergency aid though it seems many dwellings were reliable – about two dozen old houses remain.

Farming is nearly impossible, but the Manikákis family have arable land in the throat of the valley adjacent to the town, orchards, and a vegetable and flower garden. Thyme and basil sprout wild from the stone walls. Vassílis is retired now, but spent his youth working on passenger ships, as many islanders once did. The younger generation

Vasilis Manicakis, with Eyios Efstratios behind him.

has generally deserted Aghios Efstrátios now, including Vassílis's children.

Goats and hens have taken over the shell of the enormous old school. Now classes are held in a private house; the children throw a party each year to welcome the teacher from Límnos.

No one has yet excavated Aghios Efstrátios as most of the island's ruins are painfully recent. The village chapel's graves all date after 1968, the earlier ones destroyed in the earthquake. An odd pair of monuments occupy a nearby hillock: a shrine to the perished islanders, and a German soldier's grave.

Merchant shipping and fishing are the island's lifeblood. Tourists are an oddity, and must inevitably stay in the one hotel. None of the several beaches, less than an hour's walk to north or south, will likely contain another soul.

LÉSVOS: Mytilíni, the capital of Lésvos (natives call the entire island Mytilíni), has a charged, metropolitan atmosphere, and is a good place to get a reading on the temper of this proud island. In fact, many Mytilínians were born in Turkey,

returning in the 1920s ethnic exchanges. Occasionally, they now cross over to find their childhood homes. Usually, they are welcomed, despite political tension between the countries.

The core of Mytilíni town seems little changed since the 18th century, when it grew to house the pasha's shipyard workers. Its focal point, the **Old Market**, is a long, dusty street crammed with tiny shops. Mytilíni's **archaeological museum** sorts the puzzle of its past, along with the **Byzantine** and **popular art museums**. More noteworthy is the **Theophilos Museum** at Vareiá, 4 km (2½ miles) south of town. Theophilos was a gifted "primitive" painter.

The enormity of the island (Greece's third largest) means far-flung villages. Between them lie 11 million olive trees producing 45,000 liquid tonnes of oil yearly. Shipbuilding, carpentry, ouzo distilling, and ceramics are still important, but none rival the olive, especially as it complements Mytilíni's second industry: tourism. The nets are laid out in autumn, and as soon as the tourists leave, Mytilíni's black gold begins to drop into them.

The northern coastal villages and their beaches draw the most visitors. **Mólyvos** (Míthymna), wrapped around the foot of a Genoan castle, was once graphite-rich. Its homes, built of stone with pine window jambs, have frescoed or carved wood ceilings.

The preserved towers of ancient **Thermí,** which has natural spas, make it architecturally unique. In Pétra, a beach town 5 km (3 miles) south of Mólyvos, the Women's Agricultural/Touristic Cooperative promotes women's financial independence, and arranges lodging.

Further west, **Eressós** (the best beach is Skála Eressóu) was the home of Sappho. The Petrified Forest around **Sígri** was transformed by lava; the ash-dusted, hardened stumps are scattered, but the enriched soil produces wild flowers that attract furious clouds of butterflies. **Aghiássos**, a medieval hill village hidden below the island's summit of Olympos, produces traditional weaving and pottery. Ploumári, south of Aghiássos on the coast, combines Scandi-

he beach
Gera,
ésvos.

LITERARY LÉSVOS

U p at the Genoan castle a group of strolling players were doing Chekhov in Greek under floodlights. The following week, there would be a touch of Dario Fo. Not quite what you would expect at a package holiday resort. But this was Mólyvos, magnet for culture vultures on Lésvos, the cradle of the arts.

A kind of Hellenic St Ives, the village has long attracted writers, poets, artists and thinkers, reflecting the island's intellectual heritage. Beguiling as Circe, Lésvos gives off a very special vibe, an inspirational magic.

Lésvos, "where burning Sappho loved and sung", is best known as the birthplace of the extraordinary poetess, the original Lesbian. Sappho (*Sapfó* in Greek) was born in ancient Eressós, a well-educated aristocrat and a free-thinking woman – remarkable elsewhere in Greece around 600 BC. But Lésvos, known as the Red Island by other Greeks because of its Communist leanings, has always had a history of democratic ideals; a quest for knowledge and literary freedom.

Plato called Sappho the tenth muse. Her lyrical outpourings and erotica, usually written to women at her academy, however, were deemed too hot to handle by Pittacus, the contemporary ruler. Her work was ordered to be burned and only fragments of her nine books of poetry have survived, although some of her writings were discovered among papyrus rolls in Egypt only 100 years ago.

The Greeks say she had a bad press. Her condemnation was political: she was too smart for comfort, a threat to democratic reforms. Who knows? She and her pupils followed Aphrodite, warrior as well as love goddess. Whatever her sexual proclivities, Sappho was way before her time, introducing new poetic metre and, with the poet Alcaeus, giving lyric verse new depths. Yet she threw herself from a cliff on far away Lefkácla for the love of a young man. A statue of her stands in the harbour at the main port while gay women pay homage to her at Skála Eressoú.

Lésvos has always been a cultural oasis, according to the Ionian poet Anacreon: "An island with a touch of class." Mytilíni people – they don't like being called Lesvians – seem to have an almost Celtic temperament. Like the Welsh or Irish they burst into song, or tears, or dance at the drop of a hat. They are great dancers and musicians. Forget tourist Greek nights. Here it's all for real, an explosion of exuberance and heart-felt emotion.

If Sappho is the first lady of literary Lésvos then her male counterpart must surely be Aesop, he of the fables. The island also boasts the poet-musicians Arion and Terpandros, while Aristotle and Epicurus often gave lectures to students at the famous local School of Philosophy.

The Nobel prize-winning poet Odysseus Elytis came from Lésvos, as did the novelist Stratis Myrivilis, who lived in the village of Sykaminiás near Mólyvos. Apparently the writer used to sleep in the branches of the mulberry tree in the village square of Skála Sykaminiás on hot summer nights. The tiny chapel to the Mermaid Madonna, immortalised in his prose, is in the port of Skála Sykaminiás.

The village of Pétra is famous for the primitive painter Theophilos. A wandering tramp, he painted murals to earn a crust. After he died his work became internationally known thanks to the locally born critic Thériade, who lived in Paris. Most of his paintings are in the Theophilos Museum at Vareiá, just south of Mytilíni.

Poetry is alive in the mountain village of Aghiássos. The villagers wear traditional costume and uphold the old oral traditions at their fiestas. On Shrove Monday, *(Katherí Deftéra in Greek)*, there is a custom known as *Vallia* which involves impromptu exchanges of satirical verse, one poet picking up the thread from the other.

Albert Camus planned to build a house overlooking Sígri, in the west – perhaps better to comprehend the existential void posited by his friend Sartre, as there really *is* nothing at Sígri. Songwriter and national hero Mikis Theodorakis was a regular visitor to Mólyvos for a long time. Once visited, Lésvos lures you back. The Muses still haunt the olive groves. ∎

navian package tourism and an ouzo distillery among its hillside houses.

Check tourist information (Mytilíni and Mólyvos) for local feast days. Aghiássos, on 15 August, has one of the most vivid festivals; there's also a winter carnival with improvised poetry and masked jesters.

PSARÁ: Minute Psará has been on the political map since antiquity, and is first mentioned by Homer, who may have stumbled on Psará first when he left his native island of Chíos. Further, Independence hero Kanáris, who destroyed the Turkish flagship in 1822, was born here and exemplifies the courage of the islanders. When Ottoman troops came to avenge the continual harrassment of Ottoman shipping by boats from Psará, 17,000 islanders were killed.

The powder magazine in which some islanders blew themselves up rather than be captured by Turkish troops has been restored by the tourist office and turned into a taverna (run by two Psaráns with 20 years of experience in New York restaurants); several ferry or caique runs are made weekly from Chíos. There are only around 300 inhabitants on Psará. It is a sleepy, one-village island that makes a good living off the sea and is amused by the few tourists that trickle over from Chíos for a visit.

Psará is covered with dry, thorny stubble. Fig trees provide virtually the only greenery. The coastal cliffs resemble petrified wood, with narrow outcrops of red-veined marble pushing through. The coastline is pocked with caves which once made Psará popular with pirates. Just past the electric plant is a handsome beach with a smooth, sandy seafloor. Twenty minutes' walk into the interior and a left turn reveals a longer beach, graced by a wreath of tiny islands offshore; on the largest is perched a **fisherman's chapel**. The wind-buffeted beaches are covered with chalk-white seagrass and minute nautilus shells.

The climb to the highest summit at 530 metres (1,750 ft) is a dusty, windy one; the view will confirm Psará's nakedness, broken by one green plain on the west coast where corn is grown.

There is a tiny monastery, uninhabited and visited only in August, called **Theotókou** which stands at the island's northern extreme.

CHÍOS: This island (also spelled Hios) has a bitter past. In 1822, some 30,000 islanders were executed by the sultan's men and an additional 40,000 men and women were shipped to Constantinople as slaves. In the centuries preceding this bloodbath, Chíos was a highly Europeanised island. The Koraïs library was established in the capital in 1792. The **Argenti Ethnographic and Folklore Museum**, a vivid collection of folk art, costumes (each town had its own distinct dress), and tools was annexed to it in the 1980s. There is also a reproduction of Delacroix's *Massacre at Hios*, the original of which is in the Louvre.

The best of **Chíos Town** lies within the old citadel – peaceful and dilapidated, mostly car-free. From atop the walls one sees windmills strung along the coast. A mosque nearby is used as a warehouse for archaeological finds.

No two villages on Chíos are alike.

Some towns are built in roseate granite, while others are plasterwork, painted in deep ochres and pastels. The villages in the south are called **Mastichochória** (mastic villages), after the mastic trees which yield gum and derivatives used in industrial production. The mastic's vaunted sweet smell is undetectable, despite claims to the contrary. The *ksystá* (geometric etchings in plaster) that adorn the houses of **Pýrgi** are singular.

Walled **Mestá** is a weird labyrinth of a town with only a handful of gates in its perimeter, formed by the backs of its houses. **Kámbos** is an enclave of the island's wealthiest families.

The Byzantine monastery, **Néa Moní** (due west of the capital and constructed in 1049), was built on a spot where an icon of Mary is said to have appeared in a myrtle tree. Néa Moní seems to be run single-handedly by an ancient nun, daintily proud of the brilliant mosaics that escaped ruin by the Turks. There is a local bus here only twice a week; otherwise, follow the road up from **Karyés** by taxi or hired moped.

Stringing tomatoes at Pírgi, Híos.

Once weekly, the bus continues to once prosperous, stony **Anávatos**, the scene of the island's greatest tragedy: in 1822, 400 villagers leapt to their deaths from the cliff here rather than be captured by the Turks.

In the empty northwest is **Volissós**, said to be Homer's birthplace and served by one bus a day. Homer's "teaching stone" lies near **Vrontádos** on the east coast, where most of the island's population can be found.

IKARIA: Except for the brief flurry when a ferry arrives at Ikaria's main port, the traffic of **Aghios Kírykos** consists mainly of towel-draped elderly people streaming down the stairs from the nearby hot springs. On the bus to **Armenistís**, endpoint of Ikaria's only paved road, islanders disembark into what seems complete wilderness. Far-flung villages and the steep pitch of the island – the 1,000-metre (3,300-ft) **Atherás mountain** covers its length – makes some villages (like Karkinágri) more easily accessible by caique.

The wing-shaped island is named af-ter mythical Ikaros, who fell into the sea when his wax wings melted. It is one of the most undeveloped large islands in the Aegean today. **Armenistís** and **Nas**, both prime beaches, lack the packaged resort feel many travellers dread. An offshore chapel marks Yialaskári, Armenistis's eastern reach. The Naiads were believed to have lived at Nas, a deep-cut cove between two mountainous vertebrae; the **Temple of Artemis Tavropolío** here is the island's most significant pre-Christian ruin.

In the mountain towns around **Christós Ráchon**, dominoes rather than *tavli* is played, and people carry their belongings in hairy goatskin rucksacks. Southwestward, the roads become demoniacally rough. Many minor roads aren't on the map, making for navigational Russian roulette.

The uplands' naked towers of boulders are inhabited only by russet-chested hawks. Lower down, yews, beards of heather, and the exotic autumn crocus grow. Stone walls weave senselessly up empty mountainsides near the coast, but

weirdest of all are the Stone Age-like dwellings with slabs of slate forming their roofs and walls. Toward **Evdilos** (the second port on the north shore), at **Kámbos**, are remnants of the ancient city of Oenoe; Kambos's museum displays the finds.

Xsylosýrti Monastery and the beach at Fáros are the outstanding south coast sites. A ruined Venetian tower at the eastern tip looks toward Sámos, the island's long-time ally. Songs about historic sieges still survive, accompanied by violin and bone flutes.

The biggest feast day is 17 July (St Marina). On the same date in 1912, Ikarian Dr Malachias declared the island a republic; until Greek unification in the following October, Ikaria made its own coins and stamps. In subsequent years, the island's remoteness resulted in thousands of Communist exiles being sent here, a presence which is still strongly reflected in the inhabitants' voting patterns.

SÁMOS: It's dense forests may recently have been ravaged by fires, but Sámos's distinctive red-roofed houses, the variety to be found in both town and countryside, the proximity of the exotic east (Turkey lies little more than a mile off its coast) plus the pleasures of its many beaches mean many return.

Sámos Town (Vathý) has an elegance rare in most sizeable Greek towns today. Tourism is concentrated in other parts of the island, which leaves Vathý relatively free to concentrate on civic and domestic life. Its quiet suburbs at the foot of Mount Thío – a few minutes' walk from the harbour – make a convenient, restful base. The small **archaeological museum** features the finds from Hera's Temple near Pythagóreio, the ancient capital.

Pythagóreio is a cluttered resort, but this cannot dim its historical importance. Renamed in 1955 after its most famous resident, Pythagoras, the town teems with activity.

Highlights include: the Temple of Hera, the Tunnel of Eupalinius, and the harbour mole, built by slaves from Lésvos. At the time it was built (560

A remote chapel on remote Ikaria.

BC), the Temple of Hera was the largest temple in the ancient world. After it burned down, the construction of an even larger temple was ordered by Polycrates, but this was never completed. A Roman settlement borders the Sacred Way.

Riveting on its own, the place jumps to life with a visit to the **Vathý Museum**, with exhibitions of votive offerings like pomegranates, pine cones, poppies, and palm fronds, plus tales of degenerates and a tax scandal.

Most of the mountain villages are engagingly set. **Spatharaíoi** offers fine views across the island to Turkey. The village of Mytilinioi, near Vathý, has a fossil museum. Acres of pines, pierced by cypresses, undulate over most of the island except in the fire ravaged east. There are several deep gorges in the western half; roads are sometimes unpaved and many of the small coves, perfect for swimming, can be reached only on foot.

More accessible beaches lie on the south coast; a north coast favourite is **Kokkári**, and the island's most luxuriant mountain valley rises above it toward **Mount Ambelos**. Follow the road to **Vourliótes** for **Moní Vrondianí**, the island's oldest monastery, built in 1566 with vast courtyards. The footpath from Kokkári emerges inside a long storage chamber filled with firewood and tires. The monastery has been taken over by the army for use as a watchpoint, but it is still focus of a 7–8 September festival, the island's best.

Below Vourliótes, a tiny hamlet called **Pnaka** hangs over a shaded gush of water. A stone road from the coast leads past Pnaka to Vourliótes through terraced fields devoted to the grape of the celebrated Samian wine. The best variety is the bulk dry white, available directly from the cooperative which produces it in Karlóvassi.

Karlóvassi is the other major port. Behind the serviceable waterfront area, it resembles Vathý with its graceful turn-of-the-century houses funded largely by profits made from the local tanning industry.

ythagóreio
arbour.

THE DODECANESE ISLANDS

RHODES, KÁRPATHOS, KÁSSOS, KASTELLÓRIZO, CHÁLKI, ALIMIÁ, TÍLOS, SÝMI, NISSIROS, ASTIPALEA, KOS, PSERIMOS, KÁLYMNOS, TELENDOS, LEROS, LIPSI, PÁTMOS

The term "Dodecanese" is relatively new to the Greek vocabulary. For the 450 years that these far-flung islands were ruled by the Turks, they were known, incongruously, as the Southern Sporades. At the beginning of the 20th century, 12 islands (*dódeka nisiá*) banded together to protest the harsh rule of the Ottomans. The rebellion failed although the name stuck – hence the Dodecanese.

In fact, there are and always have been more than 12 islands in this archipelago. Depending on the source, 14, 18 or even 27 islands comprise this chain. The only fact on which everyone seems to agree is the number of inhabited islands is never lower than 12.

The 17 principal islands included in this chapter are divided into three sections. Rhodes is the first for it is the capital, the administrative and the economic centre of the prefecture. The collective term "Southern Dodecanese" has been coined to include the islands which fan out in all directions from Rhodes, and for which the capital is the main port of call. "Northern Dodecanese" islands, on the other hand, use Kos as a transport hub or are serenely self-contained, like the holy island Pátmos or the proverbial "inset island" Astypálaia, rarely included on any map of Greece except as a boxed insertion.

During the 8th century BC several of the islands enjoyed a period of intellectual and economic growth, sending scholars to the West and founding prosperous colonies. Two centuries later the three cities of Rhodes (Ialyssos, Líndos, and Kameiros) comprised, along with Kos, Halicarnassus and Cnidus, the influential Dorian Hexapolis. Periods of wealth and domination alternated with capitulation for the next 2,000 years.

The Dodecanese were Greece's final territorial acquisition, completing the tourist map we know today as recently as 1948. Before the Greeks came (briefly) the British; before the British but after the Turks came a reign of wartime occupation by the Italians. To walk the streets of Kos or Rhodes is to piece together a geographical and cultural jig-saw; a minaret on one corner, an Italian villa on another. As always, though, it is the sea which provides the most lasting continuity for the islands known as the Dodecanese.

RHODES

The capital of the Dodecanese and fourth largest Greek island, **Rhodes** (Ródos) has long been on the package tour trail. But the Island of Eternal Summer, smiled on by Helios the sun god almost all year round, still holds colossal surprises.

It's a duty-free port, thronged from May to September by Scandinavians in search of Valhalla via cheap booze. Stylish Italians swarm the streets in August and the British beer and *bouzouki* brigade also abound, propping up the hundreds of bars in town and the built-up outskirts.

Rhodes spells fun for the young, free and single. But far from the madding crowds in Mandráki (Rhodes New Town) and the serried ranks of umbrellas and sunbeds on the town beaches, you can find the peaceful, unspoiled face of the island.

Hop on a bus – frequent services run down the east and west coasts from beside the "New Market" – and you can get off the beaten track in under an hour. It's worth hiring a car – plenty of buggies and jeeps available – or a powerful motorbike if you really want to explore.

The island offers deserted sweeps of shingle with deep aquamarine waters; rocky coves scented with pine; castles perched above lemon groves; sylvan glades with strutting peacocks. This Rhodes is light years away from the "No Problem, No Aids" teeshirts and tawdry knick-knacks of the town.

Patchwork history: The legacy of ancient Greeks, besieging Turks, crusading knights and occupying Italians forms a fascinating architectural patchwork in Rhodes town, from the turrets of the castle to the ancient city walls. There are Doric pillars and Byzantine churches; mosques and minarets, plus the twin bronze deer guarding the waters of Mandráki Harbour where the Colossus once stood.

In mythology, when Zeus shared out the world, he forgot Helios the sun god. Helios settled for newly-erupted Ródos as his prize. He fell in love with the nymph Roda, the island's namesake, daughter of Poseidon, and their grandsons Líndos, Kámeiros and Ialyssos founded the triple Doric cities which joined forces in 408 BC to form the city of Rhodes.

Rhodes was once plagued by snakes, and Forvas of Thessaly was brought in to do a Pied Piper. Helped by local stags, who speared the serpents with their antlers, he did the trick and a deer has been the civic symbol ever since.

From the 5th to the 3rd centuries BC Rhodes was the major commercial force in the Aegean, founding colonies, minting coins and introducing maritime law. Sport and theatre flourished and the School of Rhetoric, founded in present day Rodini Park in 303 BC, was attended by great orators like Julius Caesar, Cato and Cicero.

Under Alexander the Great, Rhodes forged links with the Ptolemies, so the Rhodians refused to fight the Egyptians alongside King Antigonos. Angry, the king sent his son Dimitrios Polyorkites (the Besieger), along with 40,000 men

eft, wheels rn in Rhodes rbour.

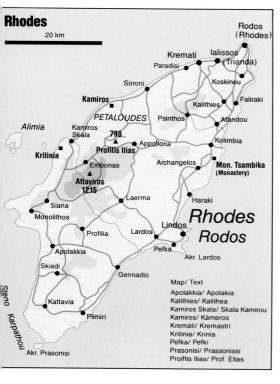

Rhodes
20 km

Rodos (Rhodes)
Kremati
Ialissos
Paradisi
(Trianda)
Soroni
Koskinou
Kamiros
Faliraki
Kalithies
PETALOUDES
Psinthos
Afandou
Alimia
Kamiros
Skala
798
Appollona
Kolimbia
Profitis Ilias
Kritinia
Embonas
Archangelos
Mon. Tsambika
(Monastery)
Attavyros
1215
Laerma
Haraki
Siana
Monolithos
Profilia
Lardos
Lindos
Rhodes
Rodos
Apolakkia
Pefka
Skiadi
Akr. Lardos
Gennadio
Kattavia
Plimiri
Steno
Karpathou
Akr. Prasonisi

Map/ Text
Apolakkia/ Apolakia
Kalithies/ Kalithea
Kamiros Skala/ Skala Kamirou
Kamiros/ Kámeros
Kremati/ Kremastri
Kritinia/ Krinia
Pefka/ Pefki
Prasonisi/ Prassonissi
Proiftis Ilias/ Prof. Elias

to attack the city with all the latest weaponry. He failed after a year and a peace treaty was signed in 304 BC.

The assorted military hardware left over was melted down or sold to make the island's most famous landmark, the giant **Colossus of Rhodes**. The work of a local sculptor named Charis of Líndos, this wondrous statue stood some 31 metres (102 ft), and was a representation of Apollo. Impressive by any standards, rumour made it even more so by describing the figure standing with one foot on either side of the harbour entrance so that ships passed between its legs. But to do so it would have to have been over 10 times its original size, an impossible architectural feat. Nonetheless this beacon to passing ships and monument to peaceful prosperity stood for nearly 70 years before it fell to the ground during an earthquake in 226 BC. The bronze was later sold off for scrap by the Arabs.

Rhodes remained at peace until, ironically, she tried to reconcile the warring Romans with the Macedonians only for it to backfire as Rome took revenge in 168 BC by declaring Délos an open port and ceding it to Athens. Rhodes lost 15 percent of its trade. This punishment forced Rhodes to give up much of its independence and become subservient to Rome. Rhodes's trading partners took a dim view of her alliance with the trouble-making Romans.

In one chapter of Roman intrigue, Rhodes sided with Julius Caesar only to have Gaius Cassius, after Caesar's murder, destroy her fleet, plunder the city and fill up Rome with her treasures. Two years later in 42 BC Octavius triumphed over Cassius who committed suicide and Rhodes regained much of its autonomy. However, its fleet was gone as was much of its wealth. But Rhodes did regain cultural influence and for three centuries was the place where many statesmen and literary leaders of the age received their education.

In AD 43 the Apostle Paul landed at Líndos bringing Christianity to the island, and in AD 395 Rhodes came under Byzantine rule.

View from the Clock Tower in the Turkish Quarter.

The Knights of St John, who had fled Jerusalem via Cyprus, captured Rhodes from the Byzantines in 1308. The Knights ruled for 213 years under 19 Grand Masters, fortifying the city against the Turks. But in 1522 they were overwhelmed by the Turk Suleiman the Magnificent, who had 100,000 warriors against their 650 knights.

The Grand Master plus 180 surviving brethren surrendered and was allowed under generous terms to leave for Malta. The Turks held the island for 390 years when churches became mosques and Greeks were banned from living within Rhodes's city walls.

In 1912, Italy occupied Rhodes while at war with Turkey. Rebuilt during the 1930s, the Grand Master's Palace was intended to become Mussolini's summer residence. But when Italy fell in 1943 during World War II, the Germans took over. Rhodes was liberated by the Allies in 1945 and the Greek flag hoisted in 1948 when the Dodecanese became united with Greece. These days, the island is still under siege – by tourists.

The present town of Rhodes divides neatly into the New Town and the Old City: neon, fast food, designer clothes and disco beat versus quaint medieval streets and a time warp.

The New Town: This is designer territory, full of smart shops. Lacoste, Trussardi and Benetton abound. Duty free umbrellas are big business and you can have any logo, from YSL to Dior. Rhodes romeos *(kamákia)* are known as "Princes" because of the brand of Danish cigarettes they smoke.

You can sit and watch the world go by and the yachts bobbing at one of the pricey and touristy pavement cafés in **Mandráki**. Better, and slightly cheaper are those inside the covered market (Néa Agorá) amongst the fishmongers, butchers and the wonderful arrays of fruit and vegetables. Little *kafeneía* announcing the owner's origins like the "Sými" and "Halki" bars, are seemingly open all hours. The market stalls offer cheap *souvlákia*, *pitta* and freshly squeezed orange juice and there's a good bakery for early morning *psomákia* (bread rolls)

The Mosque of Suleiman in the Old City.

or *kouloúria* (biscuit rings), plus very fattening doughnuts for late morning breakfast.

The harbour front buzzes night and day with artists, popcorn vendors, sponge sellers and agents hawking their daily boat trips. Most boats leave at 9am for the island of Sými, calling first at Panormitís Monastery, or down the east coast to Líndos. You can also go on barbecue cruises or take the hydrofoil to Kos. Inter-island ferries leave from the commercial harbour, which is a 15-minute walk east.

The harbour, guarded by the round fortress and lighthouse of **Aghios Nikólaos** is also part of the smart international yachting scene, like a mini Cannes, with boats for charter. In the evening it's packed with tourists taking a pre-dinner *vólta* (stroll) past the windmills down to Aghios Nikólaos. At the northern end of the harbour is the picturesque **Governor's House** with its Venetian Gothic arches, now the seat of the district administration. Next door is the **Church of the Annunciation** (Evangelismós), a 1925 replica of the old church of the Knights of St John.

A stroll along the waterfront from here towards Elli beach brings you to the grandly named **Hydrobiological Institute** at the northern tip, apparently the only aquarium of its kind in Greece.

Opposite the harbour are the Italianate public buildings. The **Post Office** and **Port Police**, the court, the town hall, the police station and the national theatre – featuring Rhodian character plays – are all next to each other in a convenient row, while the **Mosque of Mourad Reis** with its graceful minaret next door is beside the garden containing **Villa Cleobolus**, where Lawrence Durrell lived from 1945 to 47.

Palm trees wave in the municipal gardens beneath the imposing **Palace of the Grand Masters** where there are *son et lumière* performances every evening, re-enacting the siege of Suleiman the Magnificent. Pay as you enter and check with the person in the box office that a performance in your particular language is scheduled for that night.

Museum of Folk Art, in the Old Town.

Buses for Líndos and the east coast leave from outside the *son et lumière* and the helpful municipal Tourist Information Office is also just downhill, next to the taxi rank. The National Tourist Organisation and Tourist Police are on Papágou St, while the Olympic Airways Office is on Ieroú Lóckou. For flights, ferry guides, sight-seeing tours and other information regarding Rhodes, Triton Holidays just off Mandráki at Plastíra Street is an especially pleasant and helpful company.

The New Town throbs with nightlife, revellers spilling out of the bars onto the pavements in high season. One pub points out: "A balanced diet is a drink in each hand." Big spenders can head for the Casino at the Grand Hotel Astir Palace, 7pm to 3am, where smart dress and passports are required.

Just south of the town, **Rodíni Park**, home of the ancient school of rhetoric, turns up some interesting modern babble during August with a wine festival every evening. Entrance fee covers all the wine you can drink. There are lovely rose gardens, lakes and bridges, Hellenistic tombs and the grave of Ptolemy.

Monte Smith, more correctly, the **Hill of Aghios Stéfanos**, offers panoramic views over Rhodes. Named after Admiral Sir Sydney Smith, who kept watch there for the Napoleonic fleet in 1802, the hill is also the site of the ancient Acropolis with the ruined temples of Athena and Zeus.

In an olive grove on the east side are the partially restored **Temple of Pythian Apollo**, the 3rd-century BC stadium and the theatre.

The Old City: The medieval walled citadel, with its ramparts, turrets and narrow cobbled streets, is so well preserved a visitor half expects to bump into a Crusader. Step through the **Freedom Gate** (Pylí Eleftherías) into Sými Square to view the remains of the **Temple of Aphrodite** and **Inn of the Order of Auvergne**. There's a giant map of the old town at this point behind some newly laid pebble mosaics. In the corner of Argyrokástrou Square the **folklore museum** is well worth a visit for its

display of Dodecanese costumes, folk art – especially ceramic plates – and carved woodwork taken from inside local houses.

The **Byzantine Icon Museum** is opposite, situated in the former Cathedral of the Knights, now known as Panaghía Kástrou. Next stop is the 15th-century Knights Hospital, now the **archaeological museum**. Full of 6th and 7th century BC ceramics, plus coins and ornaments found in the Mycenean graves at Ialyssos, its most famous exhibit is the sea-eroded **Aphrodite of Rhodes**, the Marine Venus.

From here the **Avenue of the Knights** (Ipóton St) stretches to the Palace of the Grand Masters in medieval splendour. Preserved from commercialization and cobbled, the thoroughfare houses the inns of the various knightly orders emblazoned with heraldry and escutcheons of the Grand Masters. The Inn of the Order of France is outstanding. There are also several small churches, a Turkish school and piles of redundant cannon balls.

The **Palace of the Grand Masters**, is at the top of the street, its turreted towers as perfect as they were back in the 14th century. Destroyed when an arms store in the nearby Church of St John exploded in 1856, it was rebuilt by the Italians and was supposed to become the summer retreat of King Victor Emmanuel and Mussolini.

Inside the palace, the upper storey boasts excellent Roman and early Christian mosaics which were transferred from the island of Kos. The ground floor now houses an excellent collection devoted to Byzantine and medieval Rhodes, making it easily the best museum on the island.

For an excellent view of much of Rhodes, walk the **City Walls** from the entrance to the Grand Masters' Palace at 2.45pm Tuesday and Saturday only.

The main street of the Old City is **Socrátous**, the "Golden Mile," packed with fur and leather, jewellers, lace and embroidery stalls, ceramic stores and all kinds of tourist paraphernalia. You can see carpets being woven – rugs are

Turning heads in the Archaeologica Museum.

generally good buys. (Don't forget to haggle.) You can also pick up good bedcovers, table linen and pottery, and, of course, gold.

Socratous leads from the **Castellania** in Hippocrates Square with its impressive fountain up to the pink **Mosque of Suleiman**, conqueror of Rhodes. The mosque is currently shut for maintenance, as are most Ottoman monuments in town.

Deep in the heart of the Turkish quarter with its mazes of winding alleys, it is easy to get lost. Minutes away from the crowds you can find tiny churches with taverna tablecloths on the altars, while cobblers tap industriously away at shoes next door. Rooms are reasonable to rent in the old town though highly variable in quality. Make sure the shower works, as the **Turkish baths** on Plateía Ariónos are shut indefinitely for repairs.

Sample real Greek dancing at the **Nelly Dimoglou Theatre**, behind the baths on Androníkou and Antiokhíou Streets. The garden is open all day for refreshments and there are traditional folk dance performances nightly, except Saturdays. There are also dance courses from June to September.

West Coast: Travelling along the west coast, **Ixiá** is the first resort, all high-rise hotels and a sandy beach packed with sardine sunbathers and early morning joggers. By night there are neon signs and discos galore.

Ixiá blends into **Ialyssos**, also called Triánda, similarly commercialised. Above town, the **Filérimos Plateau** (accessible by bus) is the site of the ancient city of Ialyssos, with ruins of Doric temples. The restored **monastery**, open only to the modestly dressed, is based on a Byzantine basilica and features the Via Dolorosa with 14 icons of the Stations of the Cross plus a Doric fountain. The monks sell the local *sette* herb, made from seven different varieties. Stunning views abound – a must for photographers.

Kremastí, further along the coast, is famous for its festival of the Virgin on 15 August, otherwise notable for a Greek army barracks and a few nice tavernas.

surfeit of shepherds.

Next stop is the frenetic international airport. The village of **Paradísi** under the flight path is hardly heaven but a good place for cheap rooms on arrival.

Rhodes is also called the Island of the Butterflies and the reason why is **Petaloúdes**, the Butterfly Valley, the island's most famous beauty spot. Well worth a visit, the narrow valley with its gentle stream, criss-crossed by rickety rustic bridges like something out of an Indiana Jones movie, teems with Jersey tiger moths from June to September. Dull spotty grey when at rest, the rare species rise in clouds of vermilion as you pass. They are attracted by the *Liquidamber orientalis* trees, which exude a sweet, sticky sap. Although the scene is blissfully bucolic, under no circumstances should you drink the water from the stream.

The bus stops in the middle of the valley. Turn right and you head down to the restaurant; turn left and past the gift stalls at the end of the valley you can walk through the woods to the Monastery of the **Panaghía Kalopétras**, a tranquil resting place with stunning views over the plains.

A wooded trail from here leads to the monastery of **Aghios Soúlas** (about 6 km/4 miles from Soroní on the coast road) which has a giant fiesta on 30 July with donkey races and folk dances.

The other big tourist attraction just off the coastal road is **ancient Kámeiros**, the remains of the flourishing city excavated in 1929. Many of its treasures are in the British Museum, but you can see the 6th-century Temple of Athena, a cistern holding enough water for 400 families, public baths, and ruined houses. There are frequent buses from Mandráki, 32 km (20 miles) up the coast.

High above Kámeiros, **Profítis Ilías** is the nearest thing to a Rhodian Switzerland, 720 metres (2,400 ft) up with Alpine scenery. There's a church above the chalet style *Elafos kai Elafína* (Stag and Doe) lodge, where a stay restores body and soul; the attached restaurant is open to non-residents.

Back on the coast **Skála Kameírou** (also Kámiros Skála) is a pretty fishing

Ancient Kámeiros.

harbour now being enlarged, with good fish tavernas. Small ferries leave daily for the unspoilt island of Halki opposite.

Junoesque women: Nearby **Kritinía Castle** is well worth a visit for its breathtaking views over the rugged vineyards and lemon groves. The village, founded by Cretans, is a cluster of white houses on the hillside. Above is **Embonas** on the slopes of Mount Attávyros, famous for its fruit with vineyards, olive groves and tobacco plantations. Many of the villagers still wear national costume with long boots. The women are Junoesque and wonderful dancers; festivals at Embonas are not to be missed.

The road skirts lofty Mount Atávyros through wild scenery and herb-clad hills to the pretty village of **Siána,** famous for its honey and *soúma* – a strong grape distillate spirit that is deceptively smooth. You can sample both here at the *kaféneia.*

Further south, **Monólithos**, and its nearby Crusader castle perched on a single rock, has one of the most spectacular views on Rhodes. The path climbs up to the tiny chapel, then there's a sheer 250-metre (800-ft) drop.

The southwest coast is windy and hence undeveloped for mass tourism. There are miles of unspoilt beaches and the **Bay of Apolakkiá** is wild and undiscovered. The village is unexceptional but **Skiádi Monastery,** 11 km (7 miles) away, has a revered collection of icons worth seeing, including a miraculous one of the Virgin.

Roads are little more than tracks here, so it's unwise to "do" this part of the island by motorbike unless the machine is strong and reliable. Check insurance before you set off. Some car hire firms are touchy about damage caused by attempts at motocross.

Kattavía has a petrol station if you're exploring by car. It also has a church with remarkable frescoes and niches containing ancient sculptures. From here you can get down to the southernmost tip, **Prassoníssi**, or Leek Island, joined by a narrow sandy neck of beach – one side windy, the other calm.

East Coast: Although the east coast is

far more developed than the west, it is possible to still find unspoiled beaches, remote countryside and beauty spots, particularly beyond Líndos.

Koskinoú is worth a stop for its intricate pebble mosaic courtyards. Then head down through the pines to **Kallithéa** (Thérmes Kallithéas), with splendid arches and domed pavilions built in Moorish style by the Italians. Below the spa are a pair of sandy coves flanked by rocky headlands which are popular with divers.

Sadly, the magnificent spa buildings have long since been abandoned, and you can no longer drink the healing waters. But the attractive landscaped gardens still offer welcome shade.

Wall-to-wall hotels characterize **Faliráki**, the popular package resort bursting with the young, carefree and single. Also known as "Fairly Crappy", there are hordes of eateries, discos, a mini golf, and swinging night life. The long sandy beach offers para-gliding and all kinds of watersports.

Back on the coast, past the quaintly named Anthony Queen (*sic*) cove where Quinn starred in *The Guns of Navarone*, you come to **Afántou**, which has a long shingle beach and caves. There's a campsite on the way from Faliráki. Popular with barbecue cruise boats, the beach has enough space for glorious seclusion. The 18-hole Rhodes golf course is here, plus a castle and the church of Panaghía Katholikí with many frescoes. The village is famous for its apricots and lovely handwoven carpets.

From here, it's easy to go "over the top" via **Psínthos** to the Butterfly Valley and west coast road. A little past **Kolymbia**, a sandy beach with plenty of sports facilities, you'll come to the leafy inland glades of *Eptá Pigés* (Seven Springs). It is one of the island's most popular beauty spots. Peacocks strut beside the gurgling streams and waterfalls which run to a central pond.

You can either hit the woodland trail to the pond fed by the said seven springs, or shuffle ankle-deep in dank water down a very narrow, pitch-dark tunnel. It's quite a spooky experience and not for

Rhodes is one of the few Greek islands to house a Turkish cemetery.

the tall or claustrophobic. As a reward for this ordeal, sample charcoal-grilled meats at the taverna under the shady plane trees.

The Greek answer to fertility drugs, **Tsambíka Monastery** is perched high on the mountain opposite, overlooking the sandy namesake beach. The tiny white Byzantine church is a magnet for childless women who walk barefoot to pray for fertility at its festival on 8 September. If the stork calls, they pledge to call the child Tsambíkos or Tsambíka – names unique to the Dodecanese – in gratitude to the Virgin Mary. There are daily boat trips to the beach from Mandráki.

It's certainly well worth calling in at **Archángelos**, the island's largest village which is famous for soft leather peasant boots and hand-thrown ceramics. You can visit the potteries where traditional plates are good buys. The graveyard boasts tombs painted blue and white – patriotic to the end.

The crumbled Knights' castle of **Faraklós** looks down over **Charáki**, a fishing village with good beach tavernas. There's another vast sweep of empty beach from here to Líndos. Pick your way down through the vineyards for some tranquil sunsoaking. **Vlýcha cove** further along is sandy and ideal for families with its safe swimming and bustling tavernas.

Huddled beneath a Crusader castle, **Líndos** with its flat-roofed houses is the dream Greek village. Stunningly beautiful, with a fascinating history, its houses have magnificent doorways and mosaic courtyards. The hottest spot on Rhodes – temperature and nightlife-wise – its cobbled streets teem with trippers in high season. Donkeys (Lindian taxis) heave tourists up the steep hill from Pallas Beach to the **Acropolis** and **Temple of Lindian Athena**. It's the Temple of Tourism now, with women selling lace on the way up. A pair of sensible shoes is a must.

Ancient Líndos dates back to the Bronze Age. With the exception of Mandráki in Rhodes Town, it has the only natural harbour on the island. The

Acropolis has two re-erected Classical temples and later Byzantine and Frankish elements. Near the main square is a beautiful Byzantine church which has well-preserved frescoes inside. The water in the fountain still runs through the original pipes.

Líndos's large northerly harbour with a long sandy beach adds the finishing touch. However, it is the light that has made Líndos famous. The jagged mountains which surround the town reflect both sun and shade in a dazzling display. Italian and German painters were the first to rediscover Líndos; some moved here for good and lived a life much like the hippies of the 1960s. In addition to Líndos's better known attractions, don't miss the so-called Tomb of Kleovoulos, the philosopher king, and the 17th-century houses preserved to show Lindian life.

Líndos is now a shrine to sun, sea and sex. The beach is a watersports playground and at night the village really rocks with numerous bars and discos.

Once super-smart and home to the astrologer Patric Walker and various members of the Pink Floyd rock band, Líndos is now overrun with visitors. Supermarkets cater for your every need and tavernas even do sweets. It's hard to believe you're in Greece.

Still, the view over St Paul's Bay, the southern port, where the Apostle landed to bring Christianity, makes up for all the tourist tat. The tiny church dedicated to him celebrates with a *paniyíri* on 28 to 29 June. There's a good bus service to Líndos from Rhodes City, which lies 56 km (35 miles) up the coast, but it's far better to take a boat from the capital to enjoy the splendid scenery.

Around the limestone headland, down the road, **Péfkoi** (Péfkos) is a good deal less frenetic than Líndos; it has a long sandy beach nearby and there are several good fish tavernas.

A campsite and plentiful accommodation can be found at **Lárdos**, and the shore, miles of shingle with sand dunes as far as Yennádi, is largely deserted. However, it's earmarked for development as a major resort, so go now.

Full moon rising over Líndos.

LEISURELY LÍNDOS

índos is the last place to visit in Greece. This aphorism was endorsed in the 1960s and 1970s by a score of expatriates who found in this beautiful resort a nirvana where they would write that great novel, compose that immortal sonnet or paint that ultimate canvas. Most were British, most were in their thirties, most had had a previous career and some had enjoyed limited artistic success – a published novel, articles in a glossy magazine.

Then there were young hippies – British, Australian, American, Italian and German – to whom the mere thought of ever holding down a job was anathema. All these expats lived in modest Greek houses and were fortunate in that Costas, the corner grocer, permitted them to buy "on tick".

Rounding off the scene were transient expatriates. These included a publisher, an opera star, an art historian, and a couple of architects. They had purchased as holiday homes the magnificent old sea-captains' houses which grace Líndos.

Ars longa, vita brevis could have been the motto of the "drop-outs" and, in the privacy of their homes, pot accompanied *ouzo* and the *ménage à trois* was not unknown. Pot was tolerated by the authorities except when Greta, a German student enjoying a long vacation and really not part of the expat community, was imprisoned for possession. The consensus was that she had been incarcerated because she refused the advances of the police sergeant. Imagine the horror of her parents when they arrived to join their daughter in her Greek idyll and found her in a rural island jail.

So was any work accomplished? Did anyone make a sale?

One day Willard, an enthusiastic snorkler who, years previously had sold a novel but had since collected rejection slips, struck gold. A visiting German television producer was looking for a diving "buddy". After diving, Klaus read Willard's short stories, and knew instantly they would make great television plays. Willard now spends a lot of time in Hollywood.

And then there was David, who appeared waving a cheque for US$5,000 and smiling broadly. And Tiger with rings (made of hand-painted pebbles from the beach) on her fingers and rings on her toes; and... ■

shbacks to 1960s.

THE SOUTHERN DODECANESE

KARPATHOS: Wild, rugged and sparsely populated, Kárpathos is the second largest island in the Dodecanese marooned in the expanse of crystalline seas between Rhodes and Crete.

With miles of white sandy beaches, usually deserted, and craggy cloud-topped mountains soaring to 1,200 metres, (4,000 ft) it's a walker's paradise, especially with wild flowers and village gardens full of Madonna lilies.

Pigádia, the main town, (also known as Kárpathos) has undergone a tourist boom in the last few years, with direct flights from Amsterdam daily during the high season and many fish tavernas on the harbour. People are very friendly, in part at least because this development is so new. Many families have sought their fortunes in America, and you're as likely to hear: "Have a nice day" as "*Kalimera*".

Exploring can be difficult. Roads are rough, often with sheer drops down to the sea, and when the *meltémi* wind buffets the west coast, mopeds should be avoided. There are buses and taxis – expensive – to less remote mountain villages like **Menetés** with vine-covered streets; **Apéri**, the elegant former capital; and **Othos** where an old Karpathian house serves as a craft museum.

Olympos is the island's famous beauty spot. Clinging to the mountainside 600 metres (2,000 ft) up, the village has been accessible by road from Diafáni only in the last few years. The women still wear their traditional costume (intricately embroidered jackets, scarves and pinafores) on a daily basis as well as for festivals. They bake bread and *kouloúria* biscuits in communal ovens from flour which is still ground in the village's two 18th-century working windmills.

The old houses here are simply one divided room, built around a central wooden pole or "pillar of the house." On a raised wooden platform behind a rail are rolled mattresses, plus dowry chests of clothes. The pole is covered in em-

broideries and usually a wedding portrait of the home-owners with their *stéfano* or wedding wreath.

The rest of the room is packed with plates, lace, crochet, souvenirs and knick-knacks – a kitsch explosion of fairground colours – gathered by seafaring relatives from ports around the world. Even modern villas are decked out in the same way with the TV draped in garish, glittery mats, a shrine for family photos and icons.

Olympos is in a time-warp and the people still speak a form of Dorian-influenced Greek. They are getting used to visitors now, but life goes on and you'll see *Olýmbisses* (Olympos women) in their high leather boots.

Because the harbour is too shallow for the big inter-island ferries, you go ashore at Diafáni by caique, often with a gaggle of grannies, cartons of disposable nappies and crates of tomatoes. It is worth staying in Diafáni to visit Olympos and the care shrine of St John, which hosts a major festival on 29 August.

Just north of Pigádia, sandy **Vrónti**

beach, fringed by trees, sweeps past to the 5th-century basilica of Aghía Fotiní. Otherwise you can drive south to Amopí with its three sandy beaches, the third for nudists, which is the largest and longest established resort on the island.

Kárpathos is supposed to be the site of the legendary Clash of the Titans. The dramatic gorges and rock formations around **Apélla** on the east coast are doubtless the giants' leftovers. **Acháta** and **Kyrá Panaghía**, with its lovely pink-domed church, are also attractive beaches south of Apélla. **Arkássa** on the west side, site of a Mycenaean fort, is a resort village popular with Greeks and foreigners. **Lefkós**, up the coast, boasts three horseshoe bays of white sand, azure seas and numerous places to stay and eat.

Direct flights are available to Kárpathos from overseas; the alternative is planes or ferry from Rhodes. Once on the island, the best way to explore is by boat trip to the various beaches and, in the north anyway, on foot.

KASSOS: Just 5 km (3 nautical miles) away from Kárpathos, Kássos is the southernmost Dodecanese. Remote, gaunt and barren, it's largely depopulated with abandoned houses crumbling in its five villages where families have left to seek work. The people welcome tourists of the non-backpacking variety, especially on 17 July when there's the big festival of Aghía Marína and women wear colourful costumes in traditional patterns.

The capital, **Frý**, is a charming fishing port with a picturesque narrow entrance, set against a mountain backdrop, with a couple of hotels and tavernas, while **Emboreiós** across the bay is also picturesque. Don't miss the cave at **Seláï**, near **Aghía Marína**, filled with stalactites. Rough roads lead to the hill villages of **Arvanitochóri**, **Panaghía** and **Pólio** and there's a local bus service.

With orange and lemon trees, sheltered gardens and wild flowers, Kássos is perfect for travellers seeking rural calm. It's great walking country (stout shoes essential) and you can walk across the island through olive groves to the beach at **Chelathrós** or get a fisherman

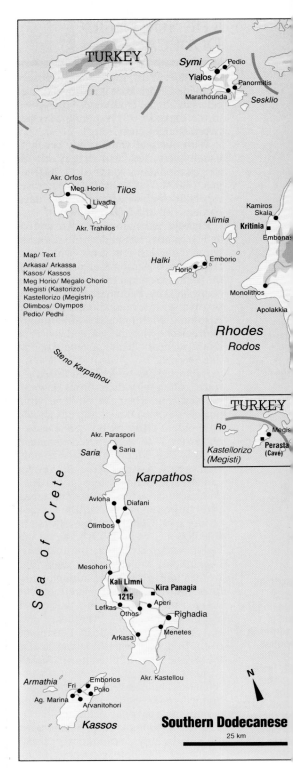

to take you to the islet of **Armathiá** which has a spectacular beach.

Frý has a tiny airstrip with planes to Rhodes, Kárpathos and Crete, but tickets are limited and the planes often full. Inter-island ferries starting from Piraeus call in at Crete, Kárpathos and Rhodes.

KASTELLORIZO: Also known as **Megísti**, Kastellórizo is laughingly called "the Biggest". The tiny island is the first – or last – in Europe, only a nautical mile across from Turkey where locals still go shopping.

The smallest in the Dodecanese chain, Kastellórizo, its harbour fringed with red-roofed houses, is topped by a red-stone Crusader castle which gives the island its Italianate name. The beautiful island, home these days to Australian Greeks from Perth and Sydney, has a rocky coastline and no beaches to speak of. But the famous Blue Grotto of **Perastá**, with stalactites and cathedral-like ceiling, rivals that of Capri. The cave is about 45 metres (150 ft) long and 28 metres (92 ft) high and the rays of the rising sun turn the water opaline. The

boat trip there takes about an hour and a half, with additional time to swim in the deep, glowing waters.

Also worth seeing is the remote monastery of Aghios Yeórgios tou Vounoú, with groin vaulting, pebble flooring, and, best of all, a catacomb with the subterranean chapel of Aghios Chará-lambos. In the port town itself is an old mosque and the worthwhile island museum, installed inside the bailey of the Knights' castle which otherwise survives only in part.

Don't go if you're in a hurry. Kastellorizo is 110 km (70 miles) from Rhodes and ferries call only two or three times a week. The tiny airstrip receives daily flights from Rhodes, though the seats are filled days in advance. Except for one expensive hotel, tourist facilities are basic; the half dozen tavernas aren't cheap because most food is imported.

CHÁLKI: An hour and a half by boat from Kámiros Skála on Rhodes, Chálki is pretty, welcoming and "arrived". The neo-Classical houses have been restored under a UNESCO-funded scheme.

astellórizo: is tiny sland is aughingly alled "the iggest".

Emborió (Halki), the fishing harbour and only settlement, has several waterfront tavernas and abundant accommodation in the restored mansions, though most of these are block-booked by two British tour companies. The island's only sandy beach is **Póndamos** with safe swimming and a good taverna. Just overhead, Chorió village is now deserted but with spectacular views from its Hospitaller fortress.

Tarpon Springs Boulevard, built with money from Halki sponge fishermen who went to Florida, is being pushed through to the monastery of **Aghios Ioánnis** on the other side of the island, otherwise it's a good 2-hour walk up. The church of **Aghios Nikólaos** has the highest belltower in the Dodecanese. There is virtually no traffic, so pebble coves like **Aréta** and **Trachiá** are reached by boat or you can walk to **Ialí**, **Aroús** or **Kánia.** Having no fresh water supply, the island is barren and harsh – but still magical.

ALIMIA: Floating between Chálki and Rhodes, the island of Alimiá has been deserted since World War II. The inhabitants aided the Allies under the very noses of the Italian forces manning submarine pens here. When detected, the islanders were deported to Rhodes and Chálki as punishment, never to return. With a **Byzantine castle**, pretty church, pebbly beaches, clear waters and ruined barracks strafed by bullet holes, the island is now a popular picnic spot, and home to Chalkian sheep.

TÍLOS: Home of the poetess Erinna, rival to Sappho, Tílos is just waking up to tourism. It's a pretty, fertile island – lovely in spring with orchards in blossom on the way to the main town of **Megálo Chorió**. The port of **Livádia** has a long shingle beach with good tavernas and several hotels.

Tranquil and unspoiled, it has 10,000 goats but only about 350 people (80 in winter). Fossilised elephant bones, now in a small museum at Megálo Chorió, were found in the grotto of **Charkádio** or **Massariá**, while at **Aghios Antónios** beach the surf washes over the petrified remains of three sailors.

Fresh vegetables often have to be imported from larger islands.

The monastery of **Aghios Pante-leímona** is well worth the journey across the island's rocky, spectacular scenery. The monastery has a beautiful fountain flanked by basil pots, and the church has important paintings and carvings. The three-day festival runs from 25 July with the famous "Dance of the Cup". The church of the Panaghía at **Polítissa** has a festival on 23 August with special boats from Rhodes the previous day.

SYMI: As you approach Sými on a day-trip boat from Rhodes, flotillas of little caiques flee the port of **Yialós** (Sými) for the beaches round the island. The foreign "residents" are escaping the daily droves of tourists.

Sými, one of the most stunning sights in Greece with its tiers of light-coloured houses, has two (if not three) faces. When the tour boats hoot, Yialós becomes a mini-Rhodes with tavernas touting for business and stalls selling local herbs, imported sponges and knick-knacks. As soon as the trippers leave, peace is restored – there's room to walk on the streets and you'll get stronger

ouzo. Yialós, in a bowl and steaming hot in high summer, is beautiful at night when the bay reflects the myriad lights from the houses above. Smart, popular with the yachting fraternity, but still relatively unspoiled, Sými has plenty of bars and tavernas downtown and uptown. It's not, however, an island for the unfit, elderly or very young.

Up the 357 steps of the **Kalí Stráta** is the village-like centre of the high town, Chorío. Even further up the maze of streets they say there are old ladies who have never been down to the bottom. On Sými you either stay up or down, or over at **Pédio**, a pretty sandy bay now fringed by a hotel and several tavernas. The fit can walk with Hugo Tyler, an Englishman married to a local girl and an island legend, who takes guided walks to meet up with the boat.

There is also a boat from Pédio to **Aghios Nikólaos**, the only natural sand beach on Sými. For walkers there's a well-marked path – follow the red paint spots – over the headland.

The town beach is **Nos**, with a taverna, and it's also worth walking to **Nimborió** (just continue along the same coastal track), where a Byzantine church floor mosaic and catacombs can be found up behind an artificial strewn sand beach.

The most important monastery is **Panormítis** in the south, a place of pilgrimage for Greeks worldwide. Opulent, and very like a movie star's bungalow in appearance, the church is packed with votive offerings from sailors. Things are tranquil again when the tour boats have gone, and you can rent a cell for whatever you wish to pay. But, if you're a woman travelling alone, beware. The priest, Father Gabriel, will insist you sleep inside the enclave and the doors are locked at 9.30pm sharp.

Symians are famous as boatbuilders – they built the legendary *Argo* for Jason – and you can still see boats taking shape on the way to Nos. The Treaty of the Dodecanese (when Sými became part of Greece again after the Italian occupation) was signed in Les Kater-inettes restaurant in 1945. There are boat trips to the beach at **Marath-ounda** and to the island of **Sesklia**.

THE NORTHERN DODECANESE

NISSIROS: Legend has it that Nissiros (Nisyros) was once joined to its larger neighbour Kos, but Poseidon, in pursuit of a giant, tore the two islands apart. This same legend credits the giant Polybetes with the creation of Nissiros's most impressive feature, a volcano 260 metres (850 ft) in diameter. Although the volcano is now extinct, its presence dominates the island, from the black pebbles which comprise several of the beaches to the spas with their therapeutic sulphurous springs.

The crater lies on the **Lakki plateau** in the heart of the island, approximately 10 km (6 miles) south of the harbour town, Mandráki. Steps lead from the rim down into the volcano, but be sure to wear sensible shoes, sun-glasses and a hat, for the temperature is hot in the centre. The air is pungent, acrid, and the floor so soft rocks must be used as stepping stones. Canary-yellow stalagmites emit a low, deep roar like Hades calling from the underworld.

Two sparsely-populated villages are perched on the ridge of the crater. **Emborios** is surrounded by greenery while the larger **Níkia**, further on, has a round *plateía* and a café. Just outside the harbour where the ferries and caiques arrive lies the old spa of **Loutra**. Since antiquity visitors have been coming to bask in its healing waters; now it is hoped they will flock to the vast new spa which has been built near the fishing village **Paloi** on the north coast.

Mandráki is the highly attractive capital and principal port. White-washed buildings sparkle next to others painted in bright colours and both are in contrast to the dark volcanic boulders which hug the shore and on which the nets of local fishermen are laid out to dry. A rambling promenade extends along the waterfront while behind are streets so densely constructed that the balconies of opposing houses meet up to filter the worst of the sun's rays.

In one of the cafés, be sure to order *soumada*, the drink made from locally grown almonds. If you prefer to buy in quantity *soumada* can also be bought in rather lethal-looking unmarked bottles which belie its alcohol-free status. Overlooking both the capital and the sparkling sea are two fortresses. Hanging onto the very edge of the cliff and within the boundaries of one of them is the monastery church of Panagía **Spilianí** which is worth a visit.

In the springtime much of the island is green and covered with wildflowers. Buses and taxis, as well as organised (expensive) excursion parties from Kos make the journey from Mandráki to the volcano. But the best way to appreciate Nissiros's rich island smells (almonds and figs) is by walking.

ASTIPALEA: This small, rocky outcrop is destined to be an "inset island," specially inserted on any Greek map. Falling mid-way between the Dodecanese and the Cyclades, Astipalea, with just over 1,000 inhabitants, technically belongs to the former island chain, yet in architecture and in culture bears more resemblance to the latter. On a clear day

eft, fish is ten sent rectly from e islands to henian food arkets. ight, the hite-hot, ack volcanic each at issiros.

it is possible to see both Amorgós and Santoríni on the horizon.

For years Astipalea was most closely observed through binoculars. Scores of visitors, enroute from Piraeus to Kos or Rhodes, would stand on the top deck of a ferryboat and subject all activity in Astipalea's harbour to a seven-minute scrutiny, the approximate time it takes to sail past without stopping. Now, boats call in more frequently, hotels have been built, discerning tour companies offer rooms on a package basis, and Athenians have discovered that a house near the **Xokastra** (old town) can be a desirable summer residence.

So far this development has had only a minor effect. The food in the tavernas and the one paved road have improved, and the houses now dazzle with even more coats of whitewash. If subsequent changes remain as modest, a pleasing time is assured.

Astipalea is shaped like the wings of a butterfly, linked by a narrow isthmus only about 100 metres (300 ft) wide. The village on the isthmus, **Maltezanas** (also called Analipsi) is said to have been named after Maltese pirates who once sought shelter in the tiny fishing harbour. Most people stay in the principal port **Pera Yalos**, with its tavernas, cafés and seasonal *bouzoúki* club.

A long flight of stairs connects **Skala** (as the port is known locally) with the old town of Astipalea, or Kástro and the ninth-century **castle of Aghios Ioannis** which dominates the hilltop. The castle is entered from the southwest and within its confines are two churches, the **Annunciation** and the church of **St George**.

In stark contrast to the whitewashed chapels is the sombre brown wall which encircles the castle, which once provided homes for the islanders. Strung out along the crest of a hill is a series of windmills in various states of disrepair. From the sea the Kastro, the windmills and the stark cubic houses provide an enchanting picture. Another fine church, dedicated to the Virgin Portaitissa, should not be missed.

Buses run from Skala to **Livadia**, a resort just over the brow of the hill. The beach, backed by citrus orchards, at-

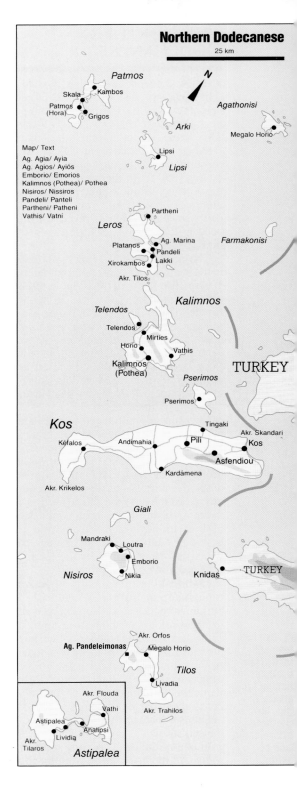

tracts insects and seaweed, but is wonderfully long. Several coves and beaches along the coastline can be reached on foot or by taxi, but the town of **Vathí**, 19 km (12 miles) northwest of Astipalea, is best visited by boat.

KOS: With an international airport, daily ferry connections with Piraeus, and an extensive system of boats, hydrofoils and caiques to neighbouring islands, Kos might well be considered the "hub" of the northern Dodecanese. The cacophony of tourists, souvenir vendors and market pedlars threatens to swamp the atmosphere of this lush, historic island; even in late spring or early autumn the buzzing of mopeds and the wail of disco music reverberates through Kos Town.

The south coast with its excellent beaches has been taken over almost exclusively by developers; hotels, pubs and cafés serving "Zombie" and "Orgasm" cocktails are much in evidence. Travellers seeking solitude should head for one of the villages in the folds of **Mount Díktaio** or for the final destination on the bus line, ancient **Kéfalos** in the southwest peninsula, but even here bungalows and hotels blur the striking view of Turkey on the horizon.

For those who enjoy the company of other foreigners, Kos's over-development has compensations. The road system is excellent, there is variety to the restaurants in Kos Town, and the range of sports facilities on the beaches – from wind-surfing to water-skiing – is good. History buffs in search of tranquillity might care to stay on one of Kos Town's tree-lined back streets in order to visit the important antiquities, then take advantage of Kos's travel communications by journeying to a satellite island like Pserimos, Tílos or Nissiros.

Kos is best known as the birthplace of Hippocrates, the father of modern medical science. But traces found at the cave of Aspropetro in the village of Kéfalos bear witness that the island has been inhabited since Neolithic times. From the 15th through the 11th centuries BC, Kos, from its ancient capital Astypalaia near Kéfalos, took part in the Trojan

stipalea
en through
e vaulting
a Genoan
stle.

War and grew into a major, influential naval power.

Together with Rhodes the island developed colonies in southern Italy and was influential in commerce and the arts. Plutarch testifies that, during the 7th and 6th centuries BC, the Koans continued to prosper, joining the holy alliance of the Dorian Hexapolis. Kos surrendered to the Persians towards the end of the sixth century, but by 480 BC the island was delivered of the Persian yoke and soon after became a member of the Athenian League.

Twin calamities forced the relocation of the capital to its present position at the other end of the island. Astyochos, Admiral of the Spartans, occupied and then sacked the old capital Astypalaia. Shortly after, an earthquake devastated the same site. Many citizens left to settle on another island which, in remembrance, was named Astipalea. Others transferred to the northern promontory and began to construct temples and beautiful buildings. The historian Strabo wrote of this new town: "She was not large but inhabited in the best way possible and to the people visiting her by sea pleasant to behold."

Cooled by sea breezes and fringed with palms, **Kos Town**'s skyline is a gracious mixture of minarets, towers and round, domed mosques. Its oldest existing quarters are those around the almost circular harbour built by the Knights of St John. The narrow neck of the harbour is guarded by the **Castle of the Knights**, most probably on the site of an older structure. Palm trees are now planted in the moat, while inside the fortified walls (a second wall was completed in 1514 after an unsuccessful raid by the Turks) can be found some remains from ancient sites.

Situated in **Lozia Square** which adjoins the Castle is the **plane tree of Hippocrates**, a handsome, gnarled tree supported by planks. According to tradition the Father of Medicine, who was born on Kos in 460 BC, used to write and teach his students under its spreading branches. This story, although delightful, is untrue, for the island capital was still located in Astypalaia during the time Hippocrates lived and the tree itself was certainly not around at the time. Nevertheless, this magnificent specimen might well live up to its other, less fanciful sobriquet, "the oldest tree in Europe."

Kos's **Archaeological Museum** is located at the Piazza of Eleftheria opposite the **Defterdar mosque**. Although some of its items have been transferred to Rhodes (notably statues and mosaic floors) its three rooms of antiquities provide an important respite away from the heat. Do not miss the regal statue of Hippocrates.

It is impossible to stroll through the streets of Kos without chancing across the island's numerous archaeological sites. Serious students will probably want to visit the ruins at mid-day, when the town slows down and contemplation is possible in relative peace.

The **portico** of the 4th or 3rd century BC, and its restored columns, the **ancient agora**, the **Roman baths**, and the **gymnasium of Xystos** are among the most notable. Theatrical performances of

Generation gap in Kos's Archaeologic Museum.

ancient legends are occasionally held in the excellently preserved Roman odeon. On the same side of the street is the restored **Casa Romana**.

Although the excavations can be loosely grouped into eastern, western and central zones, a more traditional way to view them is to follow the Greek custom of treating the sites casually. To spread a picnic with wine on a collapsed marble column and to consume lunch within the walls of history is perhaps the greatest pleasure one can find on any of the islands.

Situated in a grove of cypress trees 5 km (3 miles) southwest of Kos Town are the ruins of the **Asklépieion**, a healing institution similar to our modern hospitals. There were 300 known *aesculapiums* in antiquity; the most respected being Epidaurus and Trikki in Thessaly where the worship of the god Asklépios originated.

This sanctuary is constructed on several terraces, and the uppermost terrace offers fine views of Kos, Pserimos, Kálymnos and, northeast, the coast of Turkey. Appropriately, a temple to Apollo is thought to have stood near this spot, for it was Apollo who allegedly taught his son Asklepios the practice of therapeutic healing, an art Hippocrates and other scientists incorporated into their researches.

The oldest temple in the sanctuary is the Ionic Asklepios Temple on the middle terrace, dating from the late 4th and early 3rd centuries BC. In front of the temple is a great altar in the form of a Greek letter. The upper terrace consists of a great Doric temple to Asklepios which stands on a base of three steps, one of which is black marble.

On the lowest terrace are chambers from the Roman era. Along the exterior walls are two underground chambers, easily overlooked. A notable but unsubstantiated theory places them as treatment rooms for venereal disease.

Of the other towns on the island, **Kardámena**, 25 km (15 miles) from Kos on the south coast, is the island's second largest tourist centre. Its beach is long, sandy and very crowded. Within

FESTIVE OCCASIONS

It seemed as if the whole village had crushed into the tiny church. The air was heavy with the scent of basil framing the icon of the Virgin Mary. Hundreds of candles flickered, boosting the heat of the midsummer night, while the sweet voices of the choir – specially hired for the occasion – fought to be heard above the congregation. The priest called for hush, largely ignored. Children shoved through the crowd for their chunks of holy bread, sliced with gusto by the local taverna owner. The greengrocer's wife, dressed in her best, handed out candles and guarded the brimming collection plate.

The Assumption of the Virgin Mary, the *Panaghía*, on 15 August is the most important festival in Greece (after Easter). From mainland to the islands people flock home for the celebrations, or *paniyíria*, with feasting and dancing often all night following the religious ceremony.

The Greeks have a great knack of mixing piety with pleasure. Sombre, moving moments soon give way to rambustious carousing. Grannies, toddlers, and teenagers all join in while the macho *pallikária* – brave young men – try to out dance each other.

The festival marks the reception of the Holy Mother into Heaven. Every island has its own celebrations for the national holiday, but at most *paniyíria* the icon of the Virgin, often framed in gold or silver, or encrusted in jewels, is paraded aloft during the feast. The faithful queue to kiss the Holy image – slipping money into the collection plate for the privilege, of course – or snatch sprigs of basil for good luck throughout the year. *Vasilikó*, the royal herb, isn't used for cooking here but to adorn the church. The Greeks believe it is sacred as it grew on the tomb of Christ.

Paniyíria, equal to our *fêtes* or country fairs, stem from pagan times when ancient Greeks honoured the Gods with orgies, feasting and fertility rites, plus a bit of buying and selling. From the 4th century the *paniyíri fora* celebrated the Christian martyrs. The church frowned on the commercial aspect, although these days you'll find peddlers and market stalls selling everything from balloons to catapults, icons to amulets, crucifixes to tracts on the saints. Condoms have also been spotted among the fairground novelties.

In olden times there was often a baby boom nine months after the festival. The word stems from *pan* (all) and *agora* (market place), suggesting a public assembly. But the present Greek word to celebrate, *paniyirizo*, *pan* (all) and *yirizo* (return) seems nearer the mark when you see the exiles and expats pouring off the ferries as they return home to their islands for the big day.

On 15 August, Greeks make pilgrimages to Tínos in the Cyclades where the icon of the Panaghía Evangelistría is said to work miracles. Pilgrims flock to Pátmos, too, where St John wrote the book of Revelation. But perhaps the most colourful celebrations of the feast of the *Panaghía* are at Olympos on Kárpathos.

The village clings to the hillside almost locked away in a time warp, and until recently cut off from the world. Women wear traditional costumes every day. The black, elaborately embroidered tunic, with matching headscarf – apparently imported from Ireland – and high leather boots or *stivalia* are the hallmark of the true *Olymbissa* (Olympos women).

At festival time the *koppéles*, girls of marriageable age wear swirling skirts of vivid satin in pink, blue or green, topped by black cut-away jackets often woven by their families. Everything is smothered in embroidery, or decked with braiding, sequins and tassels. The *pièce de résistance* is a heavy collar of gold coins, a wearable dowry signifying the girl's worth.

On festival day, musicians gather beneath the village church playing traditional Karpathian music on the *tsambouna* (goatskin bagpipes). The village men lead the dancing and as they wend their way down the narrow streets the girls join in, the slow *mantinádes* giving way to the fleet-footed *soústa*. Old ladies hand out almonds in twists of net and the usual revelry ensues.

The festival attracts throngs of visitors, so beware. Transport and rooms are scarce, so make arrangements well in advance. ∎

walking distance is a fortress built around 1500 on the site of an older Byzantine fortress.

From **Pili**, in the centre, a track running for just over 3 km (2 miles) leads to **old Pylai** and a hill with the remains of another Byzantine castle. The church has well-preserved frescoes from the 14th century. The remains of a Hellenistic Doric temple and a theatre can be found in the southwest near **Kéfalos**, 43 km (27 miles) from Kos. This is the area where Astypalaia once stood, although the precise location of the ancient capital is unclear.

The beach most easily reached from Kos Town is broad, sandy **Tingáki** on the north coast. Just a cycle ride away, it is protected from northerly gales by umbrellas.

PSERIMOS: Tiny, golden Pserimos can be reached by caique from both Kos and Kálymnos. With a population of just 72 people and a main street which is actually a beach, this gem of a place is the perfect solution to the crowds and noise of Kos. At night the only sound is that of the wind rustling through bamboo groves, or the tinny tinkle of goat bells. At sunset, after the excursion boats depart, local women wade fully dressed into the sea, skirts held high, in rarely seen relaxation. The sea is perfect for children, for several hundred feet away from the shore the water is still only shoulder-deep.

A path behind the harbour leads to a simple church; a free-standing bell tower is the island's monument. The interior of the church is solemn and perfumed. Wooden carvings and icons adorned with gold watches are reflected in the light from candles which appear to remain permanently lit. Outside, beyond the tower, the cemetery chronicles Pserimos's most recent history. Beside each grave is a glass box containing plastic flowers, a photograph of the deceased, and a candle.

KALYMNOS: A reasonably prosperous island where wealth is not dependent solely on tourism, Kálymnos's income is derived from sponge-diving. Although the industry is no longer thriving – the

Left, lighting the candles at midnight on the eve of Easter Sunday. **Below**, a Greek Orthodox wedding.

Aegean seabed is being stripped bare due to demand – the absence of men in the main harbour, Póthia, signals that a fleet has departed for the annual, six-month working trip. (Female travellers might care to enquire as to the date of expected return. The port's bars and cafés become very rowdy, and plans to disappear – or participate – can then be made accordingly.)

The latter stages of the sponge-making process can be observed by asking to be escorted to a factory. If the site is an old one the operation looks medieval: under large wooden eaves stone tanks of salt water, or huge vats of scalding acid stand which bubble and steam. When the sponges are gathered they are black and contain impurities.

Men in wide-brimmed hats (or, if at sea, the divers's themselves) walk on the sponges to "milk" them of any unwanted substances. The sponges are then cleaned in the salt water tanks, bleached in acid to the soft ochre colour required by tourists (which, incidentally, weakens the fibre), then cleaned once again

with salt water. Laid out to dry in a factory's courtyard, the acres of irregularly-shaped sponges make one long for a bubble bath.

Póthia itself rises steeply up a mountain ending in a religious cross. Houses tend to be three or four stories in height with balconies looking out to sea. One church near the top has five silver domes which dazzle in the sun.

Horio, the old capital, contains a ruined castle thought to have been built by the Knights of St John. The road north runs through barren hills; visual relief is provided only by the blue wooden boxes on the slopes which are used to house honey-bees. The greyness of the landscape makes the first view of Vathí a delightful surprise. Rounding a hilltop the town appears, far below, nestled in a green fertile valley on a turquoise arm of water leading out to sea.

Vathí (which means "deep") might well be the sweetest-smelling village in the Aegean. Its principal industry is the growing and exportation of mandarin oranges, and cargo boats ply back and forth along the sparkling water with picturesque industry. Houses are white, built in the Italian style and sparkling whitewashed walls lead to a tiny chapel.

From Vathí it is a long walk or a pleasant boatride to the **Cave of the Nymphs**; in antiquity a place of worship and more recently a place of refuge from the Italians. During the last occupation, when the teaching of Greek was forbidden, it is said that secret classes were held in the cave to school the island's children in their native tongue.

Back in Póthia the route west to Mírties is green and lined with trees. Architecture is scenic and varied: windmills, ruined fortresses, a couple of private houses which resemble churches. **Mírties** itself is a busy and highly attractive resort perched on a wide bay overlooking the island Telendos.

Tavernas and *pensions* sport grape arbours and palm trees and the road to the sea, which winds through the village, is adorned with hibiscus and other flowers. The beach tends to overflow with Greek tourists as do the other two beaches at **Masóuri** and **Pánormos**.

Kálymnos is a prosperous island thanks to the sponge industry.

Intrepid bathers might like to try their luck at **Emborios**, 20 km (12 miles) northeast of Póthia, in the northern peninsula. Crowds are virtually non-existent, but so too is public transport.

TELENDOS: Until the 6th century BC Telendos was joined to the island Kálymnos. It was only after one of the Dodecanese's numerous earthquakes (535 BC) that this towering rock of an island became a separate entity. A township sank into the sea at the same time and it is claimed that the water is so clear that ancient city walls can occasionally be seen in the narrow strip between the two islands.

The caique from Mírties on Kálymnos runs every 20 minutes in the summer and (optimistically) once or twice daily in the winter. Prepare to share the boat with bulky boxes of tomatoes, loads of blankets, and other household goods. The fishermen who are the most frequent passengers are graced with wonderful manners; even if three times younger, a lady will not be allowed to stand while they remain seated.

The only hamlet, **Telendos**, lies huddled under mammoth **Mount Ráchi** which rises to 458 metres (1,500 ft). A small peninsula of pine trees attached to one side of the hill gives the impression, when approaching by boat, that the island is shaped like a gigantic snail. Telendos is more upmarket than its equally tiny neighbour Pserimos; tavernas are chic and colourful, shaded by pine trees and roofs made of straw matting. *Pensions* have interior marble steps and modern bathrooms.

The cafés are enormously pleasant; sit at one on the harbour to admire the attractive contours of Mírties on the other side of the channel, or watch the spectacle of a man in rolled-up trousers and wide-brimmed hat bashing an octopus against the wharf, presumably for someone's dinner. Three beaches lie only a five-minute walk away. **Hohlakas** is sandy and sign-posted. The two shingle beaches to the west consist of smooth, flat rocks the size of coins.

The island's houses are neat, almost suburban, decorated with trim boxes of carnations or violets. Walk through whitewashed alleyways to the church which is petite and painted pale colours; inside, the incense is overpowering after the fresh scent of flowers in town. The cool interior is dominated by a golden chandelier and 12 hand-painted saints on the wall. One of the painted panels opens to reveal an inner sanctuary for private meditation.

On the north side of the island, best reached by boat, stands a chapel of St Constantine (also known as **Aghios Vassileos**) and the abandoned ruins of a **medieval castle**.

LEROS: If given a choice, arrive by ferry at **Lakki** around midnight for a glamourous experience. The town served as a naval base during the Italian occupation and the new residents built enormous offices in the contemporary style, art deco. Towering palm trees line the harbour-front and to walk along the echoing streets, the magnificent ochre buildings illuminated by indirect light, is to feel like an intruder on the set of a melancholy Fred Astaire movie.

In daylight, Lakki's elegance is shab-

Nets drying in the sun.

bier and the streets teem with naval personnel. Still, the broad avenues and little squares tucked behind the harbour offer a faded grandeur rarely seen on Greek islands.

Leros is less popular than most islands for a variety of reasons. Mainland Greeks make crude jokes about its name (the word *"lera"* connotes dirt and unsavoury activities). Its principal business, although worthy, lacks holiday flair: Leros is the centre for the institutional care of both retarded children and intractable psychiatric cases.

Foreign visitors, seduced by the attractions of near-by Pátmos and Kos, sail straight past on the ferry, eagerly awaiting more familiar pleasures. Which means, in the end, that Leros suffers little from the ravages of tourism which blight so many of its neighbours. Although it's true that Leros enjoys a respite from souvenir shops, hawkers, and tacky cocktail bars, neither does it sparkle with tourist highlights like ancient ruins or dazzling beaches.

Its massive fortress contains an attractive church of the **Virgin of the Kastro**, but little else of singular importance. Charm lies in its friendly people and a work-a-day ambience.

The island's capital, **Platanos**, snuggled under the fortress, has spread in both directions to include the villages **Panteli** and **Aghia Marina**, names by which it is also called.

The town hall, the island museum and all the necessary shops can be found near the square. Ayia Marina is perhaps the prettiest of the three villages, approached by a steep road from Platanos which leads to a harbour fringed by fragrant pine trees.

On the way to **Alínda**, 5 km (3 miles) northwest, is a cemetery for British soldiers killed during World War II. Leros's strategic position earned it the nickname "the Gibraltar of the Med" and it was the base in turn of the navies of Italy, Germany and Britain. Alínda is a developed resort with a long beach and tourist facilities. The best beach is further on past Patheni at **Blefountis Bay.**

Patheni is thought to have derived its

Twilight ove Telendos.

258

name from the ancient word *parthenos* (chaste), an epithet of Artemis, goddess and protectress of women, who was worshipped here. The women of Leros, happily, are still protected; the ownership of all island property is inherited through the female line.

LIPSI: Also known as Leipsoi, this sparkling jewel in the Aegean is a gypsy island. Reached by daily caique (summer only) from Pátmos or by an erratic ferry service in winter, the cubic houses of its one village, **Lipsi,** have been painted bright colours which emphasise its rakish appeal. The colours, however, change frequently; one topic during the long winter months is when, and what shade to decorate each exterior, right down to the gargoyles on the façades which can be startling in reds or vivid yellows.

Lipsi's harbour-front, however, remains dignified; from the sea the town rises like a mirage. Crowned by a church with three turquoise domes, these shapes and colours are mirrored in a series of small chapels perched on the promontory. Development has meant the widening of the harbour-front and the encroachment of tourism to cater to the Pátmos overspill, so Lipsi is best appreciated after the day trippers have left on the afternoon boat.

Its beaches are sandy, the residents hospitable, and its caves a delight to explore. As the island allows few cars (although noisy farm equipment is in evidence during the day) nights are given over to the sound of the lapping sea, the crowing of errant roosters, or the occasional *bouzoúki* binge.

Three satellite islands in the area are even less developed and can be reached from Pátmos or, occasionally, Lipsi. **Arkoi** has only 68 inhabitants but nice beaches and rooms to let; **Agathonisi** has two villages, Megalo Horio and Mikro Horio. **Marathi** should only be attempted by arrangement as its facilities are seasonal and transport erratic.

PÁTMOS: If Delos, the holy island in the Cyclades, was the sacred place of worship for the ancients, its modern equivalent must surely be Pátmos, which

vo island
stimes:
noking
garettes
d sitting at
fés.

is situated roughly halfway between Ikaria and Leros. Pátmos has long been a place of pilgrimage for those who believe that this rocky island is where St John the Divine is said to have dictated the text of Revelation to his pupil Prochoros in AD 95.

Tradition identifies St John with the Apostle John, although this has never been proved. Nevertheless, in 1088 the monk Christodoulos Latrenos founded a great, fortified monastery in honour of St John, and it has been a place of scholarship and religious enlightenment ever since. At Easter and on the blessed Saint's Day, 21 May, the faithful flock to its shores to worship and give thanks.

Although the island is no longer ruled by monks, their presence, along with the fortress which looms into view at almost every turning, tempers the rowdier elements found on most holiday islands. Tourists are much in evidence, but those who elect to stay (as opposed to those who arrive by hydrofoil from Kos or Rhodes) appreciate the unique, even spiritual, atmosphere which Pátmos exudes. Conversations in the cafés tend to be elevated, night sounds are muted, and many people return season after season to enjoy what one resident calls "the classical life."

Skala, on the east coast, is the main harbour, and is best appreciated late at night when crickets serenade and the sailboats and occasional cruise ships are illuminated against a dark sky. The lights of Hora on the hill above are indistinguishable from the stars. A few paces from the sea lies a tiny cemetery. Its symmetrical tombstones, when lit by candles, provide a ghostly spectacle.

In the daytime Skala loses charm but gains in efficiency; all island commerce is here, from shops to banks to ferryboat agencies. Buses leave regularly from the main square for Hora and the monastery. Bearded priests in long, hot cassocks vie for seats on the bus with tourists in sandals and shorts; the priests, long familiar with this summer tussle, usually win the race.

Halfway between Skala and Hora is the **Cave of the Apocalypse**. A silver

The Monastery St John the Theologian

band marks the spot in the wall where St John is said to have composed Revelation; just at the mouth of the grotto is a great cleft in the rock through which the voice of God spoke.

The bus stops again at the monastery terrace where there is an unrivalled view of the Aegean. On a cloudless day it is possible to see, not only nearby Sámos, Ikaria, Kálymnos and Leros but also the far-away Cycladic isles Amorgós, Paros, Náxos and Mýkonos.

The **Monastery of St John the Theologian** is built at Hora's highest point. A brooding fortress surrounded by defensive walls, just inside is a stall where monks sell illustrated guides, well worth buying for a comprehensive interpretation. Within one of its five chapels are the relics of the Blessed Christodoulos, the monastery's founder, who lies in a marble sarcophagus.

The Treasury houses the most impressive monastic collection in Greece outside Mount Athos; priceless icons and jewellery can be viewed, even handled, by special appointment.

Of invaluable importance to scholars is the library which contains 4,000 volumes or manuscripts. It, too, requires special permission to enter but the greatest treasure, 33 leaves of the *Codex Porphyrius*, embellished with gold and silver, can be seen in the monastery museum. Written in the 6th century on purple vellum, the book contains most of St Mark's Gospel.

The silent, shuttered windows in many of **Hora's** villas highlight the fact that they are owned by Athenians. For this reason rooms are hard to come by, but Hora's discreet restaurants and, at night, silent, echoing streets are worth savouring. Taxis can be found for the return trip to Skala.

Most of the island can be visited in a day, but the most scenic way is on foot. Buses connect with the beach resort **Groikos**, whose population in winter falls to a couple of dozen people, and the fertile village of **Kambos**, which has two monasteries. Caiques from Skala call in at beaches at the **bay of Lambi, Livadi ton Kalogiron,** and **Merika.**

Young monk
St John's.

Crete, claimed by many Greeks to be the most authentic of islands, is by far the largest. This "other continent" lies in the middle of the eastern Mediterranean and provides a stepping stone between Europe and Africa. *Megalonissos* ("Great Island") is what Cretans call their home and "great" refers to much more than size.

"Great" can certainly be applied to Minoan, the first civilisation in Europe and one with which Crete is inexorably entwined. Visitors by the thousands pour into the ruins of Knossós, Phaistós, Mállia and Káto Zákros, before heading towards one of the scores of excellent beaches. With two major airports Crete could hardly be classified as undiscovered, but its size and scale manage to contain the crowds and to please visitors with divergent tastes. A car is essential for discovering the best of the island, but car hire is, unfortunately, expensive. Crete's gently shelving coastline also make it a popular choice for those holidaying with children.

Most of Crete's 500,000 people live in the north. The mountains to the south nurture a proud, rugged, independent people whose fierce mustachioed menfolk still dress in jodhpurs, black leather knee-boots and black headscarves. The mountains are honey-combed with caves – it is claimed there are more than 3,000 – with which many myths are associated. The Diktaian and the Idaian caves both claim to be the birthplace of Zeus: each has champions and detractors. Cretans have resolved the conflict with the wisdom of a Solomon, the cunning of Byzantium and the acumen of an Onassis. The conclusion? Zeus was born in the Diktaian cave and reared in the Idaian.

Unlike more integrated islands, Crete has its own songs, charac-terised by the *mantinádes* and its own dances, among them the spectacular *pentozáli*. These are almost invariably accompanied by the lyra, a ubiquitous Cretan instrument.

Mountains and beaches. Ancient ruins and modern culture. For many people, Crete is the quintessential Greek island.

Preceding pages: a heavenly view of the Cretan mountains; migrant fishermen. **Left**, catching the sun.

CRETE

The Aegean's "great island" has an east-west orientation, is 277 km (173 miles) long and has a width of between 13 and 61 km (8 and 38 miles). A massive mountainous backbone with peaks stretching skywards to over 2,400 metres (8,000 ft) dominates. In the north the mountains fall gently giving rise to fertile plains while in the south they plunge precipitously into the sea.

Deep gorges divide Crete (Kríti) into four main regions. Many gorges are now penetrated by roads which link the north and south. However, it is best to measure journeys in hours rather than in distance. (An average of 48 km/30 miles an hour is good going.)

Infinite variety: For most of the year snow lies on the highest peaks which, in spring, provide a dramatic backdrop to verdant meadows ablaze with flowers. This, as botanists and ornithologists well know, is *the* time to visit. The former

arrive to view more than 100 species which are unique to the island while the latter are thrilled by more than 250 types of birds on their way north.

These transients join such rare permanent residents as Bonelli's eagle and Eleonara's falcon. And it is in spring that the island is redolent with sage, thyme and oregano. However, *the* endemic herb is dittany. (Did you know that bathing in an infusion of dittany increases sexual desires?)

Crete, much more than other Greek islands, is a place for sight-seeing as well as for being on the beach. Minoan ruins are the major magnet but there are Greek, Roman and Venetian remains for which many tourist authorities would give their eye teeth. And, what other island has a score of museums?

There are also literally hundreds of Byzantine churches, many with rare and precious frescoes. These frescoes often have a distinct Cretan style recognisable by elongated figures and attention to detail. (Many churches are locked. Enquire at the nearest café for the key.

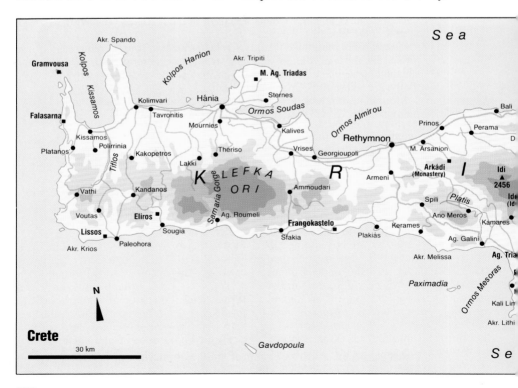

Even if you fail in your quest you will enjoy the opportunity to meet the local people.)

Dozens of monasteries have fallen into disuse but others still function and have rich treasures and histories. All occupy sites which are a real estate agent's dream. (When visiting be sure to observe a sensible dress code or you will be denied entry.)

Homer's "island of 100 towns" can also be called one of 100 beaches – the coast line is 1,050 km (636 miles) long. However, a beach is a place where a boat can be beached and not necessarily a paradise of golden sands. Yet "search and ye shall find": Crete does have superb beaches. On a few nudity, although not officially sanctioned, is tolerated. The season is long – stretching from Easter until nearly Christmas.

Minoan glory: The division of the one-and-a-half millennia of Minoan glory into several periods still causes much controversy among scholars but all agree that the apogee was the neopalatial era (1700–1380 BC). Most of the ruins vis-ited at such renowned sites as Knossós, Phaistós, Mállia and Káto Zákros are from this period when great unfortified palaces, brilliantly decorated, were built and when beautiful pottery and magnificent jewellery, used for both religious purposes and personal adornment, was produced.

The neo-palatial period had been preceded by – the proto-palatial (2000–1700 BC) which, in turn, had followed the prepalatial period (2600–2000 BC). The first palaces, which were built during the protopalatial period and of which exiguous remains can still be seen, are generally thought to have been destroyed by an earthquake. Debate still rages as to what brought the neopalatial era to an end.

By the post-palatial period (1300–1100 BC) the Minoan leadership in the eastern Mediterranean was waning and by the Early Iron Age (1100–650 BC) Crete was under the sway of mainland Greece. Surviving Minoans, Eteo-Cretans, retired to the mountains and continued to maintain their old traditions.

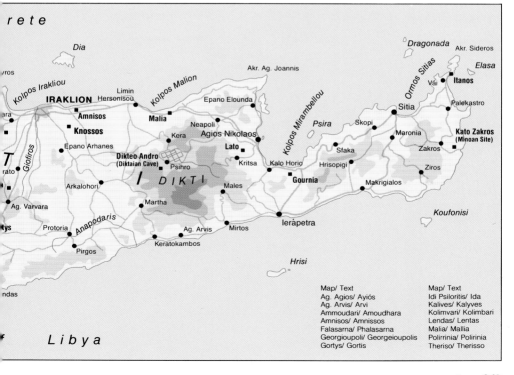

Irákleion (Iráklio, Heráklion): The capital of Crete since 1971, this city has a population of 125,000 and is the fifth largest in Greece. It boasts the highest *per capita* income of any Greek city. However, look not for elegance: much of Irákleion resembles a building site because of the propensity of its inhabitants to spend money on starting a building without the capital to complete it.

Irákleion's major attractions, other than the outstanding **archaeological museum** and the Minoan ruins of **Knossós**, are from the Venetian era, testifying that this was the most prosperous period in Crete's modern history. Visit the **restored fort** at the old harbour, whose three high reliefs of the Lion of St Mark announce its provenance, and the **Venetian arsenal**. Observe in the background Mount Yoúktas which bears a resemblance to a recumbent figure, claimed to be Zeus.

Challenging and rewarding is a complete circumambulation of the 15th-century **city walls** which, in their day, were the most formidable in the Mediterranean world. The walls stretch for nearly 4 km (3 miles) and, in parts, are 29 metres (95 ft) thick. Visit also the **historical and ethnographic** and the **religious art museums**. The latter, housed in the church of Aghía Ekateríni which is near the cathedral, contains some exquisite icons, six of which are the work of the 16th-century master, Mikhail Damaskinós.

From here, stroll north through the market redolent with tantalising smells, jammed with people and resonant with decibels. En route, stop to savour an inexpensive meal at one of the dozen tavernas which block "Dirty Alley".

Much more upmarket are the cafés and restaurants of **Venizélou** (or Fountain) **Square** which gains its eponymous name from the charming 17th-century Morosini fountain with its guardian marble lions. Overlooking the square is the handsome Venetian *loggia* flanked by the churches of **Aghios Márkos** and **Aghios Títos**. All three buildings have been heavily restored.

Since 1966, when it was returned

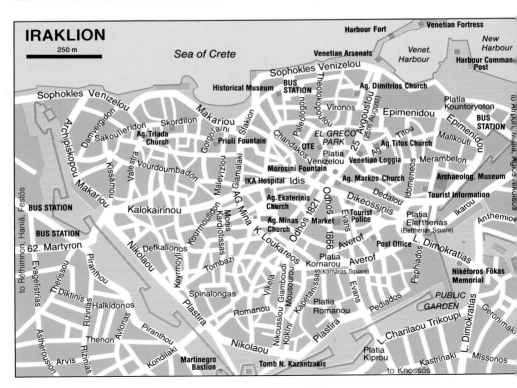

from St Mark's in Venice, Aghios Títos has housed the skull of St Titus, who was St Paul's apostle to Crete and the island's first bishop. Across town, close to the Archaeological Museum, is the less intimate **Eleftherías Square**, choc-a-bloc with cafés which are popular with both locals and tourists.

The best beaches near Irákleion are at **Amoudára**, immediately to the west and at **Amnissos** to the east. The latter, which was a port for Knossós, has the better sands and ambience.

Several short excursions from Irákleion will delight the collector of Minoan sites and provide the opportunity to view the lovely countryside and to savour village life. **Týllissos**, (13 km/ 8 miles) southwest of Irákleion, boasts three well-preserved small palaces or large villas.

Further west, the bipartite village of **Anógia**, where wool is spun and dried and where many homes have looms, is a weaving and embroidery centre. Many Anogians wear native dress with the picture-book men looking like rebels in search of a cause. This is no stage setting: Anógia has a long tradition of resistance and revolt and its men are among the fiercest and bravest in Crete.

From Anógia the road climbs to the magnificent **Nída plateau** from where it is a 20-minute stroll to the **Idaían Cave** which was the nursery, if not the birthplace, of Zeus. Here the god was guarded by the Kourétes, who clashed their weapons to drown his cries, while the nymph Amalthéai fed him with goat's milk. Climbers might wish to push on to the summit of **Mount Ida**, at 2,456 metres (8,178 ft), the highest point on Crete. A guide is advisable: allow 8 hours for the round-trip.

In and around the large village of **Archánes**, 5 km (5 miles) south of Knossós, are three churches with interesting frescoes and icons and three Minoan sites. **Turkoyeitoniá** has a Minoan palace: **Phourní** boasts the outstanding cemetery in the prehistoric Aegean and remains of a temple have been unearthed at Anemóspilia.

Human remains were found in one of

KNOSSÓS

Where else but in Crete can the visitor board a local bus in a thriving, bustling, modern city – in this case the No. 2 in Irákleion – and, 20 minutes later, be transported back nearly 4,000 years? An Irákleion merchant, Mínos Kalokairinós, discovered the site of ancient Knossós, the renowned city of the Minoans, in 1878 and, a quarter of a century later, Sir Arthur Evans purchased part of this site and began a systematic exploration.

Evans used his own fortune – sponsorship, government grants: what were they? – and, assisted by archaeologists and artists, excavated and then rebuilt Knossós in his own image rather than in that of King Minos – or so say his detractors. Still, without Evans's reinforced concrete and the brushwork of the Gilliérons, father and son, who copied and added to those frescoes (the originals are in the Irákleion Museum) the average uninitiated or unschooled visitor would be much less excited about the glories of Knossós.

What the visitor to Knossós sees are the remains of a magnificent palace and auxiliary buildings (Little Palace, royal villa, caravanserai) constructed during the so-called neo-palatial period which extended from approximately 1700 BC to 1380 BC. Exiguous remains of earlier periods (pre-palatial from 2000 BC to 1700 BC) and later periods (post-palatial from 1300 BC to 1100 BC) can also be found.

The remains cover more than 4 acres (nearly 2 hectares) and the site is usually very crowded. The best time to visit is early in the morning or just before closing time, when there are fewer visitors. Alternatively, try exploring the site backwards – by beginning at the end and walking against the flow of human traffic.

The city had a population of between 30,000 and 100,000. The Great Palace, an extraordinary complex of buildings divided by terraces, staircases and yards, had 1,300 rooms. It is easy to appreciate the legend that Knossós was a labyrinth built by Daedalos, on the orders of King Minos, to hide the half-man, half-bull minotaur conceived by his wife Pasiphaë, who had been infatuated with the white bull sent by Poseidon.

The east and west wings of the Great Palace are separated by a large central court. Was it here that the bull dancing took place? An exquisite ivory of the bull and the youthful acrobat can be viewed in the Irákleion Museum.

The Grand Staircase, with its five flights in the centre of the palace, formed the official approach to the Royal Quarters and is one of antiquity's major architectural achievements. Observe the imaginative manner in which the central light-well allowed natural light to illuminate and brighten the royal rooms. Gaze upon the original alabaster throne of Minos, guarded by a pair of painted griffins. Until the 1960s, visitors could sit on this, the world's oldest throne. Instead, in the northwest corner of Knossós, walk the Royal Road, Europe's oldest road, which was flanked by houses and workshops.

Back in the palace, observe the Queen's clay bathtub – yes, Pasiphaë did bathe here – and her lavatory, and appreciate that the Minoans were far ahead of their time in many aspects. Remains in the Queen's *toilette* suggest that there may have been running water from cisterns on a higher level and, at times, one wonders if the hydraulic technology in the eastern bastion was not much more sophisticated than that found today in many hotels on Crete.

Knossós was not only a palace for the royal family and their attendant nobles and functionaries but was also a sacred precinct as testified to by the lustral baths which were used for bathing and anointing. The complex also had workshops and storerooms where enormous *pithoi* containing wine, oil and grain were kept. These large Ali Baba jars are still made in villages such as Margarítes and Thrapsáno.

Although the names of the workmen who built Knossós are not known, they are remembered 3,000 years later by the incisions of tridents and double-headed axes on many ashlar blocks.

How did it end? Theories abound, one of which claims that after a catastrophic volcanic eruption on the island of Santoríni, a tidal wave swept away the wonder that was Knossós. ■

the rooms and it is suggested that when the temple was destroyed by an earthquake a priest was in the act of ritually sacrificing a youth. Such suggestions have outraged some scholars just as much as Nikos Kazantákis's books have outraged the established church.

A steep climb from Archánes (allow 45 minutes) leads to the summit of **Mount Yoúktas** (811 metres/2,703 ft) from where you can admire the panorama while griffin vultures swoop overhead. On the summit are a Minoan peak sanctuary, a 14th-century chapel and caves in which Zeus is said to be buried. This proves the truth of the aphorism that "all Cretans are liars" because, in the opinion of other Greeks, Zeus is immortal.

Straight on from Varvará is a breathtaking view of the lush **Plain of Mesará**. Rich soil and a benign climate make this a cornucopia where the wild flowers are said to be taller and larger than anywhere else in Crete.

After 16 km (10 miles) **Gortyn** (Górtys) is reached. This was the capital of the Romans who came to Crete in the 1st century BC to settle feuds but who stayed to conquer – how familiar! Outstanding and upstanding are the Roman odeon and a triple-naved basilica. The latter is by far the best preserved early church in Crete and was built to house the tomb of St Titus, Crete's first bishop, who died in AD 105.

However, the most renowned artefacts are some stone blocks incorporated into the odeon. About 2,500 years ago more than 17,000 characters were incised on these to produce the Code of Gortyn which consists of rules governing the behaviour of the people. The script is written in the ox-plough manner (reading left to right along one line and then right to left along the next).

Immediately before Gortyn is the almost sacred village of **Aghioi Déka** (Holy Ten) with its heavily restored medieval church into which are incorporated fragments from Gortyn. Aghioi Déka is renowned because, in AD 250, during the persecution of the Christians, 10 men were executed who are not only

ros, in the ain of esará.

ZORBA'S LEGACY

Seldom has a fictional character so engulfed its creator as did *Zorba the Greek* swallow Níkos Kazantzákis (1883–1957), the most renowned Greek writer of the modern era. (Incidentally, Odysséus Elytis, the Nobel prize-winner in literature in 1979, was also born on Crete.) Although Kazantzákis's output was large and varied, it is to the rugged, warm and happy-go-lucky Zorba, who can still be encountered on Crete, that Kazantzákis owed his reputation.

At least, that was so until another of his books was also made into a film, *The Last Temptation of Christ*. When this book was first published, the Orthodox Church sought to prosecute him. When it was screened in 1988, many church leaders the world over sought to have it banned. In Athens, priests marched on the cinemas where the movie was playing and projection screens were slashed in anger.

Common to *Zorba* and *Last Temptation* is Kazantzákis's conflict between spirit and flesh, between Christ and Dionysos. Kazantzákis lost his faith while a teenager because he was unable to reconcile Darwin's teachings with Christianity's promise of an afterlife. But he never lost his Christian convictions.

Although Kazantzákis left Crete when a youngster, it is here that he is buried – for, once a Cretan, always a Cretan; indeed, no self-respecting Cretan refers to himself as a Greek. Such chauvinism is fully justified in Kazantzákis's case: when he was born in 1883, Crete had not yet become a part of the Greek nation but was still embroiled in attempts to free itself from the Turkish yoke, a struggle which caused the Kazantzákis family to move to the island of Náxos soon after Nikos was born.

Yet, because of his non-conformist views and writings, Kazantzákis was denied burial in a Christian cemetery with the full rites of the Greek Orthodox church. He was buried in the Martinengo bastion (fortunately, one of the better maintained sections) of the Irákleion walls and his tomb carries this inscription, a testimony to his life: "I

hope for nothing. I fear nothing. I am free." A statue in Eleftherías (Freedom) Square in Irákleion honours him more than does his grave on the town's battlements.

His admirers will make for the new Kazantzákis Museum in the village of Mirtiá (24 km/15 miles) due south of Irákleion (when Kazantzákis was born here, it was called Varvári). Well arranged displays illustrate Kazantzákis's personal, literary and political life both in Greece and abroad, while one room is entirely devoted to *Zorba*.

Also worth visiting is the historical and ethnographic museum in Irákleion where a complete room has been set aside to represent a study of Kazantzákis. The Arkádi Monastery, shown on the 100-drachma note, features in *Freedom or Death*, Kazantzákis's most powerful novel.

Those who favour fiction rather than fact, frolics rather than philosophy, have much to see. Ierápetra was the home of Madame Hortense, the French courtesan who featured in *Zorba*. Visitors may be shown where her still body was washed and where, even before the body was cold, the old harpies rushed in and stripped Madame Hortense's apartment of all her possessions. And, in Ierápetra, Spyros Chrisofákes, a sprightly 60-year-old with a waxed moustache, still remembers the French courtesan who was the model for Kazantzákis's Madame Hortense and whose favours he, although a mere child, so desired. However, Spyros had to be content with gifts of candies from the beauty instead.

Much of *Zorba* was filmed in Pláka and, high above it, Kókkino Chorió, which lie on the coast midway between Réthymnon and Chaniá. Here *habitués* of the local tavernas may not recall the name of Kazantzákis but remember well that of Anthony Quinn. Then, in the northwest corner of the Akrotíri Peninsula, there is Stavrós with its pleasant beach, shallow waters and towering cliffs – known to the locals as "Zorba's Mountain" – where the film's climax was shot.

Although Kazantzákis roamed the world, Crete stayed in his thoughts. Not only are *Zorba* and *Freedom or Death* set in Crete but the story of *The Odyssey Modern Sequel* also becomes deeply interwoven with the island. ∎

among the most revered of Cretan saints but who are glorified as the first in a long line of Cretans willing to sacrifice themselves by opposing tyrannous occupiers of their beloved island.

Those in search of more classical ruins, of health and of good swimming might wish, before continuing to Phaistós, to drive south to **Léntas** over a mountainous road which provides magnificent vistas. Ancient Lebéna was the port for Gortyn and its therapeutic springs made it a renowned healing sanctuary with an Asklepiéion (temple to Asklépios, the god of healing). Traces of this sanctuary with mosaic floors and large baths can be seen.

In an attempt to equal, if not emulate, the ancients, nude bathing is popular on Léntas's best beach, beyond the headland at the western end of the village.

Phaistós (also spelled Festos), Crete's second great Minoan site, occupies a magnificent location 16 km (10 miles) south of Gortyn. Most of the remains are from the neo-palatial period although part of the floor plan of the proto-palatial palace is discernible. Staterooms, religious quarters, workshops and storerooms can all be identified. An outstanding sight is the Grand Stairway. At Phaistós those purists who bristle at Knossós's reconstruction can let their imagination run riot.

Nearby, again on a glorious site with views of the Libyan Sea, are the charming Minoan ruins of **Aghia Triáda** whose exact function still causes speculation – a palace, a villa, several villas?

And so to **Mátala**, 120 km (75 miles) from Irákleion, and practically at the mid-point of the south coast. Mátala first gained renown when the sandstone caves in the cliffs which rise above the small, excellent sandy beach became home of the world's hippies. Today, the small resort is busy, yet not frenetic. The scenic 30-minute walk to **Red Beach** is highly recommended.

Aghía Galíni, the other major south coast resort, also lies on the Gulf of Mesára but if Mátala is too boisterous then Aghía Galíni may well be the same.

The harbour, with a short wide quay

and a tiny main street jammed with tavernas and bars, is enclosed within a crescent of steep hills covered with modest small hotels. Nightlife goes on into the wee small hours. Not the place for those prone to heart attacks!

An almost mandatory pilgrimage from **Plakiás** is to the **Monastery of Préveli** (13 km/8 miles). En route, evocative ruins of the Monastery of Aghios Ioánnis are passed. Préveli has a superb position, an interesting museum with a piece of the True Cross and a courtyard fountain with the inscription, "Wash your sins, not only your face." Below the monastery is a beach from where Allied troops in World War II escaped to waiting submarines after being sheltered by the monks.

Hora Sphakíon, (Sfakiá) the centre of Sphakiá and home of the Sphákians, who are the epitome of the brave, fiery, intrepid Cretans, is another of those tiny, cliff-hanging, picturesque ports. Its *raison d'être* today – but don't tell this to the Sphákians – is to transfer exhausted tourists returning by ferry from their Samaria Gorge excursions.

Samariá Gorge: The most exciting and spectacular adventure which Crete offers the average visitor is a walk through the Samariá Gorge, the longest ravine (18 km/11 miles) in Europe. The journey starts at Xylóskalou at the end of the vast Omalós Plain by descending a steep wooden stairway.

After a mile or so, sea level is reached, then 8 km (5 miles) further along, the abandoned village of Samariá and its church come into view. Stop and admire the church's lovely 14th-century frescoes: this provides the opportunity, without loss of face, to regain your breath.

The going now gets tough and involves criss-crossing the river-bed. Be warned: flash floods can occur, so before going further check with the locals about weather conditions.

The gorge narrows and the walls soar straight upwards for 300 to 600 metres (1,000 to 2,000 ft). Soon after passing the Church of Aphéndis Christós, the Sidheróportes (Iron Gates) are reached and the gorge, scarcely penetrated by

Samariá Gorge is the longest ravine in Europe.

sunlight, is little more then 2 metres (7 ft) wide. However, it is doubtful if any but a giant can, as is claimed, stretch out and touch each side of the gorge.

If, overcome with exuberance, you feel the urge to burst into song – don't. The park is under the aegis of the Chaniá Forest Service which specifically forbids singing, among other activities.

All the while, the elusive Cretan wild goat, the *agrimi*, is watching your efforts, but it is unlikely that you will notice. On the other hand, even the most innocent of botanists will be delighted by the gorge, and ornithologists have been known to spot bearded vultures.

And so to Aghía Roúmeli and the Church of the Panaghía. However, all is not over: this is old, abandoned Aghía Roúmeli and the goal is new Aghía Roúmeli on the coast. This means a further 3 km (2 miles) of anticlimactic and hot walking before celebrating with that longed-for swim.

Refreshed, the only exit from the gorge, other than retracing the same route, is by boat eastwards to Chóra Sphakíon or westwards to Paleochóra. There are no roads.

The gorge is open from about the beginning of May until the end of October. Allow six hours for the walk.

Undiscovered gems: Other villages on the south coast which attract discerning visitors but which are not yet tourist towns are **Kalí Liménes**, **Loutró**, **Fínikas**, **Soúgia** and **Lissós**. Now may be the best time to enjoy them.

Back in Irákleion, an oleander-lined expressway runs west to Réthymnon. Some however, might prefer to travel more leisurely on the old road. Leave the former at the 22-km (14-mile) mark and in a few minutes **Phódele** (Fódele), a small village rich in orange trees and locally made embroidery, is reached. A restored house here is said to be the birthplace of Doménikos Theotokopoulos, better known as **El Greco**. Phódele's fame may be fleeting for the latest word is that El Greco was probably born in Irákleion. Back on the expressway, turn seawards at the 44-km (27-mile) mark to reach the idyllic tiny

resort of **Balí** which is clustered around three small bays at the foot of a hill.

At **Plátanes**, just before Réthymnon, turn southeast for the beautifully situated **Arkádi Monastery**, one of Crete's most sacred shrines. If the elaborate 16th-century western façade of the double-nave church seems familiar, it's because it's on the 100-drachma note.

In 1886, the monastery, sheltering hundreds of women and children, was attacked by the Turks. Rather than surrender, the abbot ordered that the gunpowder stored in the now roofless room in the northwest corner of the courtyard be ignited, thus killing both enemy and refugees (although one infant was blown into a tree and survived to become a nun). This act of defiance brought the plight of the Cretans to the public eye and gained for them the sympathy and assistance of much of Europe.

Réthymnon (Réthimno), which prides itself on being Crete's intellectual capital, still possesses an intact old town. A small, picturesque Venetian harbour, Réthymnon's major attraction is a quayside choc-a-bloc with colourful fish restaurants guarded by an elegant lighthouse. North of the harbour is the immense ruined **Fortétza**, said to be the largest Venetian castle, and from where excellent views may be enjoyed.

Réthymnon's other attractions – the **Rimóndi Fountain**, the **museum** and the **Nerandzés Mosque** – all lie between the harbour and fortress. If open, then the ascent of the Nerandzés Mosque minaret is rewarding.

Venetian houses with unexpected architectural delights can be found in the narrow streets linking these sights, while Turkish delights in the shape of minarets and overhanging wooden oriels give Réthymnon a Turkish, rather than a Greek, raffishness.

Besotted shoppers, especially those in search of leather and textiles, will find their nirvana in narrow, crowded **Paleológou Street**. Sun worshippers will make for Réthymnon's wide, flat beach with perfectly decent sands and backed by a palm-shaded promenade which starts immediately to the east of

Arkádi Monastery, which features on the 100-drachma note.

the harbour and stretches past the new part of town for several miles.

Réthymnon and Chaniá to the west are joined by an expressway and an old road. Leave the former at the 22-km (14-mile) mark and in 5 minutes enter **Yeorgioúpolis** (Georgeioupoli) at the mouth of the River Vrýsanos. This delightful hideaway has a good long beach and eucalyptus-shaded square.

Áptera, a large flat plateau above Kalýves, provides not only excellent views of the enormous **Gulf of Soúda** and the Akrotíri peninsula but also insights into Crete's history. Visit the recently restored **Aghios Ioánnis Theológos Monastery**, the massive ruined Turkish fort and the Greco-Roman remains. The name Áptera ("wingless ones") is derived from the Sirens who, defeated in musical contest by the Muses, discarded their wings and threw themselves into the bay where they became the White Islands.

Chaniá (Khaniá, Haniá), 59 km (37 miles) from Réthymnon, Crete's second city and its capital until 1971, is a larger version of Réthymnon and claims to be one of the oldest continuously inhabited cities in the world. Its jewel is the boat-free outer **Venetian harbour**. The quayside is wide and backed by charming, colourful old buildings whose reflections shimmer in the water. The ambience is of the Levant and this is *the* place for the *volta*.

The restored 17th-century **Mosque of Hassan Pasha**, the oldest mosque in Crete, stands at one end of the quay and is now the tourist office while the restored Firka Sea Fortress, which houses the **naval museum**, occupies the other end. Here the Greek flag was officially raised for the first time on Crete in 1913. The **Old Town** where artisans, especially leather workers, still occupy workshops, can be entered from this point by way of Angélou and Theotokopoúlou Streets. Both have splendid examples of domestic Venetian architecture and will please dedicated shoppers.

The **archaeological museum** occupies the church of the Franciscan Friary, one of the best preserved and the largest

of a score of still-standing Venetian churches. The **Church of St Nicholas**, as a result of various architectural as well as religious conversions, boasts both a minaret and a campanile. Another example of ecumenicalism is the small, drab **Orthodox Cathedral** built by a grateful Turkish Muslim whose son's life was saved by the intervention of the Virgin Mary.

In the **New Town** visit the lofty glass-covered **cruciform market**; the less exciting **historical museum and archives** with a collection of objects from the estate of Elefthérios Venizélos, father of the modern Greek nation.

Those with a sense of history will visit Mournies and Theriso, villages immediately south of Chaniá. The house in which Venizélos was born, now a museum, is in Mourniés. From here, a delightful journey through the **Thériso Gorge** brings the visitor to the village of that name. Much revered by Cretans is the house of Venizélos's mother which served as a revolutionary headquarters and which is now a national shrine.

Akrotíri, a limestone peninsula stretching northwards, is full of interest. First visit the **Hill of Prophet Elias**, where revolutionary Cretans gathered in 1897 to demand union with Greece. Here are the simple graves of Venizélos and his son Sophoklís.

Other graves – 1,527 of them – are found at the nearby immaculately maintained **Commonwealth Cemetery** where British and Commonwealth troops killed in the 1941 Battle of Crete are buried. (Equal honour is given to three times that number of Germans who are buried in the well-tended cemetery at **Máleme**, 16 km (10 miles) west of Chaniá.) And, on the western outskirts of Chaniá stands a massive memorial topped by a diving eagle which honours those Germans who died attempting to oppress the Cretans: surely a rare example of tolerance.

Farther out on the peninsula is the important **Monastery of Aghía Triáda**. Further on, and reached by a deteriorating road, is **Gouvernéto Monastery**, a century older. Both have many treas-

Dusk over Chaniá.

ures and shaded courtyards where the visitor can chat with monks.

From Gouvernéto a none-too-easy 20-minute downhill scramble leads to the abandoned, enchanting – and possibly enchanted – **Katholikó Monastery** hidden in a ravine populated by goats. Dating from about 1200, this is, if not the oldest, certainly one of the first monastic settlements in Crete.

The road west from Chaniá hugs the coast passing at first several busy small resorts which merge imperceptibly with each other and then arriving at the **Kolimbári** crossroads.

Proceed westwards through hilly country and emerge through a cleft to memorable views of the **Plain of Kastélli** and the **Bay of Kíssamos** enclosed within the peninsulas of Rodópou and **Gramvoúsa**. These are rather fancifully compared to a bull's horns. The road now makes a torturous descent to the plain and so to pleasant **Kastélli** with its wide, broad beach, some Roman ruins and a seldom open museum.

Turn left at Plátanos and a twisting

road, reminiscent of a corniche, leads after 32 km (20 miles) to **Váthi** and several splendidly frescoed Byzantine churches. From Váthi a poor road through a ravine hits the coast at **Stómio** from where it is another couple of miles to the **Khrysoskalítissa Convent**. The name means "Golden Stairway" and refers to the fact that one of the 90 steps descending from the terrace to a cove is made of gold. Failure to observe that step is proof that you have sinned.

From Khrysoskalítissa a barely negotiable road terminates at the broad, flat sandy beach of **Elaphonísi**, bordering what is practically a lagoon. Wade across a sandbar to an islet which has excellent beaches and you are at the westernmost point of Crete. This is possibly the best spot in the whole of the island for beach lovers: not easy to reach yet quite busy with campers.

Around the corner lies **Paleochóra**, a delightful resort which has a ruined Venetian castle.

Back to Irákleion: Return to Irákleion and continue eastwards along the ex-

hadows
the
fternoon.

A CRETAN CUSTOM

Travellers who take the road in western Crete from the town of Kastélli to the village of Ano Palaiókastro in search of the ruins of Polyrrhénia (also called Polirinía) are in for an unusual, yet typical Cretan surprise. The road climbs and twists past olive groves and, after 8 km (5 miles), terminates at Ano Palaiókastro. From here the ruins can be reached only by walking through the gardens of villagers.

The barking of an especially ferocious fenced-in dog serves not only to terrify the tourist but also to alert Mr Pirounákis to the approaching stranger. Mr Pirounákis welcomes you with *Elláte! Kathíste!* (Come! Sit down!). The greeting is timely for you are sure to be puffing and panting, completely unnerved and uncertain as to which is the route to the ruins.

Within the house all is bare and white-washed. Mr Pirounákis immediately pours for you a glass of *tsikouthiá*, Cretan fire-water, but he abstains on account of a heart condition. Sweetmeats follow and then comes the interrogation. And, be sure, no matter what country you are from – Singapore or Switzerland, England or America – Mr Pirounákis is sure to have hosted previous visitors from there. In evidence, Mr Pirounákis produces his three large guest books and hundreds of picture postcards sent by those he has entertained and who now write to him. Simple arithmetic reveals that Mr Pirounákis entertains about 500 tourists annually and dispenses many litres of the lethal *tsikouthiá*.

Mrs Pirounákis soon appears and now that her husband is comfortably settled refills your glass. It is difficult to depart and continue on to Polyrrhénia, for the Pirounákis pair believe that it is a matter of pride and honour to offer comfort to strangers. Cretans pay more than lip service to Xenios Zeus, the patron god of hospitality.

Farewells are finally permitted and you can continue your sightseeing. A stiff climb of a few more minutes and the scattered, inchoate ruins of Polyrrhénia are reached. However, it is not for the mute stones but rather for the superb views of the Gulf of Kissamos and, above all, for Cretan hospitality in the shape of Mr and Mrs Pirounákis that the traveller visits Ano Palaiókastro and Polyrrhénia. ■

Mr and Mrs Pirounákis welcome visitors from all over the world.

pressway for 24 km (15 miles). Then forget about "highway". You have reached the Cretan Riviera – a stretch reminiscent of Blackpool or Coney Island – with the resorts of **Khersónisos**, **Stalís** and **Mállia**. Search not for elegance: bars and *pizzerias* abound: ethnic it ain't. However, the beaches are among the best even although much sand is occupied by resorts.

Khersónisos has scanty Greek and Roman remains while close to the beach near Mállia is a renowned Minoan site. Stalís has to settle for palm trees.

The Palace at Mállia, traditionally associated with King Sarpendon, brother of Minos, is contemporary with that at Knossós. The ruins are not so extensive as those at Knossós and Phaistós but, even without reconstruction, are more readily understood. Remarkable are the number of store rooms and workrooms which suggest more a country villa than a palace. Recent excavations have uncovered the Chrysólakkos, the Golden Pit, from the protopalatial period (1900 to 1700 BC). The name is derived from the numerous gold artefacts found in this enormous necropolis.

Soon after leaving Mállia, the main road passes the chapel of **Aghios Geórgios Selenáris**. Public transport stops here to permit passengers to give thanks for a journey completed and to pray for a safe continuation. If you had travelled in the days of the old road, you would have been eager to do just this. Such shrines are not too uncommon at the midpoint of dangerous roads.

And so to **Aghios Nikólaos**, invariably abbreviated to Agnik, 69 km/43 miles from Irákleion, which is *the* resort – the San Tropez of Crete. This picture postcard paradise, overlooked by the eastern mountains, is magnificently situated on the Gulf of Mirabello. Here, and at neighbouring **Eloúnda**, are the island's best hotels. Unfortunately, Agnik lacks a decent beach, although there are some passable sands a couple of miles to the east. Restaurants and hotels, discos and cafés clutter around Agnik's **Mandráki harbour** and the small so-called "bottomless" lake. The latter is

oughnut ller at állia.

connected to the harbour by a canal. Hedonists have been known to tear themselves away from their sybaritic lifestyles to visit the town's **archaeological** and **folk museums**.

The **Lasíthi Plain**, at an altitude of about 840 metres (2,800 ft) is, as far as the eye can see, a regular cornucopia. Impeccably cultivated land supports potatoes and grain crops, apples and pears. The visitor can well believe that Crete was the granary of Rome and will recall Pliny's statement that whatever is produced in Crete is incomparably better than that which is produced in other parts. However, rare is the day when you will see the unfurled sails of the 10,000 windmills which irrigate the rich alluvial soil.

Proceed counter-clockwise around the plateau. Psychró is the starting point for the descent to the giant **Diktaian Cave**, supposedly the birthplace of Zeus. Guides here can be irritating but how, without one, will you be able to distinguish the nipples upon which Zeus suckled from all the other stalactites and stalagmites? Before leaving the plain try to visit **Tzermiádo** and its **Kronioan** (or Trapeza) **Cave** which is the mythical home of Kronos and Rhea, the parents of Zeus.

Clinging to the mountainside above Agnik is **Kritsá** – "the largest village in Crete". It is said to be the home of the best weavers on the island and their brilliantly coloured work hangs everywhere complementing the flowers and contrasting with the whitewashed homes which line the narrow passageways and alleys. Lovely frescoes adorn the church of Aghios Yeórgios.

Immediately below Kritsá is the church of **Panaghía Kerá** which is Crete's greatest Byzantine treasure. The entire interior is a picture book bible consisting of 12th- to 14th-century frescoes. Indicative of changing times, until a few years ago Panaghía Kerá was a functioning church: it is now a museum and charges admission.

A couple of miles beyond and above Kritsá are the ruins of **Lató**. The pleasure here lies not so much in the fairly

Pots in some of Crete's more remote areas are still made as in Minoan times.

extensive remains of a Greco-Roman city but in superb views from the northern acropolis across plains covered with an infinite number of olive and almond trees to the coast and to Aghios Nikólaos (in ancient days the port for Lató) and beyond to the Gulf of Mirabéllo and the Sitía mountains. To sit here and to absorb the view with the background music provided by the bells of unseen sheep is to feel completely chaste.

The nearby island of **Spinalónga** with its ruined Venetian fortress is readily reached from Aghios Nikólaos. Poignant memories abound on this island which was a leper colony until 1957 – the last in Europe. Onassis then considered building a casino here.

Leave Aghios Nikólaos and head eastwards for Sitía. After 19 km (12 miles) **Gourniá**, the poor man's Pompeii, is reached. Spread over a ridge, overlooking the sea, are remains, not of another palace, but of streets and houses of a Minoan town. Especially in spring, when the site is covered with a riot of flowers and their perfume fills the air, even those bored with old stones will be delighted to be there.

A further few miles and a poorly surfaced side road drops to the unspoiled fishing village of **Mochlós**. The tiny island opposite, which can be readily reached by strong swimmers, bears the same name as the village and has scanty Minoan ruins.

Someway beyond is the larger island of **Pseíra** where a Minoan town and port are being excavated. (Both islands can, on occasions, be reached by boat from Aghios Nikólaos.)

Sitía, is a somewhat laid-back town which, to the delight of visitors and the chagrin of locals, has not yet made the big time. Here are the almost obligatory Venetian fort, archaeological museum and a disappointing beach. There is also a folklore museum.

Tóplou Monastery, its tall 16th-century Italianate belltower beckoning like the minaret of a mosque, stands in splendid isolation in the middle of nowhere beyond Sitía. The monastery derives its name from a renowned cannon (*toplóu*

wo uses for ots.

is Turkish for cannon) which formerly protected it. The monks also had other methods of protecting themselves: observe the hole above the monastery gate through which they poured hot oil over their assailants.

After a further 8 km (5 miles) is **Váï**, renowned for myriad palm trees and a large sandy beach which brings to Crete a taste of far-away tropics. Don't believe it. However, the palm trees are not the species associated with desert islands and the beach is usually crowded. For a more relaxed time, better make for the quiet, palm tree-less **Itanos**, a couple of miles farther north.

Southwards along from Itanos is **Paleókastro** which hit the headlines because of outstanding finds at the largest Minoan town yet to be uncovered. Beaches about a mile away, especially at the southern end of the bay, are well worth visiting.

Further on is **Ano Zákros**, the starting point to Káto Zákros and the fourth great Minoan site. Hikers will prefer to make their way from Upper to Lower Zákros by walking through the spectacular **Ravine of the Dead**, so-called because of its caves which were used for Minoan burials.

Káto Zákros is a dig which you could fund. In the 1960s Dr Nikolas Pláton, director of the Archaeological Service, was asked by the Pomerances, a New York business couple, if any Minoan sites had still to be excavated. Yes, he told them. What then was the problem? they asked. Money, he replied. With that, the Pomerances underwrote the dig with no strings attached.

The ruins at Káto Zákros are from the New Palace era, but there are intrusions from the Old Palace era. They are often waterlogged because Crete is tipping over longitudinally with its eastern end sinking below and its western end rising above the water table. Close to the main dig, with the customary central courtyard and royal, religious and domestic buildings and workshops radiating outwards, are remains of a Minoan town and of a sheltered Minoan harbour which was ideally situated for trade with the Levant and Egypt. As at most Minoan sites, the setting is everything.

Back at Gourniá, a flat road shoots across the island's isthmus to **Ierápetra**, the largest town on the south coast and the southernmost in all Europe. Over the past decade Ierápetra has enjoyed a boom, not only because of tourism but also because of market gardening and the uncovering of archaeological sites. The town, scarcely atmospheric, has a short promenade at the rear of a not-so-good beach, the inevitable archaeological museum and a small Venetian fort.

Eastwards, the new inchoate resort of **Makriyialós**, which has a fairly good beach, can be reached. From here a side road leads to the small 14th-century **Kapsás Monastery** built snugly into the cliffs at the entrance to a gorge. Monks will show you, encased in a silver casket, the skull of Gerondoyíannis, a 19th-century faith healer, who is a kind of a cult figure.

Káto Zákros is practically around the corner but cannot be reached without returning to Makriyialós and then taking twisting mountain roads to Sitía.

Left, painting miniatures. **Right**, that elusive itch.

FOR THOSE
WITH MORE THAN
A PASSING INTEREST
IN TIME...

Before you put your name down for a Patek Philippe watch *fig. 1*, there are a few basic things you might like to know, without knowing exactly whom to ask. In addressing such issues as accuracy, reliability and value for money, we would like to demonstrate why the watch we will make for you will be quite unlike any other watch currently produced.

"Punctuality", Louis XVIII was fond of saying, "is the politeness of kings."

We believe that in the matter of punctuality, we can rise to the occasion by making you a mechanical timepiece that will keep its rendezvous with the Gregorian calendar at the end of every century, omitting the leap-years in 2100, 2200 and 2300 and recording them in 2000 and 2400 *fig. 2*. Nevertheless, such a watch does need the occasional adjustment. Every 3333 years and 122 days you should remember to set it forward one day to the true time of the celestial clock. We suspect, however, that you are simply content to observe the politeness of kings. Be assured, therefore, that when you order your watch, we will be exploring for you the physical—if not the metaphysical—limits of precision.

Does everything have to depend on how much?

Consider, if you will, the motives of collectors who set record prices at auction to acquire a Patek Philippe. They may be paying for rarity, for looks or for micromechanical ingenuity. But we believe that behind each $500,000-plus

bid is the conviction that a Patek Philippe, even if 50 years old or older, can be expected to work perfectly for future generations.

In case your ambitions to own a Patek Philippe are somewhat discouraged by the scale of the sacrifice involved, may we hasten to point out that the watch we will make for you today will certainly be a technical improvement on the Pateks bought at auction? In keeping with our tradition of inventing new mechanical solutions for greater reliability and better time-keeping, we will bring to your watch innovations *fig. 3* inconceivable to our watchmakers who created the supreme wristwatches of 50 years ago *fig. 4*. At the same time, we will of course do our utmost to avoid placing undue strain on your financial resources.

Can it really be mine?

May we turn your thoughts to the day you take delivery of your watch? Sealed within its case is your watchmaker's tribute to the mysterious process of time. He has decorated each wheel with a chamfer carved into its hub and polished into a shining circle. Delicate ribbing flows over the plates and bridges of gold and rare alloys. Millimetric surfaces are bevelled and burnished to exactitudes measured in microns. Rubies are transformed into jewels that triumph over friction. And after many months—or even years—of work, your watchmaker stamps a small badge into the mainbridge of your watch. The Geneva Seal—the highest possible attestation of fine watchmaking *fig. 5*.

Looks that speak of inner grace *fig. 6*.

When you order your watch, you will no doubt like its outward appearance to reflect the harmony and elegance of the movement within. You may therefore find it helpful to know that we are uniquely able to cater for any special decorative needs you might like to express. For example, our engravers will delight in conjuring a subtle play of light and shadow on the gold case-back of one of our rare pocket-watches *fig. 7*. If you bring us your favourite picture, our enamellers will reproduce it in a brilliant miniature of hair-breadth detail *fig. 8*. The perfect execution of a double hob-nail pattern on the bezel of a wristwatch is the pride of our casemakers and the satisfaction of our designers, while our chainsmiths will weave for you a rich brocade in gold *figs. 9 & 10*. May we also recommend the artistry of our goldsmiths and the experience of our lapidaries in the selection and setting of the finest gemstones? *figs. 11 & 12*.

How to enjoy your watch before you own it.

As you will appreciate, the very nature of our watches imposes a limit on the number we can make available. (The four Calibre 89 time-pieces we are now making will take up to nine years to complete). We cannot therefore promise instant gratification, but while you look forward to the day on which you take delivery of your Patek Philippe *fig. 13*, you will have the pleasure of reflecting that time is a universal and everlasting commodity, freely available to be enjoyed by all.

Should you require information on any particular Patek Philippe watch, or even on watchmaking in general, we would be delighted to reply to your letter of enquiry. And if you send

fig. 1: The classic face of Patek Philippe.

fig. 4: Complicated wristwatches circa 1930 (left) and 1990. The golden age of watchmaking will always be with us.

fig. 6: Your pleasure in owning a Patek Philippe is the purpose of those who made it for you.

fig. 9: Harmony of design is executed in a work of simplicity and perfection in a lady's Calatrava wristwatch.

fig. 10: The chainsmith's hands impart strength and delicacy to a tracery of gold.

fig. 5: The Geneva Seal is awarded only to watches which achieve the standards of horological purity laid down in the laws of Geneva. These rules define the supreme quality of watchmaking.

fig. 7: Arabesques come to life on a gold case-back.

fig. 11: Circles in gold: symbols of perfection in the making.

fig. 2: One of the 33 complications of the Calibre 89 astronomical clock-watch is a satellite wheel that completes one revolution every 400 years.

fig. 8: An artist working six hours a day takes about four months to complete a miniature in enamel on the case of a pocket-watch.

fig. 12: The test of a master lapidary is his ability to express the splendour of precious gemstones.

fig. 3: Recognized as the most advanced mechanical regulating device to date, Patek Philippe's Gyromax balance wheel demonstrates the equivalence of simplicity and precision.

PATEK PHILIPPE
GENEVE
fig. 13: The discreet sign of those who value their time.

your card marked "book catalogue" we shall post you a catalogue of our publications. Patek Philippe, 41 rue du Rhône, 1204 Geneva, Switzerland, Tel. +41 22/310 03 66.

Reality check. Call home.

—— *AT&T USADirect® and World Connect®. The fast, easy way to call most anywhere.* ——

Take out AT&T Calling Card or your local calling card.** Lift phone. Dial AT&T Access Number for country you're calling from. Connect to English-speaking operator or voice prompt. Reach the States or over 200 countries. Talk. Say goodbye. Hang up. Resume vacation.

Austria*†††......022-903-011	Luxembourg 0-800-0111	**Turkey***......00-800-12277
Belgium*......0-800-100-10	**Netherlands***......06-022-9111	**United Kingdom**......0500-89-0011
Czech Republic*......00-420-00101	Norway 800-190-11	
Denmark 8001-0010	Poland†◆¹......0◇010-480-0111	
Finland 9800-100-10	**Portugal**†......05017-1-288	
France......19-0011	**Romania***......01-800-4288	
Germany......0130-0010	**Russia***†(Moscow)......155-5042	
Greece*......00-800-1311	**Slovak Rep.***......00-420-00101	
Hungary*......00◇-800-01111	Spain●......900-99-00-11	
Ireland 1-800-550-000	Sweden 020-795-611	
Italy*......172-1011	**Switzerland***......155-00-11	

AT&T
Your True Choice

**You can also call collect or use most U.S. local calling cards. Countries in bold face permit country-to-country calling in addition to calls to the U.S. World Connect® prices consist of USADirect® rates plus an additional charge based on the country you are calling. Collect calling available to the U.S. only. *Public phones require deposit of coin or phone card. †May not be available from every phone. †††Public phones require local coin payment during call. ◆Not available from public phones. ◇Await second dial tone.¹Dial 010-480-0111 from major Warsaw hotels. ●Calling available to most European countries. ©1995 AT&T.

For a free wallet sized card of all AT&T Access Numbers, call: 1-800-241-5555.

Getting Acquainted

The Islands

Greece is one of the southernmost European countries, ensuring a high sunshine rate throughout much of the year. The combined population of Greater Athens and Piraeus is just over 4 million inhabitants. The most populated island is Crete, with just over half a million inhabitants, followed by Corfu (97,000), Lésvos (89,000), and Rhodes (88,000). The least populated islands covered in this book are the "Back Islands" of the Cyclades. Tiny Donoussa, Iraklia, Schinoussa and Koufonissia have only 100 to 200 inhabitants each.

Time Zones

Greek time is 2 hours ahead of Greenwich Mean Time. So, when it is noon in Greece it is 10am in London, 5am in New York, and 8pm in Sydney. Like the rest of the European Union, the clock is advanced 1 hour during summer to give extended daylight hours.

Spelling & Place Names

Syntagma Square in Athens is also known as Constitution Square. The island of Lésvos is known variously as Lesbos, Mytilene, or Mytilini. Corfu can be called by its Greek name Kerkira, or Kerkyra; Ithaki by its English name Ithaca. Attempts have been made in this book to use a system which has no national standard. If you find a place-name which is unfamiliar, check on more than one map or ask at a local ticket office if the destination has another name or spelling.

Climate

If you visit Greece in the summer months you'll want to bring lightweight, casual clothing. If you visit Greece during the winter months, bring the same kind of clothes you would wear during spring in the northern part of the United States or central Europe: that is, be ready for rainy, windy days and temperatures ranging between 40° and 60°F (3° and 16°C).

On the whole, islands are ill-equipped for visitors during the winter months. Heating can be basic or non-existent, boats infrequent, food tinned and amenities scarce. The tourist season is officially "over" in early October. Should you find yourself on the islands during this period (the first week in October for the Sporades; the second week for the Cyclades), you will be treated to a curious spectacle: an emerging ghost town. Cafés and shops close down daily, often locking their doors directly after you have left, and remaining closed for the next 5 months.

In general, the north coast of each island is subject to more gales and cooler temperatures than the protected south coast; be sure to check on a map exactly where a holiday resort is before making a final booking. Many travellers underestimate the differences in climate between individual island chains. The green, cool Ionian islands, for instance, are prey to rainy spells from mid-September through to the end of March. By contrast, the southern coast of Crete can offer swimming for the hardy as late as mid-December. A good rule to follow if planning to visit any island between mid-September through the end of April is this: the further south the island geographically, the better the sunshine rate.

Government & Economy

Greece is a republic with a president, elected by parliament, who holds ceremonial executive power. The parliament has a single chamber made up of 300 elected members and led by the prime minister.

King Constantine went into exile following the dictatorship in December, 1967, and the monarchy was abolished after a referendum held after the collapse of the dictatorship in 1974. Since then three main parties have established themselves: New Democracy (ND, conservative), PASOK (socialist and KKE (communist).

Strikes and demonstrations are a way of life in Greece. Should there not be one in Athens, consider yourself lucky

The late 1980s and early 1990s saw a huge rise in inflation throughout the country; a shock for anyone who remembers the islands as a "cheap & cheerful" vacation destination. Although the islands are no longer the place for rock bottom, cheap holidays, the drachm tends to go down against other currencies, and Greece remains good value for travellers.

Culture & Customs

Siesta

Siesta is strictly observed on many islands, when, between the hours of 2pm and 5pm, the driving of motorbikes and scooters in towns is prohibited. This provides a wonderful respite in even the noisiest of tourist towns, and is the ideal time to take a nap or extend a leisurely lunch into the afternoon. Most shops will close, perhaps to reopen again in the evening. Although the sun is fierce during these hours, anyone with a strong constitution and protective clothing will be rewarded if they choose this time to visit busy archaeological sites; crowds will have diminished considerably.

Nude Bathing

Nude bathing needs discretion. It is legal on very few Greek beaches, though socially acceptable on many. The main rule-of thumb is this: if it is a secluded beach and/or a beach that has become a commonly accepted locale for nude bathing, you probably won't be bothered by, nor offend, anyone. Avoid stripping off on beaches near towns or principal harbours. If the island you are visiting has only recently joined the mainstream ferry route also strip with discretion. Shortly after Ios, now one of the more carefree islands joined the Mýkonos/Náxos boat route two young visitors were thrown into jail for a week, then taken to a Sýros court in handcuffs, merely for removing their bathing trunks in public.

Seasonal Festivals

February–March (3 weeks before Lent) Carnival season, with special festivities in Athens, Patras, and on the islands of Skýros and Zákynthos.

June–September: Athens Festival at the Herod Atticus Theatre. Information and tickets available from 4 Stadiou Street (tel: 322 1459).

July: Réthymnon Wine Festival at the Municipal Garden on Crete. Information and tickets from 100 Kountouriotou

Street, Réthymnon (tel: 083 129148).

July–August: Daphni Wine Festival (on the outskirts of Athens). Information and tickets available from 4 Stadiou Street (tel: 322 7944).

July–August: Thássos Festival (ancient drama in an ancient theatre). Information and tickets from 2 Filellinon Street in the town of Kavala (tel: 051 223958).

September: The cricket season begins on Corfu.

There are smaller island festivals which occur most years during the summer, but details must be obtained locally. The festivals include the Rhodes Festival (May–October); the Irákleion Festival on Crete (June–August); a Music Festival on Ithaki (late-July); and the Hippokrateia Festival in Kos (August). Visitors should note that the precise dates of many festivals vary from year to year.

Religious Festivals

The Greek Orthodox Church exerts enormous influence on contemporary life, both in Athens and on the islands. Sunday is the official day of rest, and even in midseason (May and September) on some tourist-laden islands, shops and activities will be suspended on the Holy Day. Excursion boats to other islands might well be running to schedule, but what no one bothers to point out is that nothing on the destination island will be open when you arrive; enquire beforehand to avoid disappointment.

The most important holiday in Greece is Easter, celebrated by the Greek Orthodox calendar and usually several weeks later than Christian Easter. Traditional foods include *tsoureki*, plaited bread with red eggs inside, and *mayeritsa*, tripe and lettuce soup. It is advisable to find out before booking a spring holiday exactly when Easter might be, as services, shops and even airplane flights experience disruptions during the week before and the week after Easter.

On 15 August, the Assumption of the Virgin Mary, many islands hold a *paniyiri* (celebration) to mark the reception of the Holy Mother into heaven. Greeks make pilgrimages from all over the country to Tinos in the Cyclades where the icon of the *Panaghia Evangelistria* is said to work miracles. Pilgrims flock to Patmos, too, where St John is said to have written the book of Revelations. The most colourful festival of the Virgin, however, takes place on 15 August in the hillside town of Olympos on the island of Karpathos, where the women wear brilliant traditional dress and the *paniyiria* can last for days.

Other important celebrations include St Spyridion in Corfu, when the relics of the patron saint are paraded around the streets (Palm Sunday and 11 August); the *Theophania* (Epiphany) on 6 January with a big ceremony in Piraeus and on Crete where the seas are blessed and boys dive for the cross thrown into the waves; the Feast of St George on 23 April, where especially on Kos and Limnos the patron saint of Greece is remembered in festivities, and the celebration of St John the Baptist on 29 August. Worthwhile festivals, with their origins in religion but now basically secular, are the spring Tavrus or Bull Festival at Aghia Paraskevi on Lesvos; on 17 July, when the first grapes are ready for harvest, *Aghios Sotiris* (celebrated on some Dodecanese islands on 12 August), when it is the custom to have fights with eggs, flour and yoghurt, and *Aghios Demetrios* on 26 October, when the first wine is ready to drink.

Nearly every day is a cause for celebration for someone in Greece. Instead of marking birthdays, Greeks have *yiortés*, name days, which celebrate Orthodox baptismal names. When the day is to commemorate a popular name like John or Helen, practically the whole nation has a party. You'll hear locals say: "*Yiortazo simera*" (I'm celebrating today). To which you may reply: "*Chrónia pollá*" (Many years).

Planning The Trip
Getting There
By Air

Quite a few of the more popular islands have international airports. These include Crete, Rhodes, Corfu, Kos, Skiáthos, Mýkonos, Lésvos, and Zákynthos and new channels open each season. Most people, however, fly to Athens first; then take a ferryboat or a domestic airplane to the island of their choice.

Greece has good air connections with all five continents and is serviced by numerous international airlines. There are different ways of flying at a much lower cost than the standard airline ticket (APEX, stand-by, last-minute seats, "bucket shops"), and you may want to inform yourself of the different possibilities and of their related advantages and disadvantages, before buying a ticket. By far the cheapest way to travel to Greece is by buying a seat on a charter flight, which can cost as little as £100 return from London. These usually arrive in the middle of the night (and depart in the middle of the night), are uncomfortable and can be chaotic. But they are very cheap nonetheless.

Athens has two air terminals. The East Air Terminal is for international and charter flights; the West Terminal is for Olympic Airways flights and flights to the islands. Taxis or buses connect the two.

During the peak summer season it is impossible to walk through the East Terminal hangar which services charter flights without tripping over sleeping bodies and rucksacks. All part of the fun.

Reservations

The dual perils of Greek civil aviation strikes and package tour operators' double-booking practices means nothing should be left to chance. Confirm travel arrangements and hotel accommodation with your tour operator or travel agent approximately 3 days before leaving for Greece. When returning home, call the airline or the appropriate authority before setting off for Athens to catch a flight home. Inexpensive charter flights are often subject to several hours' delay, so be sure to slip a good novel or a pack of cards into your hand luggage and be prepared to sit it out, probably on the floor of the airport. For information on transfer to the islands domestic airlines, or of how to reach Athens or Piraeus from the airports, see the section called *Getting Around*.

By Sea

The majority of visitors entering Greece by sea do so from the west, that is, from Italy. You can catch a boat to Greece from Venice, Ancona, and Bari, but the most regular service is from Brindisi. Daily ferry lines (somewhat less frequent in the low-season) connect Brindisi with the three main western Greek ports: Corfu, Igoumenitsa and Patras. Corfu is a 9-hour trip, Igoumenitsa 11 hours; and Patras 16 hours to 18 hours, depending on whether it is a direct boat or one making stops in Corfu and Igoumenitsa. From Corfu it is possible to get a ferry, then a bus directly to Athens (about 11 hours), but Patras is best for travelling to Athens as regular buses and trains connect the two (about 4 hours by bus). If you plan to take your car with you on the boat, you should make a reservation well in advance. Otherwise, arriving a few hours before the departure time should suffice, except during peak seasons when booking in advance is advisable.

Italy and the west, however, are by no means the only provenance for Greece-bound sea travellers. Southward, boats connect Alexandria and Piraeus once every 10 to 15 days: eastward, boats run weekly between Haifa, Limassol and Piraeus, and once every 5 days between Volos, Cyprus and Syria, not to mention the numerous crossing-points between the East Aegean islands and the Turkish coast. Northward, frequent boats connect Piraeus and Istanbul, and in the summer boats run twice a month between Odessa (Russia) and Piraeus.

By Road

The overland route from northwestern Europe to Greece is a long one – some 3,000 km (1,900 miles) from London to Athens. It is an arduous and impractical travel option if you're just trying to get to Athens for a brief vacation, but it can be an interesting trip if you make the journey a part of your vacation. There are also inexpensive bus services, along the lines of the famous Magic Bus, which connect Athens and Thessaloniki with many European cities – a 3½-day trip from London. The various trains that you can take from northwest Europe will take about as long as the bus, will cost considerably more, but may get you to Greece feeling more intact.

If you're travelling to Greece from Asia you'll pass through Istanbul and cross into Greece at the Evros River. The recommended route is by car or bus. The road is good and the journey from Istanbul to Thessaloniki takes approximately 15 hours; various bus companies run the route. The train has the mythical appeal of running the route of the old Orient Ex-

press, but unless you're a great train fan, the travel may be prohibitive: some 25 hours from Thessaloniki to Istanbul. This trip crosses the fascinating region of Thrace; a fine adventure if you have the time and the spirit for it.

Visas & Passports

With a valid passport, citizens of the European Union, the United States, Canada, Australia and New Zealand can enter Greece and stay in the country for up to 3 months. No visa is necessary. To stay longer than 3 months, you must obtain a permit from the Aliens Bureau in Athens (Alexándros Avenue, tel: 770 5711). Citizens of other countries should contact the nearest Greek embassy or consulate with regard to visa requirements.

The following do not need a passport:

1. Holders of a United Kingdom "British Visitor's" passport.
2. Holders of National Identity Card nationals of Austria, Belgium, France, Germany, Italy, Luxembourg, Netherlands and Switzerland.
3. Holders of either a Military Identity Card (issued by NATO) or of Laissez Passer (issued by the United Nations).
4. Seamen, travelling on duty, who hold a Seaman's book.

No visa is required for citizens of the following countries:

For a stay of 3 months: United Kingdom, United States of America, Australia, New Zealand, Canada, Andorra, Argentina, Austria, Bahamas, Barbados, Belgium, Brazil, Cyprus, Denmark, Finland, France, Gambia, Germany, Granada, Ireland, Iceland, Israel, Italy, Japan, Luxembourg, Liechtenstein, Malta, Mexico, Monaco, Morocco, the Netherlands, Norway, South Korea, Spain, Sweden, Switzerland.

For a stay of 2 months: Portugal, Republic of South Africa, Venezuela, Chile, Colombia, Dominican Republic, El Salvador, Haiti, Honduras, Guatemala, Ecuador, Kenya, Mozambique, Nicaragua, Panama, Paraguay, Peru, Uruguay, Zambia.

For a stay of 1 month: Tunisia and Hong Kong.

Currency

The Greek unit of money is the drachma. The Bank of Greece issues bank notes of

50, 100, 500, 1,000, and 5,000 drachmas and coins of 50, 20, 10, 5, 2, and 1 drachmas. A 10,000 drachma note is said to be in the works.

Exchange Rates

Rates of exchange go up or down daily. To find out the current rate of exchange check with the newspapers; you can read the tables even in Greek.

Credit Cards

The plusher hotels, shops and restaurants of Athens and larger islands all recognise the major international credit cards, but many tavernas will not. Stickers in the front windows will advise on which cards are acceptable, but be sure to check *before ordering* or buying that the arrangement is still valid. Generally, visitors to small islands are likely to encounter problems with credit cards.

Travellers' Cheques

As with credit cards, only the more popular islands will have facilities to cash travellers' cheques. This can be done in banks and in larger hotels by submitting proof of identity such as a passport. Be sure to retrieve it from your hotel reception desk before going to the bank.

Cash

Every island, no matter how remote, will have some form of banking system. Some islands set up temporary banking facilities in tourist shops, post offices and OTE (telephone) offices and hours are irregular, never over weekends. Cash is often the only currency which is guaranteed legal tender on these far-flung islands. If you plan to island-hop, jump ship or follow up on any itinerant whims, carry quantities of both drachmas and your native currency. Islanders are honest and your cash will almost certainly be safe, but be careful.

Customs

If arriving from EU countries: You are allowed to import anything free of duty, as long as it is not for resale. The guidelines given are: 400 cigarettes or 200 cigars or 400 cigarillos or 1kg of tobacco; 10 litres of spirits or 90 litres of wine; and 60 ml of perfume.

If arriving from non-EU countries: You are allowed to import free of duty: 200 cigarettes or 50 cigars or 100 cigarillos or 250 grams of tobacco; 1 litre of spirits or 2 litres of wine; 50 grams of perfume and gift items to a total value of 7,000 drachmas.

It is prohibited to import narcotics, medicine (except limited quantities prescribed by a licensed physician for your own use); explosives and weapons. Computers or wind surfers (yes, that's right) will be registered in your passport so you will not sell them but take them out of the country when you leave.

For other specific restrictions regarding the importation and exportation of such things as animals, plants, shotguns, pleasure craft and antiquities, contact the nearest Greek embassy, consulate or tourist organisation.

On Departure

Leave plenty of time to reach Athens for your international flight home, especially if you are visiting a remote island. Any situation involving more than one Greek vehicle (plane, boat, taxi) is courting disaster, so leave nothing to chance. If the distance is far, or merely complicated, it might be an idea to break the journey into "laps" to prevent calamities along the way. On Chálki or Sými, for instance, it would be wise to arrive on Rhodes the day before your flight departs; 2 days before if flying back from Athens via Rhodes.

Animal Quarantine

Dogs and cats require health and rabies inoculation certificates issued by a vet in the country of origin before being allowed to enter Greece. The certificate must be issued not more than 12 months in advance in the case of dogs and 6 months in the case of cats (and not less than 6 days prior to arrival). Parrots and other birds must have a health certificate stating they are free from psittacosis.

Health

Residents of EU countries are eligible to receive free emergency medical care. In Britain, it is necessary to obtain a form from the DHSS before leaving home, so check this out beforehand. Medical insurance is always a good idea for additional coverage. Be sure your policy covers the cost of an air taxi as this is the quickest way, in an emergency, off the smaller islands to the nearest hospital. If you plan to hire a car, a motorcycle or a moped, ensure that your policy covers all motoring accidents. The number of accidents, especially on mopeds, mounts annually.

Drinking water

Carrying a large plastic bottle of mineral water is as common a sight on Greek islands as is carrying a *baguette* around Paris. Although tap water is essentially safe to drink, having a private water supply is much handier, as drinking fountains are few and the sun is fierce. Bottled water can be bought almost anywhere that sells food, even in beach cafés and tavernas.

Insects & Pests

Snakes and scorpions can be found in rocky areas. They tend not to attack unless disturbed, but always dress in long trousers and socks when hill walking. Jellyfish (*médusas*) are less common these days but can still occasionally be seen (and should be avoided) near the shores of some beaches. Spiny sea urchins can give painful stings if stepped on in the water; a local Greek remedy is to rub the wound with olive oil and then gently massage the foot until the spines pop out. This rarely works, so wear plastic shoes when walking in shallow water.

The most common pest is the mosquito, which loves virgin white skin. Avoid perfumes and deodorants (it attracts them even more) and invest instead in either of two items. The first is a coil, which, when lit and placed by the window, acts as an effective means of combat by smothering the mosquito in foul-smelling smoke. Even the smaller islands sell these coils in chemists or grocers. The second method is more modern: a plug-in electric coil which burns smokeless tablets called *Spira*. Practically odourless, it's worth seeking out in chemists or hardware shops.

Sunburn

Each year hundreds of tourists are badly burnt by ignoring the obvious rule: do your tanning slowly. For the first few days wear a sunhat and a sun block. Observe, like sensible Greeks, the afternoon siesta when the sun is at its hottest, and stay on the beach for just a couple of hours in the mornings and the early evenings. Gradually work up to staying out longer, and remember to reapply suntan lotion whenever you come out of the sea. It's possible to get burned while swimming or sightseeing too. Wearing a tee-shirt over your swimsuit for the first couple of days or when touring the island, and dressing in dark colours and long sleeves, avoids senseless burning.

Drugs

All prescribed drugs should be packed in their original bottles, carefully labelled and marked. Failure to do so could result in an arrest for the possession of dangerous drugs. Greek authorities take the unauthorised use of drugs very seriously indeed; this is not the country in which to store cannabis, no matter how small the quantity. Err on the side of caution at all times.

What To Wear

On the whole, island life is casual. It's possible to get by without offending anyone by dressing simply, in a tee-shirt dress and sandals (if a woman) or long trousers and a tee-shirt (if a man). Bathing costumes can be slipped on underneath. Disco clothes or wash-and-wear cottons are sold on most larger islands.

Like any other country, Greece has a set of codes, both stated and implicit, which defines the socially acceptable range of attire. The Greeks will not expect you as a tourist to dress as they do. However, in certain places and regions you will encounter requirements or conventions concerning dress which do reflect on you as a visitor.

To enter a church, men must wear long trousers and women, sleeved dresses. These will occasionally be provided at the church entrance if you do not have them. Not complying with this code will be taken as insulting irreverence on your part. It's also important to conform to the socially acceptable dress code of the region you are visiting. On Mýkonos, for example, male and female tourists alike will shock no one by wearing shorts, a swimsuit or going bare-chested, even in many public places. But this same dress will be severely alienating if worn in a mountain village in Crete. The best approach is to observe what people around you are wearing and to dress accordingly.

Footwear

Sandals are appropriate day or night. Plastic shoes are invaluable for walking in shallow water containing rocks, garbage or sea urchins; also for walking on the red-hot volcanic beaches of Santoríni and Níssyros. Plastic shoes can usually be bought on the islands themselves. Sturdy walking shoes are required for mountain climbing or uphill strolls to monasteries as snakes are common in the hills. Three pairs of socks should suffice; one pair to wear while walking, one pair to dry in the hot sun, and one pair to wear at night; temperatures in the evenings can be surprisingly chilly.

What To Bring

These items should appear on every dedicated island hopper's checklist, but again, most can be bought in Athens or the larger island cities: binoculars (invaluable, entertaining and often overlooked), tin opener, corkscrew, sharp knife, plastic fork and spoon (a good Swiss army knife includes most of these domestic items), folding drinking cup, torch (very important for steep island paths late at night), thermos flask, face cloth (unavailable in Greece), towel, beach towel, soap, little bags of soap powder, sticking plasters, antiseptic cream, sink plug, portable clothes line and pegs, insect repellent, aspirin, indigestion tablets, earplugs, an alarm clock and/or a watch. These last items are for catching ferries, caiques and island buses; no two island clocks tell the same time and ferries wait for no one.

Baggage

The old saying which applies to travellers everywhere applies especially to those travelling on Greek islands: pack your suitcase, then unpack it and leave half the contents behind. Nothing ruins a holiday more than having to heave a heavy suitcase around unsuitable terrain, i.e. hills and ferryboat decks. Only the poshest hotels have mini-bus services to/from the harbour or airport; if you plan to find accommodation on the spot, plan to carry your suitcase or stash it somewhere while you look around. (A few of the more popular islands offer temporary luggage storage facilities near the harbour.) If your suitcase is still too heavy for prolonged island hopping, consider investing in a suitcase trolley which can be bought

in the shopping arcades around Syntagma Square in Athens, or from a department store on Rhodes, Kos, Crete or Corfu.

A handy tip: carrying a basket or packing a smaller suitcase inside a larger one can be useful. The smaller one can be brought out for the beach or for short trips to other islands, while the larger one and its contents stay safely stored in the hotel.

Left Luggage

There are no left luggage facilities at either of the Athens Air Terminals. Most hotels in Greece, however, will be willing to store locked suitcases for up to a week if you want to take any short excursions. This is a free service, and the hotel accepts no responsibility in the highly unlikely event of theft. Commercial left luggage offices operate in many harbour towns on the islands. For a small charge space can be hired by the hour, by the day, by the week or longer. Although contents will probably be safe, take any valuables with you.

Useful Addresses

Greek National Tourist Offices
Australia & New Zealand: 51–57 Pitt Street, Sydney, N.S.W. 2000 (tel: 241 1663).
Austria: Karntner Ring 5, 1015 Vienna (tel: 525 317).
Belgium: 62–66 Blv. de I'Imperatrice, 1000 Bruxelles (tel: 513 0206).
Canada: 1233 rue de la Montagne, Montreal, Quebec H3G 1Z2 (tel: 514 871 1535); 80 Bloor Street, Suite 406, Toronto Ontario M5S 2V1 (tel: 416 968 2220).
Denmark: Vester Fartmagsgade 3, DK 1606, Copenhagen (tel: 123 063).
Finland: Stora Robertsgatan 3–5 C38, 00120 Helsingfors Helsinki 12 (tel: 607 552).
France: 3 Avenue de l'Opera, Paris 75001 (tel: 260 6534).
Germany: Neue Mainzer Str, 22, 6 Frankfurt/Main 1 (tel: 236 562); Pacelli Str, 2, 8000 Munich 2 (tel: 222 035); Neuer Wall 35, 2000 Hamburg 36 (tel: 366 910).
Italy: Via L. Bissolati 78–80, 00187, Rome (tel: 474 4249); Piazza Diaz 1 (Ang. Via Rastrelli), Milan (tel: 860 470).
Japan: 11 Mori Building, 2-6-4 Toranomon, Minato-Ku, Tokyo 5 (tel: 503 5001).
Netherlands: Leidsestraat 13, NS Amster-

dam (tel: 254 212).
Norway: Ovre Slottsgatan 15B, 0157 Oslo 1 (tel: 426 501).
Saudia Arabia: Embassy of Greece, Madina Road, City Centre, P.O. Box 1326 Code No. 21493, Jeddah (tel: 667 6280).
Spain: Alberto Aguilera 17, Madrid 1 (tel: 248 4889).
Sweden: Birger Jarlsgaten 8 IV, 2 P.C. Box 5298, 10246 Stockholm 5 (tel: 20 802).
Switzerland: Gottfried Kellerstr 7, 800 Zurich (tel: 251 8487).
United Kingdom & Ireland: 4 Conduit Street, London W1R 0DJ (tel: 0171 73 5997).
USA: Olympic Tower, 645 Fifth Avenue New York, N.Y. 10022 (tel: 212 42 5777); 611 West 6th Street, Los Angeles California 90017 (tel: 213 626 6696); 16 North Michigan Avenue, Chicago, Illinois 60601 (tel: 312 782 1084); Nationa Bank of Greece Building, 31 State Street Boston, Mass 02109 (tel: 617 227 7366).

Practical Tips

Emergencies

Pharmacies

In Greece there are certain pharmacie which are open outside normal shop hour and which work on a rotating basis. I you need a pharmacy after hours or o weekends, you can find out which ones ar open either by looking at the card post ed in any pharmacy's window (which give details on 24-hour pharmacies), or b consulting a local newspaper.

In Athens, the doctor's roster can be obtained by dialling 105; the 24-hou pharmacy roster can be obtained b dialling 107.

Hospitals

In case of a medical emergency requirin hospital treatment in Athens, tel:166. for some reason this fails, call the loca Tourist Police. They should speak Englis and will have information as to whic hospitals have emergency facilities.

The Greek health system will be bewildering to the tourist who needs to make use of it, particularly in an emergency. Perhaps most important in emergencies is to find a competent speaker of both Greek and English who can make the necessary manoeuvrings for the patient's safety and inform you of what is going on. If entirely helpless, try calling your embassy. US citizens can call the "emergency" number 21 2951 in Athens.

Security and Crime

Crime is rare on the islands, and the petty theft which does occur might well be the result of other tourists, rather than locals. Although it is not advisable, luggage left on quay sides or temporarily in cafés will probably be left undisturbed. If something has been left in an Athens taxi or bus, call 523 0111. Should trouble arise, each island has a police number which can be rung in emergencies. Special officers known as "Tourist Police," whose duties are concerned solely with visitors, are also assigned to some islands and can even help with accommodation. Tourist Policemen usually speak English. The police numbers listed here are preceded by the code from Athens:

Ionian Islands:
Corfu, tel: (0661) 39503/30265
Paxos, tel: (0662) 31222
Léfkas, tel: (0645) 92696
Cephalonia, tel: (0671) 22200
Zákynthos, tel: (0695) 22550

Saronic Gulf Islands:
Aegina, tel: (0297) 23333
Hydra, tel: (0298) 52205
Póros, tel: (0298) 22256
Salamis, tel: 465 1100
Spétses, tel: (0298) 73100

Cyclades Islands:
Amorgos, tel: (0285) 71210
Anafi, tel: (0286) 61216
Antiparos, tel: (0284) 61202
Andros, tel: (0282) 22300
Folegandros, tel: (0286) 41249
Ios, tel: (0286) 91222
Kéa, tel: (0287) 51205
Kimolos, tel: (0287) 51205
Kíthnos, tel: (0281) 31201
Mýkonos, tel: (0289) 23990
Milos, tel: (0287) 21378
Náxos, tel: (0285) 22100
Páros, tel: (0284) 23333
Santoríni, tel: (0286) 22649

Serifos, tel: (0281) 51300
Sífnos, tel: (0284) 31210
Sikinos, tel: (0286) 51222
Sýros, tel: (0281) 22620
Tínos, tel: (0283) 22255

Sporades Islands:
Alonissós, tel: (0424) 65205
Skiáthos, tel: (0427) 21111
Skopelós, tel: (0424) 22235
Skýros, tel: (0222) 91274

Northeast Aegean Islands:
Chíos, tel: (0271) 23211
Ikaria, tel: (0275) 22222
Lésvos, tel: (0251) 22776
Limnos, tel: (0254) 22200
Psará, tel: (0272) 61222
Sámos, tel: (0273) 27980
Samothraki, tel: (0551) 41203
Thássos, tel: (0593) 22500

Dodecanese Islands:
Astipalea, tel: (0242) 61207
Chálki, tel: (0246) 71213
Kálymnos, tel: (0243) 22100
Karpathos, tel: (0245) 22218
Kassos, tel: (0245) 41222
Kastellorizo, tel: (0241) 26068
Kos, tel: (0242) 22222
Leros, tel: (0247) 22221
Nissyros, tel: (0242) 31201
Patmos, tel: (0247) 31303
Rhodes, tel: (0241) 27423
Sými, tel: (0241) 71238
Tilos, tel: (0241) 53222

Crete:
Aghios Nikólaos, 17 Kon. Paleologou Street, tel: (0840) 22251
Chaniá, 44 Karaiskaki Street, tel: (0821) 94477
Irákleion, Vas. Konstantinou Street, tel: (081) 282243
Réthymnon, 29 Iroon Politehniou Square, tel: (0831) 28156
Sitia, 24 Mithonos Street, tel: (0843) 22266

Police stations in Athens/Piraeus:
24-hour Tourist Police number, tel: 171
4 Leoharous Street, tel: 323 0263
58 Sokratous Street, tel: 522 6067
37 Iroon Politehniou Street, tel: 412 0325
East Air Terminal, tel: 969 9523
West Air Terminal, tel: 981 4093

Electricity

220 AC is the standard household electric current throughout Greece. This means that appliances from the US require converters. Greek outlets and plugs are different from both American and most European types, so you'll probably need an adapter as well.

Business & Banking

Business Hours

The schedule for business and shop hours is a complicated affair, varying according to the type of business and the day of the week. The main thing to remember is this: if shopping for something important, buy it between 10am and 1pm. The store may or may not be open that afternoon; it may well open in the evening. Again, it may not. Athens is experimenting with "straight" hours during the winter to bring the country more in line with the EU. Whether this will catch on and spread to the islands is anyone's guess.

Winter opening hours – Athens: Nonfood shops: Open Monday, Wednesday 9am–5pm; Tuesday, Thursday and Friday 10am–7pm; Saturday 8.30am–3.30am. Food shops: Monday 9am–2.30pm; Tuesday to Friday 9am–6.30pm; Saturday 9am–3.30pm.

Summer opening hours – Athens: Monday, Wednesday, Saturday. Most businesses open Tuesday, Thursday, Friday 8am–2.30pm. Most businesses open from 9am–1.30pm, then reopen from 5–8.30pm.

The shops in Athens' Plaka district remain open until 10pm or longer to take advantage of anyone who wants to browse. Tourist shops (selling clothes, sandals, suntan oil) and kiosks will almost always be open until midnight on popular islands like Corfu, Rhodes, Páros, Mýkonos and Kos.

Dry cleaners and specialty shops have yet another schedule of opening hours, which is not covered here. Chemists operate on a rota system so there will be at least one open for emergencies; check in the window of the nearest pharmacy for the list.

Banking Hours

All banks are open to the public from Monday to Thursday 8am–2pm; Friday 8am–1pm. In heavily touristed areas like central Athens and the popular islands, however, you may find at least one bank open on some summer evenings and/or weekends for currency exchange. This will always be in or around the main harbour area. On the small, rarely visited islands, expect only the minimum of banking facilities so travel with emergency cash.

Around Syntagma Square in Athens, at the time of going to press, these banks offered extended hours: General Bank of Greece, 1 Ermou Street (tel: 324 6451), and the National Bank of Greece, 2 Karayiorgi Servias Street (tel: 323 6481).

The East and the West Air Terminals in Athens have several banks each, all with extended opening hours:

EAST AIR TERMINAL
Agricultural Bank of Greece, tel: 962 2791. Open daily 24 hours.
Commercial Bank of Greece, tel: 961 3611. Open daily 8am–8pm.
General Bank of Greece, tel: 961 3700. Open daily 7am–9.30pm.
National Bank of Greece, tel: 961 2728. Open daily 7am–11pm.

WEST AIR TERMINAL
Agricultural Bank of Greece, tel: 984 1282. Open daily 8am–8.30pm.
Commercial Bank of Greece, tel: 981 1093. Open daily 8am–7pm.
Ionian Bank of Greece, tel: 982 1031. Open Monday–Friday 8am–2pm.
National Bank of Greece, tel: 982 4699. Open daily 7am–11pm.

Athens is the headquarters for banks with international branches, and money can often be deducted straight from your account at home into your pocket in Greece by visiting the appropriate headquarters. The industrial disputes which plague Greece can lead to local banks locking their doors for days at a time. Knowing the Athens headquarters of your domestic bank can, quite literally, mean the difference between having money to eat and having nothing.

American Express Bank, 31 Panepistimiou Street (tel: 323 4781-6).
Athens Bank, 3 Santaroza Street (tel: 321 2371).
Bank of America, 39 Panepistimiou Street (tel: 325 1901-9).
Bank of Nova Scotia, 37 Panepistimiou Street (tel: 324 3891-8).
Bank Paribas, 39 Panepistimiou Street (tel: 325 5021).
Banque National de Paris, 5 Koumbari Street (tel: 364 1880).
Barclays Bank International, 15 Voukourestiou Street (tel: 364 4311).
Chase Manhattan Bank, 3 Korai Street (tel: 323 7711-9).
Citibank, 8 Othonos Street (tel: 322 7471); Kolonaki Square (tel: 361 8619).
Credit Bank, 2 Stadiou Street (tel: 322 0141); 9 Panepistimiou Street (tel: 323 4351-5).
Credit Commercial de France, 20 Amalias Avenue (tel: 324 1831).
Ergobank, 36 Panepistimiou Street (tel: 360 1011).
Grindlays Bank, 7 Merlin Street (tel: 362 4601).
Midland Bank, 1A Sekeri Street (tel: 364 7410).
National Westminster Bank, 24 Stadiou Street (tel: 324 1562-7).
Société Générale, 23 Ipokratous Street (tel: 364 2010-9).

Rush hours: One reason for turning to "straight" opening hours is to combat Athens' horrendous rush hours. The twin perils of traffic jams and pollution reached such heights in Athens that a law was introduced: on even days of the month only cars with even-numbered licence plates are allowed into the city centre; on odd days only those cars with odd-numbered licence plates.

Public Holidays

1 January	New Year's Day
6 January	Epiphany
variable	Shrove Monday
25 March	Feast of the Annunciation/ Independence Day
1 May	Labour Day and Flower Festival
variable	Good Friday
variable	Greek Orthodox Easter
15 August	Assumption of the Holy Virgin
28 October	Ochi Day (when Greece said "no" to Mussolini)
25 December	Christmas Day
26 December	Boxing Day

Tipping

Most restaurants and tavernas add a 15 percent service charge to the bill, so a tip is not expected, although it is customary to leave the small change on the plate after a bill has been paid. If the waiter (mikrós) has been particularly good about clearing away empty plates, etc., reward him separately by placing change on the table rather than on the plate. The waiters rely on tips as a supplement to rather meagre wages. Just as important as any gratuity, however, is your appreciation of the food. Greek restaurant owners are pleased when you tell them you like a particular dish.

Postal Services

Signs denoting post offices are usually bright yellow, as are post boxes. Post boxes are tiny and can be hard to find; often they are on the outside walls of tavernas or shops obscured by flowers. Look carefully. Island post offices can be large and efficient (on Rhodes, there are separate mail slots to separate European destinations), or tiny and chaotic. If on a remote island, mail your postcards on the return journey on a larger island; it will arrive home quicker. Opening hours of post offices vary, but can most often be visited Monday to Friday between 8am and 2pm. The main post office in Syntagma Square, Athens, is open usually from Monday to Saturday 7am–8.30pm; and on Sunday 9am–1pm.

Stamps can be bought at post offices and most kiosks *perptera*, although occasionally a service tax may be added by the kiosk. If sending the attractive, large-format postcards, additional postage may be required, so it's best to have them weighed first.

Parcels sent abroad must be inspected by the post office, so do not wrap them beforehand. Brown paper can be bought from some kiosks. If you're sending home bought goods, get the store to do it for you. The mail service is riddled with discrepancies: three parcels containing identical contents were sent to London at the same time. The sender was charged three different postal rates. Why? This is Greece. Give in gracefully.

Telephone/Telegrams

All large islands and most small ones have OTE offices (Greek Telephone Exchange) which are open in the evening in most days. OTE offices are the cheapest way to make local or international calls. To do so, walk in and wait for a booth to be free. A desk operator will switch on the phone, the meter registering zero units. After dialling, talk for as long as you like either locally or internationally. At the end of the call, the desk operator will

resent you with a bill in drachmas. Con-
ections from the islands vary, but perse-
ere. Telegrams can also be sent from OTE
ffices. Two OTE offices in Athens are
cated at 15 Stadiou Street, just behind
yntagma Square, open Monday to Satur-
ay 9am–10pm; Sunday 9am–8pm, and at
monia Square, open 24 hours.

Local and international calls can also
e made from many kiosks. Although
ere is often a queue (island teenagers
lling their friends), it is very romantic
talk to loved ones only a few feet from
e sea and with a full moon.

ALLING CODES

he dialling code from Greece to the UK
0044. From Greece to the USA or
anada it is 001. Calls made from hotels
pensions are often subject to extra tar-
s, so it is cheaper to use OTE offices.
otels, however, are likely to contain the
ly telex and fax machines around. From
e UK to Greece the code is 0030. For
thens 00301.

Media

The Press

iosks on the major islands receive most
ritish newspapers the day after publica-
on; two days after weekends. The *Inter-
tional Herald Tribune* can sometimes be
ught on the day of publication. Rhodes,
rete, Corfu and Kos produce local
What's On" guides (several languages in
ch publication) which can be found in
osks or information centres.

English-language newspapers can be
rchased around Syntagma Square in
thens from kiosks; again, the British
ess and a smattering of American papers
e well represented. Several local publi-
tions provide news and information in
nglish for both tourists and residents
ike. The daily *Athens News* contains a
attering of world news taken from wire
rvices, Greek news coverage plus inter-
ting small ads. *The Athenian* is a month-
magazine providing literate coverage on
rious aspects of life in Greece (politics,
lture, travel) and useful information on
hat's happening in the arts; a solid read
ith a wry approach. The *Odyssey* is a
arterly, well worth getting. *Greece's
eekly* concentrates on business and fi-
nce for the English-speaking communi-
. All these publications are readily
ailable from kiosks in areas of Athens
equented by tourists. The tiny *Week in

Athens has been published for 41 years by
the National Tourist Organisation of
Greece. It contains a list of useful addresses of amenities and entertainments. Pick
up one free at any NTOG desk.

Radio & TV

Athens, naturally, offers the best English-
speaking communications. Most hotels
now broadcast satellite TV. Channel 3 is
Sky (movies and sit-coms); Channel 4 is
Super (mainly music); and Channel 7 is
CNN (news). There may be a fee for private TV if staying in a posh hotel; otherwise a communal set in the lobby is
available free for visitors' pleasure.

The two state-owned and -operated TV
stations in Athens are ET1 and ET2. In
Thessaloniki it is ET3. These channels
often transmit English-speaking movies
and programmes with Greek subtitles.

ERT 1 and ERT 2 are the two Greek
radio channels. ERT 1 is divided into three
different "programmes". First (728 KHz)
and Second (1385 KHz) both have Greek
popular music and news, some foreign pop
and occasional jazz and blues. Third Program (665 KHz) plays classical music.
ERT 2 (98 KHz) is much like the first two
programmes. News can be heard in English, French, German and Arabic on the
First Program every morning of the week;
in English twice a day on ERT 2 at 2pm
and 9pm. The BBC World Service offers
news on the hour (plus other interesting
programmes and features). To find out the
best short wave (MHz) frequencies on
which to pick up the BBC, ask at your
hotel reception.

Libraries

The following libraries in Athens contain
books in English, French, German, Span-
ish or, in the case of Greek institutes,
perhaps all the above. Call for opening
times (and/or an appointment) as hours
are subject to change. A tip: in the case
of the smaller libraries, be sure to take the
complete address, i.e, 17 Valaoritou
Street. As with much of industrialized
Athens, libraries do not necessarily look
like libraries from the outside and specific
places can be difficult to find.

American Library, American-Hellenic
Chamber of Commerce, 22 Massalias (tel:
363 8114). Two libraries, one on the
fourth floor; one on the seventh floor.
Benaki Museum Library, 1 Koumbari

Street (tel: 362 6462).
Blegen Library, American School of Clas-
sical Studies, 54 Souidias Street (tel: 723
6313).
British Council Library, Kolonaki Square
(tel: 363 3215).
French Institute Library, 31 Sina Street
(tel: 362 4301).
Gennadius Library, American School of
Classical Studies, 61 Souidias Street (tel:
721 0536).
German Archaelogical Institute, 1 Fidi-
ou Street (tel: 362 0270).
Goethe Institute Library, 16 Omirou
Street (tel: 360 8114).
Italian Institute Library, 47 Patission
Street (tel: 522 9294).
Loberdios Library, Othonos & Eleftheri-
ou Venizelou, Kifisia (tel: 801 3861).
National Library of Greece, Panepistimi-
ou (tel: 361 4413).

Bookshops

Most popular islands have at least one
bookshop located near the harbour with
books in English. Don't expect grand
literature, however, the stock-in-trade
tends to be dire thrillers, international
best-sellers, and bodice-ripping romanc-
es. Many island kiosks (as in Athens) sell
second-hand paperbacks throughout the
summer, probably rescued from beaches
and hotels. These can be found in a heap
on the pavement and are even more
down-market in quality than the bookshop books.

Athens has numerous bookstores which
sell quality books in English. Distributors
often import from America, so some
books unavailable in Britain can be found
on sale in Athens.

The Bookstall, 6–10 Har. Trikoupi (tel:
361 9933). Modern shop in swish complex; good on Penguin classics.
Compendium, 33 Nikis (tel: 322 1248).
Friendly and helpful, owner is an expat
with good taste.
Eleftheroudakis, 4 Nikis, behind Syntagma Square (tel: 322 9388). A comprehensive, convenient shop.
Kakoulides – The Book Nest, 25–29
Panepistimiou (tel: 322 5209). Upstairs in
this old-fashioned shop in the Stoa Meg-
arou Athinon arcade are shelves and tables
piled high with books. Good for publications in French and other languages, too.
Pantelides, 11 Amerikis (tel: 362 3673).

Tourist Information

In Greece

The 24-hour Tourist Police number in Athens is **171**.

The Athens headquarters of the Greek National Tourist Organisation (GNTO or EOT in Greece) is located at 2 Amerikis Street (tel: 322 3111-19). Visiting hours are from Monday–Friday 12–2.30pm. There is also an information desk at the East Air Terminal which is open during the day and displays ferryboat sailings even when closed. Most general literature (maps, hotel information, etc.) can be obtained from the two information bureaus located in Syntagma Square, which also post daily sailings of ferries from Piraeus.

Inside the National Bank of Greece, 2 Karageorgi Servias Street (tel: 322 2545). Open Monday–Friday 8am–2pm and 3.30–8pm; Saturday 9am–2pm. Piraeus: Marina Zeas, ntog building (tel: 413 5716/413 4709).

Island Tourist Offices

At least one-third of all the islands operate unofficial tourist information centres from June until September. These are prominently sited in the centre of the main harbour town and often located in picturesque buildings, i.e. a windmill on Páros, a clocktower on Symi. They serve the usual function of all tourist information centres, and some can even help with accommodation. These information centres are not to be confused with the numerous ticket and tourist agencies at every port and promenade. The latter are run by private individuals, usually to promote excursions and activities of their own. Although they may be helpful and provide details when asked, information from tourist agencies is not comprehensive. Occasionally, this will be the only office on an island where anyone speaks English.

Most islands also devote a special section of the police force to deal solely with visitors and their requirements. This division of the police force is called the Tourist Police. They, too, can help with accommodation. For a list of Tourist Police telephone numbers on the islands, see the section on *Emergencies*. The larger islands have proper, authorised tourist information centres. Although opening times vary with the island and the season, a weekday visit in the morning between 9am and 1pm is sure to find them open.

Corfu: The Governor's House, Diikitirion Kerkyras (tel: 0661 30298/30360).
Cephalonia: Information Office, Argostoli (tel: 0671 22847).
Sýros: Ermoupolis (tel: 0281 26725/22375).
Kos: Information Office, Akti Koundourioti (tel: 0242 28724/24460).
Rhodes: Archbishop Makarios & Papagou Street, Rhodes Town (tel: 0241 23655/23255/27466); City of Rhodes Information (tel: 0241 35945); Lindos Information Office (tel: 0244 31428).
Sámos: Central Tourist Office (tel: 0273 28582/28530).
Crete: Hania: 40 Kriari Street (tel: 0821 26426/42624).
Irákleion: 1 Xanthoulidou Street (tel: 081 228203/228225). Information office tel: (081) 228203.
Réthymnon: El. Venizelou Av (tel: 0831 29148/24143).

Embassies

All embassies are open from Monday through Friday, usually from 8am until 2pm.

Argentina: 59 Vas. Sofias Avenue, Athens (tel: 722 4753).
Australia: 37 D. Soutsou Street, Athens (tel: 644 7303).
Austria: 26 Alexandras Avenue, Athens (tel: 821 1036).
Belgium: 3 Sekeri Street, Athens (tel: 361 7886-7).
Canada: 4 Genadiou Street, Athens (tel: 723 9511-9).
China: 2a Krinon Street, Paleo Psihiko (tel: 672 3282).
Cyprus: 16 Herodotou Street, Athens (tel: 723 7883).
Denmark: 7 Vasilissis Sophias Avenue (tel: 360 8315).
Finland: 1 Eratosthenous Street, Athens (tel: 701 2122).
France: 7 Vas. Sofias Avenue, Athens (tel: 729 0151-6).
Germany: 10 Vas. Sofias, Maroussi (tel: 36941).
India: 4 Meleagrou Street, Athens (tel: 721 6227).
Ireland: 7 Vas. Constantinou SE, Athens (tel: 723 2771).
Israel: 1 Marathonodromou Street, Paleo Psihiko (tel: 671 9530-1).
Italy: 2 Sekeri Street, Athens (tel: 361 1722-3).
Japan: 2–4 Mesogeion Avenue, Athens (tel: 775 8101-3).

Morocco: 14 Mousson Street, Paleo Psihiko (tel: 647 4209).
Netherlands: 5–7 Vas. Constantino Street, Athens (tel: 723 9701-4).
New Zealand: 15–17 An. Antosha Street Athens (tel: 641 0311-5).
Norway: 7 Vas. Constantinou Street, Athens (tel: 724 6173-4).
Portugal: 19 Loukianou Street, Athen (tel: 729 0096).
Spain: 29 Vas. Sofias Avenue, Athens (tel: 721 4885).
Sweden: 7 Vas. Constantinou Street, Athens (tel: 729 0421).
Switzerland: 2 Iassiou Street, Athens (tel: 723 0364-6).
Turkey: 8 Vas. Georgiou Street, Athen (tel: 724 5915-7).
United Kingdom: 1 Ploutarchou Street Athens (tel: 723 6211-9).
United States of America: 91 Vas. Sofias Avenue, Athens (tel: 721 2951-9).

Getting Around

From The Airport

To Athens

By taxi: From the airport the taxi fare to Athens costs around 2,000 drachmas Many charter flights to Athens arrive at the East Terminal in the early hours of the morning. For each piece of luggage there is an extra drachma charge.

By bus: From the East Terminal, Express lines A and B travel into Syntagma or Omonia Squares every 20 minutes from 6am to midnight. The fare is 300 drachmas. From midnight to 6am the buses run every hour and the fare is 300 drachmas. From the West Terminal the fares and the hours are the same; the buses, however are marked A and B with a diagonal slash through each letter.

To Piraeus

By taxi: From the East and West Terminals to Piraeus the taxi fare costs about 2,000 drachmas. From the centre of Athens to Piraeus, expect to pay around the same amount.

By bus: From the East Terminal to Piraeus the Express line No. 19 runs every [ ] minutes from 6am to 12 midnight. [f]rom 12 midnight to 6am buses run eve[ry] 90 minutes. From the West Terminal, [ca]tch the same No. 19 bus, as the Express [li]ne makes one continuous "loop". The [jo]urney is a slow one, but the only alter[n]ative is a taxi.

By metro: It is possible to get to Piraeus in about 25 minutes by catching one [of] the clean, tidy and safe metro trains. [T]he stations nearest centre of Athens are [V]ictoria, Omonia, Monastiraki, Thissio. [T]he fare is cheap and the metro is open [un]til around midnight.

Domestic Travel

[T]ravelling on one of the domestic planes [o]perated by Olympic Airways to an island [is] a delightful alternative to the ferryboat. [T]he air fare, by European standards, is in[ex]pensive, and the time saved is huge: it [ca]n take up to 8 hours to sail from Piraeu[s] to Mýkonos; only 50 minutes to fly. [T]he flights are fun, too; the planes too [ti]ny (sometimes only 16 seats) to treat the [jo]urney as anything but a bus ride in the [sk]y. Carry your own luggage aboard, [st]ore it where possible, then grab a win[d]ow seat for a magnificent view of low[-ly]ing hills, sparkling seas, and evocative [is]lets crowned by chapels. Upon arrival, a [m]odern or a dilapidated bus will transfer [y]ou to the principal harbour town. There [is] sometimes a fee, sometimes not.

There are drawbacks to inland air [tr]avel, however. Demand can be greater [th]an the number of seats, and having a [ti]cket doesn't guard against being uncer[e]moniously bumped when you arrive at [th]e West Terminal. (During the summer, [A]thenians with island homes "block [b]ook" seats, often more than 2 months [a]head. Tourists rate as a low priority [w]hen it comes to check-in.) The domes[ti]c terminal itself is chaotic and confus[i]ng; check-in desks seem to appear or [d]isappear at whim. Remote islands like [K]assos can, at the height of the season, [b]e almost impossible to reach, as planes [a]re cancelled due to bad weather, indus[t]rial action or at the whim of the gods. [W]hen they do take-off, it is occasional[l]y ahead of schedule, so be sure to arrive [w]ell in advance. Ferryboats are more [r]eliable in every respect.

Having said that, if you approach do[m]estic air travel as a treat rather than as [a] necessity and actually do achieve take-

off, the experience is a delight. Early morning flights have the most advantages. Not only do you gain extra time to book on the next flight if you get bumped, but flying into the sun as it rises over the Aegean, or arriving on Mýkonos in time to watch the revellers go to bed and the old ladies sweep the streets clean, is an island adventure on its own. Pick up a timetable and reserve seats at any Olympic Airways office. The headquarters is at 96 Syngrou Avenue (tel: 929 2111). The most central office is at 6 Othonos Street, Syntagma Square (tel: 929 2489). Major credit cards accepted.

Water Transport

Ferries

Advanced ferry schedules are listed in the *Greek Travel Pages* which can be purchased in the bookstore Eleftheroudakis at 4 Nikis, behind Syntagma Square. Revised ferry schedules are published weekly, and given out at Tourist Information Offices. Most offices hang a schedule in a conspicuous place, so even though the desk itself might be closed the information is still obtainable.

Unless you want a berth or first class seat, there is no need to buy a seat in advance. Simply arrive at Piraeus a couple of hours before departure and cruise the various ticket agencies. Agencies handle different boats which are often sailing to the same destinations at the same times. Many agents will claim "their" boat is the quickest, most powerful, sometimes the only way to get to an island that day. Do some shopping around; it pays off. Cynical travellers will add at least 1 hour to the time any Greek claims it takes to sail to a specific destination.

Once aboard, position yourself on the top deck for sun-bathing *after* the boat has left the harbour and turned around; otherwise, you may find yourself in the shade. Food, bought beforehand, is a better idea than eating in one of the snack bars, although should you find yourself on a long cruise in an older ferry, dinner in the first-class dining room provides a touch of shabby ambience. Bring plenty to read, and prepare for a mild dose of seasickness on any journey longer than 8 hours; the Aegean can be rough.

Although the situation is improving, catching a ferry on one island to sail to a distant island can be a frustrating experience. Ferries may arrive 2, 3, even 5

hours late, but to leave the port is to chance missing the boat entirely. Just occasionally, the boat can arrive early, and there is no guarantee it will wait until the scheduled departure time to leave. The only way to guarantee accurate, up-to-the-minute information on the erratic ways of ferryboats is to contact the Port Authority, which can (and does) monitor the movements of individual boats. Port Authority offices are usually located on the far end of the waterfront of each island's principal harbour, away from the cafés and boutiques. It would help to ask a Greek-speaking person to do the enquiring, as English is not widespread.

Port Authority telephone numbers are as follows (if dialling from Athens, locate the island area code in the *Emergency* section under island police stations on page 311).

Ionian Islands:
Corfu – tel: 39918
Ithaki – tel: 32909
Cephalonia – tel: 22224
Paxos – tel: 31259
Zákynthos – tel: 22417

Saronic Gulf Islands:
Aegina – tel: 22328
Hydra – tel: 52279
Póros – tel: 22274
Salamis – tel: 465 3252
Spétses – tel: 72245

Cyclades Islands:
Andros – tel: 22250
Ios – tel: 91264
Kéa – tel: 31344
Kýthnos – tel: 31290
Mílos – tel: 41607
Mýkonos – tel: 22218
Náxos – tel: 22300
Páros – tel: 21240
Santoríni – tel: 22239
Serifos – tel: 51470
Sífnos – tel: 31617
Sýros – tel: 22690
Tínos – tel: 22348

Sporades Islands:
Skiáthos – tel: 22017
Skópelos – tel: 22180
Skýros – tel: 91475

Northeast Aegean Islands:
Chíos – tel: 23097
Lésvos – tel: 28647
Límnos – tel: 22225
Sámos – tel: 27318

Samothraki – tel: 41305
Thássos – tel: 22106

Dodecanese Islands:
Astypalea – tel: 61208
Kálymnos – tel: 29304
Kárpathos – tel: 22227
Kassos – tel: 41288
Kos – tel: 28507
Leros – tel: 22224
Nissyros – tel: 31222
Patmos – tel: 31231
Rhodes – tel: 27690

Crete:
Ag. Nikólaos – tel: 22312
Chaniá – tel: 22600
Irákleion – tel: 82002
Kasteli – tel: 22024
Sitia – tel: 22310

The telephone number for the Port Authority in Piraeus is 451 1311 or 452 7107 (Zea Marina). For more information on island hopping by ferry, see *Island hopping* on page 76, and *Coping with Piraeus* on page 118.

Hydrofoils

Hydrofoils ("Flying Dolphins") are twice as quick and twice as expensive as ferryboats. A service between Piraeus and the Saronic Gulf Islands continues throughout the year. Seasonally (from around May to October), hydrofoils connect islands in the Sporades and northern Dodecanese, and eastern Aegean (Rhodes to Patmos, Sámos, Kos, Chíos, Lésvos, Límnos). Modern hydrofoils show videos and have bar facilities, but rough seas and bumpy rides are common. As hydrofoils need a calm sea to travel, they are prone to cancellation due to weather or technical difficulties.

Public Transport

Buses

Island buses can be converted school buses or modern coaches, or even farm equipment called into service to transport tourists. Some drivers ricochet through mountain roads at death-defying speeds; accidents, however, appear to be rare. Just stow your luggage carefully to be on the safe side.

Almost without exception, a bus of some description will meet arriving ferryboats (even if a boat is delayed) to trans-
port passengers up the hill to the island's Chóra, or capital. Bus stops are usually in main squares or by the waterfront in harbours and vehicles may or may not run to schedule. A conductor dispenses tickets on the bus itself; often the fare required and the stamped ticket will not be the same price. This isn't a con, but merely a practice. Island companies use pre-printed tickets until the supply is gone, which may take several years.

Taxis

Taxis in Greece, especially in Athens, merit a guidebook to themselves. It may well be that your taxi "experience" will figure among the most prominent memories of your holiday. Perhaps the Greek taxi experience is best divided into three stages for analytical purposes.

First: getting a taxi. It's nearly impossible at certain times of the day, and probably worst before the early afternoon meal. When you hail a taxi, try to get in before stating your destination. The drivers are very picky and often won't let you in unless you're going in their direction. If you have to say it, say it loudly and clearly (and with the right accents) as they may well otherwise just pass you by. If you see an empty taxi, run for it, be aggressive – otherwise you'll find that some quick Athenian has beaten you to it.

Second: the ride. Make sure the taxi meter is on when you start out, and not on "2" – that's the double-fare which is only permitted from 1am to 5am. Once inside, you may find yourself with company. Don't be alarmed. It is traditional practice for drivers to pick up two, three, even four individual riders, provided they're going roughly in the same direction. In these cases, make a note of what the meter-count is. In fact, because taxis are so cheap they can end up functioning as mini-bus services. Packed in with a Greek mother with her shopping bags overflowing with groceries, a chic businessman and a radical bohemian university student, you may find yourself in the middle (literally) of some rather interesting conversations. If, however, you are alone you may find yourself chatting with an ex-seaman who tells you a few yarns from his days in the United States, or perhaps with a driver who speaks no English at all.

Third: paying up. If you've travelled with company, make sure you aren't paying for that part of the trip that happened before you got in. Otherwise the meter
will tell you the straight price which may be adjusted according to the following tariff regulations.

Some drivers will quote you the fair price, others will try to rip you off. If the price is clearly above the correct price, don't hesitate to argue your way, in whichever language, back down to a normal price.

Obviously these rules apply more to Athens than to the islands, although it's still necessary to be pretty aggressive on Crete and Rhodes. On the smaller islands expect to share your taxi, not only with the aforementioned group of passengers but also an animal or two.

In recent years various Radio Taxi services have started up in Athens. They can pick you up within a short time of your call. These taxis, however, are more expensive than the regular ones.

Private Transport

Cars

Car hire and petrol is expensive in Greece and taking your car to the islands is not recommended. Only Crete, Rhodes and perhaps Lésvos, Kos and Corfu could benefit from having a car at your disposal, otherwise it's more fun to rely on island buses and taxis. At island airports and at the ticket agencies on the waterfront are desks manned by the major car hire firms. Shop around for the best price.

The Automobile and Touring Club of Greece (ELPA) provides foreign motorists with assistance and information. Offices in Crete can be found in Chaniá at Apokoronou & Skoula streets (tel: 082/26059) and in Irákleion at Knossós Avenue & G. Papandreou Street (tel: 081/289440). In Athens ELPA offices are located at 2–4 Messoghion Avenue (tel: 779 1615) and at 6 Amerikis & Panepistimiou streets (tel: 363 8632).

Driving a car in Athens is unpleasant and confusing. Greek tempers are short and road signs practically non-existent. Cars are, however, fun for daytrips out of the city. Avis, Hertz and Budget cars all have rental desks at both the East and West air terminals. Otherwise, head for Syngrou Avenue in town, which is choc-a-block with car hire firms.

Avis, 46–48 Amaias Avenue (tel: 923 8822/922 3760).
Budget, 8 Singrou Avenue (tel: 921 4771-3).

Hertz, 12 Singrou Avenue (tel: 922 102-4).

Just Rent A Car, 43 Singrou Avenue (tel: 923 9104).

Speedo Rent A Car, 8 Singrou Avenue (tel: 922 6102).

Thrifty Rent A Car, 24 Singrou Avenue (tel: 922 1211-3).

Motorcycles, Bicycles and Scooters

On most islands you'll find agencies that rent small motorcycles, bicycles and various types of scooters. For a reasonable price they give you the freedom to wander independently and also to delight in the smell of a place, impossible on buses or in cars. For longer periods, rates are cheaper than for 1-day rentals. Before setting off, however, make sure your vehicle actually works. Ask to take it for a test spin down the street (be on the lookout for lethal "staircase" alleys). Otherwise you may get stuck with a lemon or, worse, they may hold you responsible for its malfunctions when you return it. Above all, be careful. More than one holiday in Greece has been ruined by very nasty moped accidents. Wear protective clothing and check that your holiday insurance covers any problems.

In Athens, motorbikes and bicycles can be hired from two companies: Meidanis Rent A Moto at 4 Dion, Areopagitou Street (tel: 323 2346), and at Motorent, 5 Falirou Street (tel: 923 4939).

Where To Stay

Hotels

The Greek National Tourist Organisation governs the construction and classification of all hotels. The classification awarded is determined by the size of the rooms, size of public area including lobby, decor and furnishings of the rooms and services provided by the hotel. All hotel accommodation is divided into classes: deluxe (luxury class), then classes A–E. The price in each category is fixed, i.e., an A-class hotel will always cost more than a B-class hotel, even with seasonal variations in price. As

the classifications are so formal, anyone who rates charm above lobby space, or yoghurt and honey above an all-inclusive breakfast, will probably be just as happy in a lower-class hotel as in one of the deluxe versions; almost all accommodation from C-class upwards can be guaranteed to have a high standard of cleanliness.

NTOG offices around the world can help with accommodation. See *Useful Addresses* on page 310 for names and addresses of international NTOG offices. All NTOG offices receive pamphlets on each island chain which gives information on hotels in the A–C classes; these are available free to anyone who asks for them.

Hotel reservations can be made in writing directly to the hotel; in writing to the Hellenic Chamber of Hotels, 6 Aristidou Street, Athens; or in person by calling in at the Hellenic Chamber of Hotels at 2 Stadiou and Karageorgi Servias Street, inside the National Bank of Greece at Syntagma Square.

There is normally a 10 percent increase for a stay less than 3 nights and a larger increase for an extra bed in the room. Tax and VAT are added.

Athens

DELUXE CLASS

Astir Palace, Vas. Sofias & El. Venizelou corner, 10671 Athens. Syntagma Square area (tel: 364 3112). All rooms with TV and video, newsstand, sauna, health care, beauty parlour, conference and banquet facilities, gourmet restaurant, bar and coffee shop.

Athenaeum Inter-Continental, 89–93 Syngrou Avenue, 11745 Athens (tel: 902 3666). Air-conditioned throughout, two bars, three restaurants, swimming pool, TV in all rooms with in-house movies, health studio, bank facilities.

Athens Hilton, 50 Michalakopoulou Street, 11528 Athens (tel: 724 8322). Air-conditioned, central heating, American bar, restaurant, coffee shop, discotheque, bowling.

Grande Bretagne, Syntagma Square, 10563 Athens (tel: 323 0251). Lovely building with a distinguished history. 450 rooms plus 25 suites. Air-conditioned, central heating, two bars, three restaurants, convention and function facilities.

Ledra Marriott Hotel, 115 Syngrou Avenue, 11745 Athens (tel: 952 5211). All rooms have individual climate control, radio and colour TV, in-room movies, mini-bar, rooftop swimming pool, hy-

drotherapy pool, three restaurants and a ballroom.

CLASS A HOTELS

Acropolis View, 10 Galli & Webster streets, 11742 Athens (tel: 921 7303). Small hotel with roof garden, central heating, air-conditioning, bar, restaurant.

Electra Palace, 18 Nikodimou Street, 10557 Athens (tel: 324 1401). Swimming pool and rooftop garden, cosy, nicely furnished bedrooms, which are air-conditioned throughout, pleasant bathrooms.

Golden Age, 57 Michalakopoulos Street, 11528 Athens (tel: 724 0861). Near the Hilton Hotel, air-conditioned, mini-bar in every room, restaurant and taverna.

Novotel Mirayia Athenes, 4–6 Michail Voda Street, 10439 Athens (tel: 862 7133). An underground car park, roof garden with swimming pool, mini-bar in rooms, satellite colour TV and radio in all rooms.

Zafolia, 87–89 Alexandras Avenue, 11474 Athens (tel: 644 9012). Bar, restaurant, roof garden, swimming pool, room service.

CLASS B HOTELS

Acropolis House, 6–8 Kodrou, Plaka (tel: 322 2344). A favourite with academics and writers, this pension was once a family mansion. Warm, friendly atmosphere with good conversation in the lobby.

Adonis Hotel, Voulis & 3 Kodrou, Plaka (tel: 324 9737). Just across the pedestrian street from the Acropolis House, this sweet and functional pension serves breakfast on the roof which overlooks the Acropolis. The reception staff are unfailingly helpful and friendly.

Athenian Inn, 22 Haritos, Athens (tel: 723 8097). Just two blocks from fashionable Kolonaki Square, this family-run pension is pretty and rustic, with an open fire, paintings on the wall by local artists, and wall-to-wall carpets in the bedrooms.

Athens Gate, 10 Syngrou Avenue, 11742 Athens (tel: 923 8302). Near the Temple of Olympian Zeus and not far from Syntagma Square, this modern hotel has a roof garden restaurant with a stunning view, spacious rooms (some with terraces offering the same panorama), and serving American-style buffet breakfasts.

Omiros Hotel, 15 Apollonos Street, 10557 Athens (tel: 323 5486). In a street filled with hotels just on the edge of Plaka, this handy little place has the charm of an old world taverna and is efficient, too.

CLASS C HOTEL

Aphrodite Hotel, 21 Apollonos Street, 10557 Athens (tel: 323 4357). A better-than-average C class hotel, with air-conditioning (uncommon even in many B class hotels), polite staff, room telephones, large lobby with bar and good, buffet-style breakfast for a small fee. The rooms on the top floors in the rear offer lovely views of tiled roofs and the Acropolis. Roof garden in summer.

Attalos Hotel, 29 Athinas Street, 10554 Athens (tel: 321 2801). All rooms have a balcony, telephone, and some a view of the Acropolis. Roof garden bar.

Nicola, 14 Olenou Street, 11362 Athens (tel: 883 7911). Bar on a 24-hour basis, room service, attractive roof garden, TV and video room.

Phaedre Hotel, 16 Cherefontos Street, Athens (tel: 323 8461). The relatively large rooms in the front overlook towering palm trees and a lovely church; the scene is so tranquil during siesta it's impossible to believe the hotel is only a couple of blocks from the noisiest part of Plaka. But the olde worlde charm continues inside the hotel, too – unfortunately, none of the rooms has a private bathroom, just a sink.

The Ionian Islands

Corfu

Avoid the hotels on Kanoni, too close to the airport for peace.

Corfu Palace Hotel, in town (tel: 0661 39485). Plush, expensive.

Arkadion, in town (tel: 0661 37671). Quite basic.

Aiolos Beach bungalows at Perama, just 8.5 km (5 miles) south of Corfu town. Private beach, bungalows.

Léfkas

Léfkas Hotel (tel: 0645 23916). Almost kitsch architecture, relatively new, clean, and the less expensive.

Nirikos Hotel next door, both in town (tel: 0645 24132).

Ithaki

Nostos Hotel, Frikes (tel: 0674 31644). New, simple, good.

Hotel Kioni, in Kioni (tel: 0674 31362). New, simple, good.

Rooms available through **Greek Islands Club** (tel: 0932 220 477).

Cephalonia

Mouikis Hotel, Argostoli (tel: 0671 23032). Very nice.

Miramare Hotel, Argostoli (tel: 0671 25511).

Zákynthos

Hotel Diana, Zákynthos town (tel: 0695 28547). Good, inexpensive.

Hotel Bitzaro, Zákynthos town (tel: 0695 23644).

Villa Meltemi, Limni Keriou (tel: 0695 33366). Beautiful location.

Saronic Gulf Islands

Aegina

Nafsika Bungalows, edge of Aegina town (tel: 0297 22477).

Danae Hotel, edge of Aegina town (tel: 0297 251 47).

Póros

Seven Brothers Hotel, in Póros town near harbour (tel: 0298 23412). Clean, well run, reasonable price.

Pavlou Hotel, 2 km (1 mile) from town (tel: 0298 22734).

Hydra

Orloff Guest House (tel: 0298 525 64).

Spétses

Spétses Hotel (tel: 0298 76202).

Cyclades Islands

Santoríni

Atlantis, Fira (tel: 0286 22232). Elegant hotel with magnificent view.

Galini, Firostefani, (tel: 0286 22336).

Atlantis Villas, Oia (tel: 0286 71214). Luxurious.

Bellonia Villas, Kamara (tel: 0286 31138). On the black beach.

Folegandros

Polikantia, in Chora (tel: 0286 41322).

Sikinos

Porto Sikinos (tel: 0286 51220). Bungalows on beach, good, reasonably expensive.

Kamares (tel: 0286 51281). Less expensive

Náxos

Chateau Zevgoli, Chora (tel: 0285 22993).

Anixi, Chora, Kastro (tel: 0285 22112).

Páros

Xenia, Paroikia (tel: 0284 21394).

Pandrosos, Paroikia (tel: 0284 22903).

Svoronos Bungalows, Naoussa (tel: 0284 51211).

Antíparos

Galini Hotel, Chora (tel: 0284 61420).

Mykonos

Kouneni Hotel, Chora (tel: 0289 22301). Quiet, with garden.

Despotiko Hotel, Chora (tel: 0289 22009).

Elysium, near Chora (tel: 0289 23952). Luxurious.

Cavo Tagoo, San Stefano (tel: 0289 23692). Jet set luxurious.

Syros

Omiros, Ermoupolis (tel: 0281 24910). In old mansion, port view.

Europe, Ermoupolis (tel: 0281 28771).

Nisaki Hotel, Ermoupolis (tel: 0281 28200). Convenient, inexpensive.

Tínos

Meltemi Hotel (tel: 0283 22881). Inexpensive, convenient, attractive.

Alonia Hotel, on the road east out of Chora (tel: 0283 23541).

Andros

Perrakis, between Gavrion and Batsi (tel: 0282 71456). On beach.

Epaminonda's, in Batsi (tel: 0282 41177).

Mílos

Venus Village, in Adamas (tel: 0287 22030).

Kapetan Tasos Apartments, Pollonia (tel: 0287 41287).

Sífnos

Artemonas Hotel, in Artemonas (tel: 0284 31587). Simple, beautiful.

Platys Yialos Hotel, in Platys Yialos (tel:

284 31224). Large, Cycladic style hotel at far end of beach.

Sporades Islands

Skiáthos

Atrium Hotel, in Platanias (tel: 0427 49345). Casual elegance, with traditional architecture, resembles monastery. Chic, beautiful, expensive.
Bourtzi Hotel (tel: 0427 21304) and **Pothos Hotel** (tel: 0427 22694), both in Skiathos town, clean, simple moderate price.

Skópelos

Kyr Sotos Hotel, in town (tel: 0424 22549). Remodeled family house set on the waterfront, inexpensive, casual and tiny rooms.
Adrina Beach, Panormos (tel: 0424 233 73-5). Casual elegance, private beach, expensive.

Alonissos

Galaxias Hotel, in Patitiri (tel: 0424 65251).
Paradeisos Hotel, in Patitiri (tel: 0424 65160).

Skyros

Skýros Palace, Yirismata Beach, at Molos (tel: 0222 91994).
Xenia, at Molos, on beach (tel: 0222 91209).
Ask at Skyros Travel (tel: 0222 91123) for a place to stay.

NE Aegean Islands

Límnos

Akti Myrina, in Myrina (tel: 0254 22681). Elegant, very expensive bungalows.
Aphrodite Apartments, in Myrina (tel: 0254 23489).

Lésvos

Villa 1900, Mytilini town (tel: 0251 23448). In restored neoclassical mansion.
Vatera Beach, in Vatera (tel: 0252 61212).

Sámos

Olympia Beach, Kokkari (tel: 0273 92420). Small hotel facing beach.

Olympia Village, Kokkari. Apartments, same management as Olympia Beach.
Christian Hotel, Ano Vathy (tel: 0273 23084).
Galini Hotel, Pythagorio (tel: 0273 61 167). New, small, quiet hotel.

Dodecanese

Rhodes

Andreas Hotel (tel: 0241 34156).
Casa de la Sera (tel: 0241 75154).
S. Nikolis Hotel (tel: 0241 34561), in ascending order of price, are probably the best three choices of perhaps two dozen in the old town.

Kárpathos

Blue Bay Hotel, in Pighadia (tel: 0245 22479). Comfortable and near the beach.
Kárpathos Hotel, inland (tel: 0245 22347). More modest.
Aphrodite, in Olympos (tel: 02435 51454).

Kassos

Anessis (tel: 0245 41234) and **Anagenessis** (tel: 1245 41495), modest though they are, represent nearly half the beds available.

Kastellorizo

Megisti Hotel (tel: 0241 49272) is overpriced but the only really luxurious place, at the north end of the waterfront.
The **Mavrothalassidis** (tel: 0241 49202) pension in town is the only more modest place with en suite plumbing.

Tilos

Eirini Hotel, Livadia (tel: 0241 44293). Best hotel on island, used by tour groups.
Livadia (tel: 0241 202), newly upgraded, is good value, especially the upper floor "suites".

Symi

Chorio, in the Chorio (tel: 0241 71800).
Aliki (tel: 0241 71665). Swankier, next to the clocktower on the quay.

Chálki

The Captain's House (tel: 0241 57201), English-and-Greek-run, is good.

If full of tour groups try **Pension Kleanthi** (tel: 0241 37648).

Nissyros

Porfyris Hotel, Mandraki, inland (tel: 0242 31376). Comfortable, with a good swimming pool.
Pension Drosia, Mandraki (tel: 0242 31328). Simple, right on the sea.

Kos

Pension Alexis, in main town (tel: 0242 28798).
Afendoulis, in main town (tel: 0242 25321).

Kálymnos

The Panorama (tel: 0243 23128) lives up to its name at moderate prices.
Greek House Pension, nearby in the same district of Amoudhara (tel: 0243 23752). Doesn't have views but is excellent value.

Telendos

Most establishments here – surprisingly numerous for such a small place – are taverna-accommodation combos. Try **Uncle George's** (tel: 0243 47502) or **Foukaina Galanomati** (tel: 0243 47401).

Leros

Pension Cavos, in Pandeli (tel: 0247 23247). Reasonable and well sited.
Eleftheria Hotel, in Platanos (tel: 0247 23550). A fairly quiet, comfortable establishment.

Leipsoi

Rooms Panorama (tel: 0247 41279).
Rena's Rooms (tel: 0247 41363).

Patmos

Summer Hotel, in the Hochlaka district of Skala (tel: 0247 31769).
Blue Bay Hotel, just out of Skala on the way to Grikou (tel: 0247 31165).

Crete

Chaniá

Amphora (tel: 0821 42998).
Doma (tel: 0821 21772).

Réthymnon

Hotel Réthymnon Bay (tel: 0932 22859).
Theartemis (tel: 0831 21991). New.

Irákleion

Astoria (tel: 081 229002).
El Greco (tel: 081 181071).
Esperia (tel: 081 288512).
Gramboles (tel: 081 241207).

A list of D and E class hotels can be obtained from offices of the Greek National Tourist Organisation.

Private Rooms

On the islands, the most widespread type of inexpensive accommodation is renting private rooms (*domátia*). These are rented out by local residents at prices controlled by the tourist police. In general, when looking for any kind of accommodation, the tourist police can be of considerable help. If you arrive without any accommodation and none seems to be available, inquire at their office. If you'd like to make a reservation or arrangement in advance call them and they'll often be able to help. For a list of police telephone numbers on individual islands, see *Emergencies* on page 311.

Except at the height of summer, when rooms are scarce, *domátia* can be secured just by stepping off the ferryboat. Housewives meet any and all ferries until late into the evening. "Room? Room?" they will inquire, and a deal is struck there on the spot. The price is normally for the room itself, rather than per bed; a single, therefore, costs the same as a double. Within 10 minutes of the ferry departing the women and the rooms have disappeared. As most accommodation on the islands is clean and perfectly acceptable, upon arrival it might be an idea to take the first room offered for 2 nights (cheaper than 1 night) and shop around in the meantime. Men with rooms to offer, or when a car journey is involved, often bring their children along, a gesture which makes women travelling alone feel more secure.

Pensions

A pension tends to be a casual, family-run establishment, falling somewhere between a private room and a hotel. As the accommodation has been purpose-built, many rooms have balconies and, whenever possible, a sea view. As with hotels, they are divided into classes A–E, but rates tend to be less expensive than hotels. First class pensions are listed in the NTOG hotel guide and can be pre-booked directly. Lists of pensions in lower categories can only be obtained on the spot through the Tourist Police. See *Emergencies* on page 311 for numbers.

Villas & Apartments

Self-catering is increasingly popular in Greece, especially for those holidaying with young children. Villas and apartments are clean, and comfortably, if sparsely, furnished. These, too, are graded according to fixed-price categories. Expect to pay just under the same amount of money for a first class apartment as for a deluxe hotel room.

Rental Agencies

Accommodation Centre, 3 Filelinon Street (tel: 322 0000). Flats in Athens.
Alexander Travel, 4 Stadiou Street (tel: 322 7668). Flats throughout Greece, especially Skiáthos and Corfu.
Ameridian Ltd, Room 63, 3 Filelinon Street (tel: 323 2608). Houses throughout Greece and villas in caves.
Corfu Sun Club (tel: 0661 33855). Self-catering on Corfu.
Polytravel, No. 60, 25th August Street, Irákleion (tel: 081 282476). All types of accommodation throughout Crete.
Skópelos Tours (tel: 0424 22721). Self-catering on Skópelos in the Sporades.
Ikos Travel (tel: 0424 65320). Self-catering on Alonnisos in the Sporades.

Camping

A certain portion of tourists who come to Greece decide to "rough it", although this type of holiday is now being discouraged by the NTOG. Those who want to camp at organised campsites with facilities will find scores of them all over the islands, some run by the NTOG, some by the Greek Touring Club, and many privately. The most beautiful campsites, however, are usually the ones you find on your own. While in most places it is officially illegal just to lay out your sleeping bag or pitch a tent, if you're discrete you'll probably not be bothered. That means asking permission if you seem to be on private property, avoiding "unofficial" campsites set up in popular tourist areas, and always leaving the place looking better than when you came. For a list of official sites contact the NTOG.

Youth Hostels

A member's card is required in order to stay in a Greek Youth Hostel. An international membership card can be obtained by applying to the Greek Youth Hostels Association located at 4 Dragatsaniou Street, 10559 Athens (tel: 323 4107).

Athens

Athens Youth Hostels are located at:
1, Agiou Meletinou & 57 Kipselis Street, Kipseli (tel: 822 5860).
Alexandras Avenue & Drossi Street (tel: 646 3669).
52 Peoniou Street, Stathmos Larissis (tel: 883 2878).
75 Damareos Street, Pangrati (tel: 751 9530).
YWCA Youth Hostel, 11 Amerikis Street (tel: 362 6180).

Crete

Chaniá Youth Hostel, 33 Drakonianou Street (tel: 0821 53565).
Irákleion Youth Hostel, 24 Handakos Street (tel: 081 222947).
Malia Youth Hostel, Malia Beach (36 km/22 miles from Iraklion) (tel: 081 285075).
Réthymnon Youth Hostel, 4 Therissou Street (tel: 0831 22848).

Ionian Islands

Kontokali Youth Hostel, Kontokali beach, Corfu (tel: 0661 91202).

Cyclades Islands

Santoríni Youth Hostel, Kontohori, Aghios Eleftherios (tel: 0286 22722).

Monasteries/ Settlements

Monasteries and convents can occasionally provide refuge for the adventurous and solitary traveller. Enquiries must be conducted on the spot, or through a specific island's Tourist Police (see page 314). Remember that you must dress and behave according to their rules; no shorts and skirts for women. The doors may be closed as early as sunset and some kind of donation may be expected.

Traditional settlements are villages recognised by the Greek government as forming an important part of the national heritage. Buildings in these villages have been restored and set up by the NTOG for tourist use. At the moment there are four on the islands: on Santoríni, on Chíos, on Cephalonia, and on the tiny islet Psará. For information write to the NTOG at EOT Diéfthynsis Ekmetalefseos, 2 Amerikis Street, Athens 10564 (tel: 322 3111-7).

Eating Out

What To Eat

Dining out in Greece is a social affair. Whether it is with family or *parea*, that special circle of friends, a meal out is an occasion to celebrate, a time for *kefi*. This may have something to do with the fact that eating out continues to be affordable and popular, not something restricted to those who have American Express cards. And the predominance of the taverna, that bastion of Greek cuisine, reflects this popularity. These casual eating establishments have more or less the same style and setting throughout Greece, and the menu is similar. Which is to say no frills, no packaging which tries to convince the "consumer" that this taverna is different from the others, special, distinct. The place, and your being there, is somehow taken for granted: you eat the good food at Yanni's or Yorgos's, you enjoy yourself, and you don't pay an arm and a leg for it.

There is, of course, some variation. The taverna is by no means the only kind of eating establishment. You'll also encounter: the *estiatório*, a more conventional restaurant – fancier and more polished than the taverna, with linen tablecloths and higher prices; the *psistariá*, a barbeque-style restaurant which specialises in lamb, pork or chicken on a spit; the *psarotavérna* which specialises in fish; the *ouzerí* which is mainly an establishment for drinking, but which also serves *mezédes*, snacks of various types; the *yíros*

stand with *hiro* sandwiches and the ubiquitous *souvláki* stand, sometimes a sit-down place with salads, sometimes a take-away on the corner.

There's also regional variety in Greek cuisine and you should keep an eye out for those specialties of the house which you haven't seen before. Another thing is how strikingly different the same dish can be when it's prepared well or prepared badly, for example, a *meletzanosaláta*, or stuffed tomatoes. It's worth shopping around in heavily touristed areas for the best taverna, asking the locals where they eat. Even better – invite a Greek to dinner; the food is bound to improve immeasurably.

A few notes about Greek eating habits. The main meal is eaten at midday, between 1.30pm and 2.30pm and is usually followed by a siesta break lasting until 6pm. The evening meal can either be another full meal, or an assortment of *mezédes*. This is eaten late, between 9pm and 11pm. (Breakfast in Greece is rather meagre, usually consisting of bread, butter, jam and coffee. Try ordering yoghurt and honey as a delicious alternative.)

Greeks never simply "go out drinking". Even if an evening involves heavy drinking of retsina or ouzo, there will be accompanied by food – a habit which minimises the effects (and after-effects) of the alcohol. When it comes to ordering wine, check to see if they serve wine from the barrel (ask for *chíma*). *Aspro* is white wine, *mávro* is red, and *kokkinélli* is rosé.

Greek Foods

Here is a partial list of the more popular foods you'll find in Greece.

Starters

Starters are usually eaten as appetizers with bread (*psomí*).

kolokithákia – deep-fried courgette (zucchini)
melitsanosaláta – aubergine (eggplant) dip
rossikisaláta – cold potato salad with lots of mayonnaise
taramasaláta – fish roe pate/dip
tzatzíki – yoghurt/cucumber dip, heavy on the garlic

Vegetables

anginares – artichokes
arakádes – peas
bámies – okra

dolmádes – stuffed grape leaves
fasolákia – snap beans
choriátiki – "Greek" salad
maróuli – lettuce
patzária – beetroot (beets)
yemistés – stuffed tomatoes or peppers
yígandes – large haricot beans

Meats

Note the following terms: *psitó* – roasted; *sti soúvla* – barbecued on the spit; *tiganitó* – fried; *sto foúrno* – baked; *skáras* – grilled; *vrastó* – boiled; *kapnistó* – smoked
arní – lamb
biftéki – beefsteak
brizóla – pork or beef chop
keftédes – meatballs
kokorétsi – stuffed innards, spit-roasted
kotópoulo – chicken
loukániko – sausages
mialó – brain
paidákia – lamb chops
sikóti – liver
souvláki – chunks of lamb or pork, spit-roasted

Soups & Specialities

avgolémono – chicken stock with egg and lemon
fasoláda – bean soup
moussaká – aubergine (eggplant) and ground beef casserole
pastítsio – macaroni casserole
patsás – tripe stew sold at special stalls
salingária – snails
stifádo – any kind of stew, stewed meat
soutzoukákia – baked meat rolls
yiouvarlákia – meat-and-rice balls

Seafood

astakós – lobster
bakaliáros – cod
galéos – shark meat
garídes – shrimp
glóssa – sole
kalamária – squid
ksifías – swordfish
ktapódi – octopus
péstrofa – trout
sinagrída – red snapper

Desserts

Rarely will you find dessert served where you eat dinner. You'll find sweets instead at *zacharoplastía* (sweet shops) and some *galaktopolía* (dairy stores).

baklavá – fillo dough leaves, honey, nuts

kataífi – nuts and honey wrapped in shredded wheat

kréma – plain custard

loukoúmi – Turkish delight

moustalevriá – grape pudding (autumn)

rizógalo – rice pudding

Snacks

kalambóki – corn

kástana – roast chestnuts, sold at stalls

kouloúria – sesame-sprinkled "pretzels"

kreatópita – meat pie

spanakópita – spinach pie

tirópita – cheese pie

tost – toasted sandwiches sold at stalls

Other Useful Words

aláti – salt and *pipéri* (pepper)

boukáli – bottle

potíri – glass

piroúni – fork

koutáli – spoon

machéri – knife

katálogo/lista – menu

to logariasmó – the bill

Where To Eat

Island cuisine can be more than just *moussaká*. Stelios Platonos, the proprietor of the two excellent restaurants called Kalamaras in London's Notting Hill Gate, is passionate on the subject of Greek home cooking, and plans to open a food museum on his native island of Páros. But island cooking holds a few surprises. Seafood can be difficult to find, even impossible on some remote islands, and is quite expensive by local standards. The Aegean has been over-fished, and often the proceeds of a successful day are sent straight to Athens or the large island hotels. The most sensible thing to do is to walk into the café kitchens and see what's cooking. This is a respectable island practice, although it must be said that in out-of-the-way tavernas, the evening meal might merely be luncheon dishes heated up. To enjoy the meal of a lifetime you must stay on one island for some time, and strike up a friendship with a fisherman. The rewards will be worth it: the best of a daily catch often goes straight into the fisherman's family pot.

Athens Restaurants

For an extensive listing of tavernas and restaurants in Athens, see *The Athenian* monthly magazine.

Apotsos, Penepistimious Street, No. 10 in the arcade (tel: 363 7046). Classic lunchtime place, good food; great decor. Open only at lunchtime. Closed Sunday.

Bajazzo, Ploutarchou and Dinokratous, Kolonaki (tel: 729 1420). Unusual food which combines nouvelle cuisine and traditional Greek dishes. Full wine list and expensive by Greek standards but cheap by world-wide standards for innovative, high-quality food. Open for lunch and dinner. Closed Sunday.

Gerofinikas, 10 Pindarou (tel: 362 2719). Cosmopolitan Greek cuisine with Constantinople specialities included. Fresh fish, lamb with artichokes and tantalising deserts. Pricey but recommended. Open lunch and dinner.

Kostoyiannis, 37 Zaimi (Pedion Areos), Exarchia (tel: 821 2496). Large selection of appetisers. Main dishes include rabbit stifado and quail. Good spiced quince with whipped cream and walnut cake for dessert.

Themistokles, 31 Vas. Georgiou, Pangrati (tel: 721 9553). Fine taverna fare on the first floor of an old Athenian dwelling.

Island Restaurants

THE IONIAN ISLANDS

CORFU

Tripa restaurant in village of Kinopiastes in the hills 20 minutes south of Corfu town. One reasonably high, set price per person for a seemingly endless series of dishes. This is very much on the tourist route, but also popular with Corfiotes.

Yanni's, near church of Saints Iason and Sosipater, at Anemomilos, just south of the town.

LÉFKAS

Regantos's. A couple of blocks off the main square. Unpretentious island establishment.

Eftychia's. In the alley opposite the small fountain on the main road between the canal and the main square. Good standard fare, low prices. Best for lunch.

ITHAKI

Gregory's outside town on the northeast end of the bay for dinner.

CEPHALONIA

Sto Psito, Argostoli

Kypos, Argostoli

ZÁKYNTHOS

Arekia taverna, Zákynthos town. Wonderful, with singing.

Oraia Ellas, Zákynthos town

Village Inn, near Strata Marina hotel. Good, expensive French food.

Skorpios taverna, in Bokhali.

SARONIC GULF ISLANDS

AEGINA

Vostitsano, in Aegina town.

Any of the numerous fish tavernas in Perdika.

POROS

Dolphin, in town near post office. Good seafood taverna.

HYDRA

Three Brothers taverna, in town, up from the harbour.

Kseri Elia, in town, up from the harbour.

SPÉTSES

Siouras, in Paleo Limani, in the old harbour. Taverna over the water, popular, noisy, expensive.

Il Padrino Bar and Pizzeria, on the water, in the old harbour.

Patralis, near the Spétses Hotel. Usually good, often excellent fish.

CYCLADES ISLANDS

SANTORINI

Nikolaos, Fira. Fine old taverna, very popular locally.

Selene, Fira. Elegant garden restaurant overlooking Caldera.

Camille Stefani, Kamari, right on the black beach.

SIKINOS

Ostria, affiliated with Kamares Hotel (*see Hotels*).

NAXOS

Elli, Chora. Good Greek restaurant with fine view of temple.

Castro, Chora, Kastro.

PAROS

Porphyra, Paroikia. Seafood.

Tamarisko, Paroikia.

Tsitanis, Prodromos. Local favourite for Greek food.

Kargas, Naoussa harbour. Old ouzeri, picturesque, seafood on charcoal.

ANTIPAROS
Galini Hotel, Chora. Good taverna in hotel (see *Hotels*).
Pepinos, Aghios Yorgos. Fresh fish.

MYKONOS
Katrin, Chora. Excellent but expensive French restaurant.
Antonini, by taxi square on quay. Good Greek food since 1955.
Sesame Kitchen, Chora, next to Maritime Museum. Inventive international food.
Osteria del Pesce da Lu, near Kalafati. One of Greece's best authentic Italian restaurants, excellent food.

SYROS
Eleana, Ermoupolis. First-rate Greek cuisine.
Lilis, Ano Syros. Greek taverna.

TÍNOS
Ksinari, Chora, on main shopping street. Greek food with a Lebanese accent.
Tsambia, in Kionia, near Tínos Beach Hotel. Typical Greek taverna food.

ANDROS
Yiannouli's, on beach between Gavrion and and Batsi. Popular place for lunch, home cooking.
Stamatis, in Batsi, up the stairs at far end of town.

MILOS
Irapatsellis, in Adamas.
To Diporto, in Plaka.

SÍFNOS
Manganas, in Artemonas, near bus stop. Simple, good Greek food.
Liotrivi, in Artemonas. First-rate Greek food in beautiful garden.

SPORADES ISLANDS
SKIÁTHOS
Asprolithos taverna in town, and **Asprolithos taverna** in Megali Ammos, just outside town. Both restaurants with the same name, great variety, fresh food, excellent cuisine.
Chez Julien, in town. French restaurant, seafood.
SKOPELOS
Spyros taverna in town on waterfront. Inexpensive, popular.
Perivoli, in town. Refined Greek cooking. Moderate price.

ALONISSOS
Astro Fengia, at entrance to Chora. Old

family house, innovative cuisine.
Paraport, at base of castle in Chora. Stunning view, grill.
To Kamaki, just up from port. Ouzeri.

SKYROS
Christina's, in the Chorio. Gourmet cooking, original dishes, in garden setting. Reasonably priced.
Margetis, in the Chorio. Best taverna in the village.
Anna's at the windmill on the beach. Wonderful lobster.

AEGEAN ISLANDS
LIMNOS
Platanos, traditional restaurant in the bazaar beneath two plane trees.

LÉSVOS
The Captain's Table, in old harbour, Molyvos. Greek and Australian-run fish restaurant.
Bennett's, Skala Eressou, waterfront.

SAMOS
Steve's, Karlovassi waterfront.
Apanemia Ouzeri, Vathy.
Ta Dilina, Paleokastro.

DODECANESE ISLANDS
RHODES
Le Bistro, in the old town. A genuine French-run bistro.
Algaion, old town. Good seafood.
Palia Istoria, new town, is one of the island's best.
O Yiannis, in Koskinou 5 km (3 miles) south of Rhodes town. Very reasonable *mezedhes* and bulk wine.

KARPATHOS
Olympia, in Pighadia, on the waterfront but away from the quay, does reasonable grills.
Kali Kardhia, in Pighadia around the point, is good for fish.

KASTELLORIZO
Ouzeri Megisteas, behind the arcaded market building. Best value for money.
Little Paris on the waterfront for fish.

TILOS
Blue Sky, in Livadia. Good grilled fish.
Irina, on the shore. Excellent Greek oven dishes.

SYMI
Giorgos's, up in Chorio. An island institution, decades old and still very good.

Tholos, past the Charani shipyards. A tasty ouzeri with an excellent view of town.

NISSYROS
Taverna Nissyros, inland, still going strong after more than 20 years.
Aphroditi, in the port of Pali, is even better.

KOS
Miramare, eastern waterfront.
Hamam, in old Turkish bath just off Plateia Diagoras. Atmospheric but expensive.

KÁLYMNOS
Psarouzeri O Kambourakis. Excellent seafood.
Ksefteris, inland. Good traditional oven dishes.

LEROS
Zorbas's in Pandeli. Good and reasonably priced for the quantity of food you are served.
Garbo's in Aghia Marina. English run, is good for a change of pace.

LEIPSOI
Delfini, by the police station.
Mangos Brothers, under the Hotel Calypso.

PATMOS
Grigoris in Skala, on the waterfront.
Vangelis in Chora on the square.

CRETE
CHANIÁ
Karnaghio, in old harbour.
Pafsilipou, in old town.
Akroghialia, in Nea Chora. Good for fish.

RÉTHYMNON
Agrimia, Cretan food.
Famagusta, Cypriote and Cretan food.
IRÁKLEION
Knossos, traditional, reliable.
Maxim's, also reliable, Cretan food.

Drinking Notes

Greek wines will never obtain the status of their French counterparts, but much local wine can be quite palatable. Some of the better Greek labels are: *Rotonda, Cambas, Boutari, Calliga*.

Retsína: the best-known Greek wine. Flavoured with the resin from pine trees and an acquired taste. Inexpensive.

Deméstica: the popular alternative to retsina. White is the most common; also comes in red and rosé.

St Helena: a reliable medium-dry white wine which can be found in many restaurants.

Cava Clauss: a full-bodied dry red wine, aged in oak barrels.

Chateau Clauss: another vintage from the Achaia Clauss bottlers. Goodish dry red wine.

Nemea: a palatable red table wine; can be found on many menus.

Danielis: slightly spicy dry red wine, less common than Nemea.

Bon Viveur: a newish dry white wine with a fruity taste.

Patras: a robust white wine made from the grapes of the Patras region.

Island Wines

Many islands bottle (or take from the barrel) wines which are sold only locally. Although island wines tend to be rough and ready, they're very cheap and certainly authentic. You may have to ask around for the following:

Ionian Islands

Corfu. Theotoki is the local wine (red or white); the speciality of the island is a very sweet orange liqueur called Kum Kwat.

Antípaxas. The local grapes are much appreciated; ask for wine from the barrel.

Zákynthos. Try the wines made from grapes grown in Zákynthos's lush green vineyards: Comouto rosé or the white Verdea.

Cyclades Islands

Náxos. Ariadne wine is delicious; also white, red or rosé Promponas. Tastings are also held of the lemon-based local liqueur Kitrou.

Páros. Of the two major locals, Kavarnis is more expensive (and better) than Lagari. All in red, white and rosé.

Santoríni. Two white wines: Visanto (sweet) and Nichteri (dry).

Serifos. A full-bodied retsina called Marko. Try it from the barrel.

Sporades Islands

Skópelos. Plums are the speciality here,

and their dried-up cousins, prunes. Locally produced plum wine is delicious; that produced from prunes is disgusting.

Dodecanese Islands

Rhodes. A visit to one of the numerous off-licences in Rhodes Town will find a whole range of locally-produced drinks; wines from Rhodes are consumed all over the Dodecanese. Ilios (named after the sun god) is the most popular, drunk by fishermen and tourists alike. Belvasia retsina is an alternative, as are the red Chevalier du Rhodes and the white Muscat or Grand Maitre. Rhodes champagne is exported to many islands and can also be found in Athens.

Sámos. Samos is one of the few islands to export, not only to the mainland but also abroad. A number of drinks are produced locally, but the best-known Samian wine is the refreshingly light Samaina.

Nissyros. Produces a non-alcoholic drink called Sumada made from almonds.

Lésvos. Quite a few local ouzos; Epom is the principal distillers of wines.

Crete

White wines include Regalo (dry) and Vilana (medium dry). Minos bottle a number of reds and whites of varying quality. Red wines include Castello, Mantiko and Saint Antonio. There are also local variations on brandy, ouzo, and the lethal raki.

Attractions

Cruises

Apparently one in six of all visitors to Greece embarks on an Aegean cruise. Cruises can range from 1-day trips to the Saronic Gulf islands, to 21-day packages on a "floating hotel" departing from Piraeus and taking in Gibraltar, Morocco, and Barbados. Many people elect for the 7-day excursion, which offers an opportunity to see a couple of islands in the Cyclades, a few Dodecanese islands, and a stop-over in Turkey or Morocco for good

measure. Accommodation, prices and standards vary widely and it might be an idea to shop around for a good price.

Ticket agencies in Athens are the places to visit, with cruise opportunities prominently displayed in windows. (Although, if you have ever been at Mýkonos harbour when the ships arrive and watched the frantic preparations of shop managers adjusting their prices upwards, it may change your mind about a cruise entirely.)

Sun Line are one of the most comprehensive companies and are accustomed to dealing with foreigners. Details can be found from any travel agent or by contacting Sun Line's headquarters at 3 Iasonos Street, Piraeus (tel: 452 3417).

A more casual atmosphere can be found aboard the boats used by Viking Tours, a long-established company with a fine reputation. Only 36 passengers can be carried in Viking's 35-metre (118-ft) ships, so the feeling is more like travelling on a private yacht than being aboard a mammoth ship. It's the type of holiday where you make new friends – and keep them. For more information contact Viking at 3, Filellinon Street, in Athens.

Excursions

If a tourist island boasts a major attraction, it has scores of package trips to view it/visit it/swim off it. It's even possible to make a day trip to. Athens from Skiáthos, in the far-flung Sporades. Ticket agencies promote excursions aggressively, so you can pick and choose at your leisure. Unless you enjoy the company of gregarious strangers, the site is of premier importance, or if time is limited, it's often nicer to make your own way to attractions as local transport is usually available, too.

If embarking on an excursion, be sure to check that you will not be arriving at a destination during siesta or on a Sunday; if so, there may not be a great deal to do upon arrival.

A tip: lots of "excursion" boats offering daytrips to neighbouring islands leave and depart at the same time as regular ferryboats. The difference? Excursion boats are twice as expensive.

Sound & Light Spectacles

Throughout the summer, Athens, Corfu and Rhodes offer "sound and light" shows projected onto the frontages of their ancient ruins. These performances are perfect for children, and the lights are exciting to watch from the comfort of a nearby terrace-top. The words, however, are dire. Try attending a show in a language other than your own.

Athens: 9pm (English); 10.15pm (French – except for Tuesday and Friday); 10pm (German – Tuesday and Friday only). Tickets available at the Pnyx before the show. Information from 332 1459.

Corfu: 9.30pm (English – except Saturday and Sunday); 9pm (French – Sunday); 9pm (Greek – Saturday). Ticket price includes Greek folk dances. Reduced rates for students. Information from (0661) 30520.

Rhodes: The spectacle at the Palace of the Knights is performed several times each evening in English, French, German and Greek. Information, tel: (0241) 23255.

Tour Guides

A tour of the island Kálymnos is fondly remembered by one traveller as the highlight of her trip to Greece. The guide, an ebullient former seaman, arrived at her hotel in a battered '68 Chevy, and for the rest of the morning kept up a steady stream of repartee and island facts in a Greek/Australian accent.

A tour guide is a good idea for anyone who wants to study an island in detail, who has no transport, or who enjoys the idea of spending several hours in close proximity with a local. Whether all the "facts" are actually true remains anyone's guess, but an entertaining companion can be worth the price. Guides generally hire themselves out by the half day, full day or even week; enquire at the Tourist Police (see page 314) or ask around at various ticket agencies. There are no set fees and few regulations governing the tour guide business, so negotiate everything in advance, including petrol and lunch.

Cultural

Museums

Museums and archaeological sites permit the taking of photos if a portable camera is used. Foreign students are allowed into most sites for half the price on production of their student cards. If an archaeological site is particularly crowded, try walking around it in reverse, against the crowds. All opening hours are subject to change without notice and most island attractions are closed on Monday and afternoons. Please check before setting out.

ATHENS

The Acropolis (tel: 321 0219). Open daily 8.30am–4.30pm. Entrance fee.

Acropolis Museum, on the Acropolis (tel: 323 6665). Open as above. Closed on Tuesday. Entrance fee.

Ancient Agora Museum in the Stoa of Attalos, entrance from Thisseon Square & 24 Andrianou Street (tel: 321 0185). Open daily 8.30am–3pm. Closed Monday. Entrance fee.

Athens City Museum, 7 Paparigopoulou Street (tel: 323 0168). Open Monday, Wednesday, Friday 9am–1.30pm. Entrance fee. Free on Wednesday.

Benaki Museum, 1 Koumbari Street and Vass. Sophias Avenue (tel: 361 1617). Open daily 8.30am–2pm. Closed Tuesday. Entrance fee.

Byzantine Museum, 22 Vass. Sophias Avenue (tel: 721 1027). Open daily 8.30am–3pm. Closed Monday. Entrance fee.

Cycladic Arts Museum, 4 Neof. Douka Street (tel: 724 9706). Open daily 10am–4pm, Saturday 10am–5pm. Closed Tuesday & Sunday. Entrance fee.

Epigraphical Museum, 1 Tossitsa Street (tel: 821 7637). Open daily 8.30am–3pm. Closed Monday. Admission free.

Greek Folk Art Museum, Plaka (tel: 321 3018). Open daily 10am–2pm. Closed Monday. Entrance fee.

Hellenic Theatre Museum & Studies Centre, 50 Akademias Street (tel: 362 9430). Daily except Saturday 9am–3pm; Monday 5–8pm; Sunday 10am–1pm. Entry fee.

Historical and Ethnological Museum, Stadiou Street (tel: 323 7617). Open Tuesday–Friday 9am–2pm; Saturday & Sunday 9am–1pm. Closed Monday. Entrance fee. Admission free on Thursday.

Kanellopoulos Museum, Theorias & Panos streets, Plaka (tel: 321 2313). Daily 8.30am–3pm; Sunday & holidays 9.30am–2.30pm. Closed Monday. Entrance fee.

Keramikos Museum, 148 Ermou Street (tel: 346 3552). Open daily 8.45am–3pm; Sunday & holidays 9.30am–2.30pm. Closed Tuesday. Entrance fee (includes fee to the archaeological site).

Keramikos Archaeological Site, Ermou & Pireos corner (tel: 346 3552). Open daily 8.45am–3pm. Closed Monday. Entrance fee.

Municipality of Athens Tradition & Folk Art Centre, 6 Hatzimihali Street, Plaka area (tel: 324 3987). Open Tuesday & Thursday 9am–9pm; Wednesday, Friday, Saturday 9am–1pm & 5–9pm; Sunday 9am–1pm. Admission free.

National Archaeological Museum, 1 Tossitsa Street (tel: 821 7717). Open daily 8am–5pm; Saturday, Sunday & holidays 8.30am–3pm; Monday 11am–5pm. Entrance fee (includes fee to the exhibits from Fira & the Numismatic Museum).

National Gallery and Alexandros Soutsos Museum, 46 Vass. Sophias Avenue (tel: 721 1010). Daily 9am–3pm; Sunday & holidays 10am–2pm. Closed Monday. Entrance fee.

National History, 13 Levidou Street, Kifissia (tel: 808 6405). Open daily 9am–2.30pm. Closed on Friday, Sunday & holidays. Entrance fee.

Numismatic Museum, 1 Tossitsa Street (tel: 821 7769). Open daily 8.30am–3pm. Closed Monday. Entrance fee.

Roman Agora, End of Eolou Street (tel: 321 0185). Open daily 8.45am–3pm. Closed Monday. Entrance fee.

Temple of Hephaistos and Ancient Agora (tel: 321 0185). Open daily 8.30am–5pm. Entrance fee.

Temple of Olympian Zeus, Olgas and Amalias Avenue (tel: 922 6330). Open daily 8.30am–3pm. Entrance fee.

Theatre of Dionyssos, D. Areopagitou Avenue (tel: 323 6665). Open daily 8.30am–3pm. Entrance fee.

War Museum of Greece, Vass. Sophias Avenue (tel: 729 0543-4). Open daily 9am–2pm. Closed Monday. Library open: Tuesday–Saturday 9am–2pm. Admission free.

PIRAEUS

Maritime Museum of Piraeus, Akti Themistokleous (tel: 451 6822). Open daily 9am–12.30pm; Sunday & holidays 10am–1pm & 5–8pm. Closed Monday, Tuesday & Friday. Admission free.

Piraeus Archaeological Museum, 31 Char. Trikoupi Street (tel: 452 1598). Open daily 8.30am–3pm. Closed Monday. Entrance fee.

SITES NEAR ATHENS

Daphni Monastery (tel: 581 1558). Open daily 8.30am–3pm. Closed Monday. Entrance fee.

Epidavros Archaeological Site and Museum (tel: 0753 22009). Open daily 8am–5pm; Saturday, Sunday & holidays 8.30am–3pm. Museum open Monday 11am–5pm. Archaeological site closed Monday. Entrance fee.

Elefsis Museum (tel: 554 6019). Open daily 8.30am–3pm. Closed Monday.

Kaissariani Monastery (tel: 723 6619). Open daily 8.30am–3pm. Closed Monday. Admission free.

IONIAN ISLANDS
CORFU
Archaeological Museum (tel: 0661 30680). Open daily 8.30am–3pm. Closed Monday. Entrance fee.

Museum of Asiatic Art (tel: 0661 23124). Open daily 8.30am–3pm. Closed Monday. Entrance fee.

SARONG GULF ISLANDS
AEGINA
Temple of Afaia (tel: 0297 32398). Open daily 8am–5pm; Saturday, Sunday & holidays 8.30am–3pm. Entrance fee.

Island Museum (tel: 0297 22637). Open daily 8.30am–3pm. Closed Monday. Entrance fee (including fee to the Temple of Apollo).

CYCLADES ISLANDS
ANDROS
Archaeological Museum (tel: 0282 23664). Open daily 8.30am–3pm. Closed Monday. Entrance fee.

Museum Basil & Elisa Goulandris (Modern Art) (tel: 0282 22650). Open daily 10am–1pm & 5–8pm. Closed Monday. Admission free.

DELOS
Archaeological Site (tel: 0289 22259). Open daily 8.30am–3pm. Closed Monday. Entrance fee.

Island Museum (tel: 0289 22259). Open daily 8.30am–3pm. Closed Monday. Entrance fee.

MILOS
Archaeological Site & Museum (tel: 0287 21620). Open daily 8.30am–3pm. Closed Monday. Entrance fee.

The Catacombs (tel: 0287 21620). Open daily except Wednesday & Sunday 9am–2.30pm. Entrance fee.

SANTORINI (THIRA)
Akrotiri Thira Archaeological Site (tel: 0286 81366). Open daily 8.30am–3pm. Closed Monday. Entrance fee.

Archeological Site (tel: 0286 22217). Open daily 8.30am–3pm. Closed Monday. Admission free.

Island Museum (tel: 0286 22217). Open daily 8.30am–3pm. Closed Monday. Entrance fee.

NORTHERN AEGEAN ISLANDS

SAMOTHRAKI
Archaeological Site (tel: 0551 41474). Open daily 8.30am–3pm. Closed Monday. Entrance fee.

Island Museum (tel: 0551 41474). Open daily 8.30am–3pm. Closed Monday. Entrance fee.

DODECANESE ISLANDS
KOS
Asclepieion & other Archeological Sites (tel: 0242 28763). Open daily 8.30am–3pm. Closed Monday. Entrance fee.

Island Museum (tel: 0242 28326). Open daily 8.30am–3pm. Closed Monday. Entrance fee.

Kos Castle (tel: 0242 28326). Open daily 8.30am–3pm. Closed Monday. Entrance fee.

Restored Ancient Dwelling (tel: 0242 28326). Open daily 8.30am–3pm. Closed Monday. Entrance fee.

LESVOS
Eressos Archaeological Museum (tel: 0251 22087). Open daily 8.30am–3pm. Closed Monday. Admission free.

Mytilini Archaeological Museum (tel: 0251 22087). Open Wednesday & Thursday 3–6pm; Saturday & Sunday 9am–6pm. Entrance fee.

Theofilos Art Museum (tel: 0251 28179). Open daily 9am–1pm & 4.30–8pm. Closed Monday. Entrance fee.

PATMOS
Island churches and other monuments, admission free.

Monastery of St John & Library, Vestry (tel: 0241 21954). Open daily 8.30am–3pm. Closed Monday. Admission free.

RHODES
Rhodes Acropolis, Theatre and Stadium (tel: 0241 21954). Open daily 8.30am–3pm. Closed Monday. Admission free.

Acropolis of Ialyssos (tel: 0241 21954). Open daily 8.30am–3pm. Closed Monday. Entrance fee.

Acropolis of Lindos (tel: 0241 21954). Open daily 8.30am–3pm. Closed Monday. Entrance fee.

Decorative Collections (tel: 0241 21954). Open daily 8.30am–3pm. Closed Monday. Admission free.

Island Museum (tel: 0241 21954). Open daily 8.30am–3pm. Closed Monday. Entrance fee.

Kamiros Archaeological Site (tel: 0241 21954). Open daily 8.30am–3pm. Closed Monday. Entrance fee.

Palace of the Knights (tel: 0241 21954). Open daily 8.30am–3pm. Closed Monday Entrance fee.

Medieval Walls (tel: 0241 21954). Open to visitors accompanied by a guide on Tuesday & Saturday from 3–5pm. Visitor should gather in the courtyard of the Palace of the Knights. Entrance fee.

CRETE
Ag. Nikólaos Museum (tel: 0841 22462). Open daily 8.30am–3pm. Closed Monday. Entrance fee.

Aghia Trias Archaeological Site (tel: 0892 22631). Open daily 8.30am–3pm. Closed Monday. Entrance fee.

Chaniá Museum (tel: 0821 94418). Open daily 8.30am–5pm; Sunday & holidays 8.30am–3pm; Monday 11am–5pm. Entrance fee.

Gortys Archaeologicial Site (tel: 081 226092). Open daily 8am–5pm; Saturday, Sunday & holidays 8.30am–3pm. Entrance fee.

Irákleion Archaeological Museum (tel: 081 226092). Open daily 8am–5pm; Saturday, Sunday & holidays 8.30am–3pm; Monday 11am–5pm. Entrance fee.

Irákleion Harbour Fortress (Koules) (tel: 081 286228). Open daily 8.30am–3pm. Closed Monday. Entrance fee.

Knossós Archaeological Site (tel: 081 231940). Open daily 8am–5pm; Saturday, Sunday & holidays 8.30am–3pm. Entrance fee.

Mallia Archaeological Site (tel: 0897 31597). Open daily 8.30am–3pm. Closed Monday. Entrance fee.

Phaestós (Festos) Archaeological Site (tel: 0892 91316). Open daily 8am–5pm; Saturday, Sunday & holidays 8.30am–3pm. Entrance fee.

Réthymnon Museum (tel: 0831 29975/23653). Open daily 8.30am–3pm. Closed Monday. Entrance fee.

Tylissos Archaeological Site (tel: 081 224267). Open daily 8.30am–3pm. Closed Monday. Entrance fee.

Zakros Archaeological Site (tel: 0841 22462). Open daily 8.30am–3pm. Closed Monday. Entrance fee.

OTHER ARCHAEOLOGICAL SITES
St Titus, Gournia (tel: 081 226092). Open daily 8.30am–3pm. Closed Monday. Admission free.

Outdoor Movies

One of the delights of an island evening is to sit under a starry sky and enjoy an outoor movie. Like an American drive-in without the cars, Greece's outdoor cinemas do not attempt to compete with mainstream movie houses, screening instead old Westerns, Hollywood war movies and films you've never heard of. Usually in English with Greek subtitles, the noise in the theatre (Greeks talk through screenings) often makes the movie dialogue incomprehensible but doesn't spoil the evening out a jot. Take snacks, a blanket or warm jacket and wear lots of anti-mosquito spray.

Nightlife

Most island nightlife consists of strolling from taverna to *zacharisplastion* to a café on the promenade. Having said that, discos abound on any island with a sizable influx of tourists. The best are out of town and out of doors; dancing under the stars is an unforgettable Greek experience. Canny managers of discos located some distance from the port hire a nightly minibus which transports revellers to the premises. Discos on small islands are the most fun when, around midnight, the Rolling Stones give way to traditional island music and older folks join young foreigners on the dance floor. For a more sophisticated evening out, both Rhodes and Corfu have casinos.

Greek Folk Dances

Athens, Corfu and Rhodes have regular performances of Greek folk dancing during the summer months. In Athens, the renowned Dora Stratou Group perform at the Philopappou Theatre most nights at 10.25pm. On Wednesday and Sunday there is an extra performance at 8.15pm. Information from 324 4395. Performances are held each evening at 9pm on Corfu at the Old Venetian Castle. The ticket price includes the Sound and Light spectacle. Information from (0661) 39730. On Rhodes, the Nelly Dimoglou Group holds sway at the old and attractive Rodini Theatre most evenings at 9.15pm. Information by calling (0241) 27524.

Shopping

What To Buy

Most Greek tourist tat is instantly forgettable; it also takes up room on ferries and airplanes. Much better to concentrate on small local items like sponges from Kálymnos, leather bags from Rhodes, hand-

made pottery from Sífnos, herbs from Symi, and extremely attractive silver jewellery from a number of islands. Much of this jewellery is made by local craftmen, and styles range from the traditional to the fashionable.

Other good buys include baskets, copper pots and other copperware, honey, olive oil, and the ubiquitous *loukoumia* (Turkish Delight), made on Sýros but exported to other islands too. The Dodecanese islands are particularly rich in fur coat shops and are also a source of inexpensive booze, both local and imported.

Hydra, Mýkonos and Páros have some of the most fashionable boutiques to be found in Greece. Much of their stock outrivals Athens; but not, unfortunately London, Paris or New York.

Bargaining is expected in market places and stalls. In these places, even if an item has a price tag, try offering a lower price. Even better, show interest and then walk away. (You can always return if the ploy doesn't work. It usually does.) Bargaining is unacceptable in department stores, chain stores and most boutiques.

Department stores implement a complicated service system not recommended for anyone in a hurry. If you happen to go to a large stationers to purchase a notebook, a pencil, a couple of envelopes and perhaps a birthday card, you could find yourself standing in six different queues: one for each department (where an assistant writes a receipt for each item), one to pay the cashier the total amount, and one for delivery of the goods. If you're lucky, all four items will have arrived from their various departments (only a few steps from each other) at the delivery desk to be wrapped or placed into a bag with four separate receipts taped on top.

PERÍPTERA (KIOSKS)

Always open days, nights, holidays and Sundays, life in Greece would be unmanageable without a neighbourhood *periptero*. Although they may appear limited by their diminutive structures, kiosks are really multi-purpose powerhouses. Besides filling the function of newsagent and tobacconist, these businesses, many family-run, also double as mini amusement parks with kiddie rides, sporting goods stores, ironmongers, locksmiths, and for many customers with problems, the proprietor may dispense psychiatric or medical advice. Here, too, is a quick place to buy tourist requisites: shampoo, nail clippers, postcards.

There are over 3,000 kiosks in Athens alone. It is not unusual for a *periteró* to work shifts of 12 hours in conditions which vary from furnace-like in summer to chill and damp in winter. The kiosks started as gifts from the government to wounded veterans of the Balkan and First World Wars. Many people remark on the similarity between the architecture of kiosks and that of military guardposts such as those used by the honour guard in front of Parliament on Syntagma Square.

Sports

Many of the larger hotels have tennis courts and facilities for water-skiing. Major beaches can provide surf boards, water bikes, snorkelling and windsurfing equipment; there's even scope for parascending on Crete, Rhodes, Kos and Skiáthos.

Golf

Greece has a few golf courses dotted around the country. In Athens, the course is at Glyfada (tel: 894 6875). Rhodes' golf course is at Afandou (tel: 0241 51255). Corfu's Ermones Bay golf club (tel: 0661 94220) is particularly nice. Lessons and rental equipment available at all courses.

Yachting

The NTOG publishes an excellent booklet called *Sailing the Greek Seas*. Included is information on weather, coastal radio telephone stations, entry and exit regulations. The pamphlet is particularly detailed on marinas, bunkering ports and supply stations. There are four marinas within striking distance of Athens. Information on services or facilities may be obtained by calling:

Vouliagmeni Marina – tel: 896 0012.
Zea Marina – tel: 451 3944.
Alimos Marina – tel: 982 8642.
Flisvos Marina – tel: 982 8537.

If you prefer to charter a yacht, the NTOG can provide lists of yacht brokers and consultants. All charter agreements have to be made in the manner and on the official form prescribed by the Greek government. The following organisations can also offer help and advice:

Greek Yacht Brokers & Consultants Association, 7 Filellinon Street, 105 57

Athens (tel: 323 0330).

P. Faliro (tel: 981 6582).

Greek Yacht Owners Association, 10 Lekka Street, 185 37 Piraeus (tel: 452 6335).

Hellenic Professional Yacht Owners Association, 43 Freatidos Street, Zea Marina, 185 36 Piraeus (tel: 452 6335).

Anyone planning to sail independently around the islands is advised to become familiar with the list of Port Authorities (see *Getting Around*). The Port Authority Harbour Police are the only people who can provide up-to-the-minute information on conditions concerning a specific island. Fuelling facilities and other provisions are available at: Adamas (Mílos); Aegina; Aghios Nikólaos (Kea); Aghios Nikólaos (Crete); Argostoli (Kephalonia); Corfu Port; Ermoupoli (Sýros); Chánia (Crete); Chios; Hydra; Kálymnos; Kamares (Sífnos); Kapsali (Kythera); Kastellorizo; Kastro (Andros); Katapola (Amorgos); Kos; Lakki (Leros); Léfkas; Linaria (Skýros); Mirina (Límnos); Mytilini (Lésvos); Mýkonos; Náxos; Paroikía (Páros); Pigadia (Kárpathos); Póros; Mandraki (Rhodes); Skala (Patmos); Skiáthos; Skópelos; Spétses; Tínos; Vathí (Ithaki); Zákynthos.

Special Information

Islands for photographers: Santorini, Crete, Nissyros, Delos, Sými, Skýros.

Islands for hikers: Crete, Cephalonia, Chios, Samothraki.

Islands for children: Crete, Skiáthos, Rhodes, Pserimos.

Islands for fun-lovers: Mýkonos, Corfu, Paros, Kos, Crete.

Islands for privacy-seekers: The "Back Islands", Pserimos, Telendos, Astypalea, Ithaki.

Islands for academics: Lésvos, Crete, Rhodes, Kos, Patmos, Aegina.

Islands with spas: Kythnos, Léfkas, Andros, Nissyros, Ikaria.

Islands for the disabled: For a list of hotels with facilities suitable for handicapped people, write to the NTOG Information Office, 2 Amerikis Street, Athens.

Language

Useful Words & Phrases

yes	*né*
no	*óchi*
okay	*en dáksi*
thank you	*efcharistó*
(very much)	*pára polí*
excuse me	*signómi*
it doesn't matter	*dhen pirázi*
nothing	*típota*
certainly	*málista*
good day	*káli méra*
good evening	*káli spéra*
good night	*káli níchta*
goodbye	*addío*
Greetings!	*yá sou, yá sas* (plural or formal)
"health to you!" (a toast)	*yá sou, yá sas* (plural)
bon voyage	*kaló taksídhi*
welcome	*kalós ílthathe*
good luck	*kalí tíchi*
How are you?	*ti kánis, i kánete* (plural or formal)
fine (in response)	*kalá*
so so (in response)	*étsi kétsi*
pleased to meet you	*chárika*
Have you...?	*échete...?*
Is there...?	*éxchi...?*
How much does it cost?	*póso káni?*
It's (too) expensive	*íne (polí) akrivó*
How much?	*póso?*
How many?	*pósa?*
Do you have a room?	*échete éna domátio?*
Can I...?	*boró na...?*
When?	*póte?*
Where is...?	*póu íne...?*
Do you speak English?	*milás/miláte angliká?* (sing./plural or formal)
Do you understand?	*katálaves?*
What time is it?	*ti óra íne?*
What time will it leave?	*ti óra tha fígi?*
I don't	*dhen (plus verb)*
I want	*thélo*
I have	*écho*
today	*símera*
tomorrow	*ávrio*
now	*tóra*
here/there	*edhó/ekí*
near/far	*kondá/makriá*
small/large	*mikró/megálo*
quickly	*grígora*
slowly	*argá*
good/bad	*kaló/kakó*
warm/cold	*zestó/krío*
shower with hot water	*douz me zestó neró*
hotel	*ksenodhochío*
bed	*kreváti*
key	*klidhí*
entrance	*ísodhos*
exit	*éksodhos*
toilet	*toualéta*
women's	*ginekón*
men's	*andrón*
store	*magazí*
kiosk	*periptero*
open/shut	*aniktós/klistós*
post office	*tachidromío*
stamp	*grammatósima*
letter	*grámma*
envelope	*fákelos*
telephone	*tiléfono*
bank	*trápeza*
marketplace	*agorá*
pharmacy	*farmakío*
doctor	*yiatrós*
hospital	*nosokomío*
police	*astinomía*
station	*stathmós*
boat	*karávi, vapóri*
bike/moped	*podílato/ motopodílato*
on foot	*me ta pódhia*
ticket	*isitírio*
road/street	*drómos/odós*
beach	*paralía*
church	*eklisía*
ancient ruins	*archaía*
centre	*kéntro*
square	*platía*
sea	*thálassa*

Numbers

1	*énna*
2	*dío*
3	*tría/tris*
4	*téssera*
5	*pénd*
6	*éksi*
7	*eptá*
8	*ochtó*
9	*ennéa*
10	*déka*
11	*éndeka*
12	*dódeka*
13	*dekatría*
14	*dekatéssera*
20	*íkosi*
21	*íkosi énna*
30	*triánda*
40	*saránda*

312

0	*penínda*
0	*eksínda*
0	*evdomínda*
0	*ógdhónda*
0	*ennenínda*
00	*ekató*
50	*ekatopenínda*
00	*diakóssia*
00	*triakóssia*
00	*tetrakóssia*
,000	*chília*

Days of the Week

Monday	*deftéra*
Tuesday	*tríti*
Wednesday	*tetárti*
Thursday	*pémpti*
Friday	*paraskeví*
Saturday	*sávato*
Sunday	*kyriakí*

Untranslatable Words

kéfi – to be in good spirits, having a good time with your *paréa*

paréa – one's group of close friends, your "gang"

kaimós – the opposite of *kéfi*, one's long-suffering or sadness

palikári – a good fellow (honourable, brave, intelligent, etc.)

filótimo – adjective meaning literally "love of honour"

mángas – a "toughie", a "cool dude", macho

re – short for *moré*, meaning baby, kid, dummy; a word thrown in when addressing a buddy in the typically male Greek rough-affectionate manner; not, properly, polite

malákas – literally "masturbator"; often combined with re (re malákas); can be directed to one's friends affectionately or to others more antagonistically. Be careful: the term is offensive.

pedhiá – the "boys", fellows, guys

alítis – a bum, roughly the opposite of *palikári*

lipón – well, so, now then

éla! – Come! Come on!

oríste (?) – Yes, can I help you?

po po po! – Well well! What have we here!

ópa – Look out! also, at a music taverna for instance, "way to go!" "all right!" etc.

The Language of Gestures

Greek is a gestural language; you don't speak it with your hands in your pockets or with your head still. The body and its movements are signs which form an integral part of the communicative process. You can learn this aspect of Greek only through close observation. Two of the most common of these gestures are those indicating "yes" and "no". "No" is often communicated by jerking the head and chin up and back sharply. This is a very slight movement, but emphatic. Sometimes, in fact, only the eyebrows or eyes make this upward gesture. The gesture indicating "yes" is a rather gentler one, a slow downward angling of the head.

Further Reading

History

Booth, C.D. and I.B. *Italy's Aegean Possessions*. London: 1928.

Cheetham, Nicholas. *Medieval Greece*. New Haven, 1981.

du Boulay, Juliet. *Portrait of a Greek Mountain Village*. Oxford: Clarendon Press, 1974.

Finley, M.I. *The Ancient Greeks*. Harmondsworth/Penguin, 1963.

Hamilton, Edith. *Mythology*. New York: New American Library, 1969.

Hopkins, Adam. *Crete: Its Past, Present and People*. London: Faber & Faber, 1977.

Mazower, Mark. *Inside Hitler's Greece*. OUP, 1994

Specialist Travel & General Background

The Aegean Islands: The Cyclades, or Life Among the Insular Greeks. London: Argonaut, 1965.

Constantine, David. *Early Greek Travellers and the Hellenic Idea*. Cambridge: CUP, 1984.

Durrell, Lawrence. *The Greek Islands*. London: Faber and Faber.

Freeley, John. *The Cyclades*. London: Jonathan Cape, 1986.

Harris, Andy. *A Taste of the Aegean*. Pavilion, 1992.

Karpodini-Dimitriadi, E. *The Greek Islands*. Athens: Ekdotike Athenon S.A., 1987.

Leigh Fermour, Patrick *Roumeli* and *Mani*, Penguin, 1984.

Kazantzakis, Nikos. *Zorba the Greek* and *Report to Greco*.

Stavrolakes, Niki. *Poros*. Athens: Lycabettus Press.

Stone, Tom. *Patmos*. Athens: Lycabettus Press.

Zenfell, Martha Ellen. *Guide to the Greek Islands*. London: Robert Nicholson, 1986.

Foreign Writers & Greece

Andrews, Kevin. *The Flight of Ikaros*. Harmondsworth/Penguin, 1984.

Boleman-Herring, Elizabeth. *The Other Side of the Road*. Lycabettus Press, 1988.

Durrell, Lawrence. *Prospero's Cell, Reflections on a Marine Venus, Bitter Lemons*. London: Faber & Faber.

Fowles, John. *The Magus*. London: Cape, 1977.

Gage, Nicholas. *Eleni*. London: Collins, 1983.

Kitroeff, Alex. *The Bananaless Republic*. The Athenian Press, 1988.

Levi, Peter. *Hill of Kronos*. New York: Penguin, 1984

Miller, Henry. *The Colossus of Maroussi*. New York: New Directions, 1958.

Renault, Mary. *The Last of the Wine*. London: Sceptre, 1986

Salmon, Tim. *The Unwritten Places*. Lycabettus Press, 1995.

Other Insight Guides

Other *Insight Guides* highlight destinations in this region. and titles include Greece, Athens and Crete as well as Cyprus and the Turkish Coast. Apa Publications has two other series of guide books: *Insight Pocket Guides,* which give detailed tours and daytrips, and *Compact Guides,* which are mini encyclopedeas. There are *Pocket Guides* to the Aegean Islands, Athens, Rhodes and Crete and *Compact Guides* to Greece, Crete and Rhodes.

314